MEXICO AND THE NORTH AMERICAN FREE TRADE AGREEMENT

Also by Victor Bulmer-Thomas

AN ECONOMIC HISTORY OF LATIN AMERICA
  SINCE INDEPENDENCE

BRITAIN AND LATIN AMERICA: A Changing Relationship
  (*editor*)

INPUT–OUTPUT ANALYSIS FOR DEVELOPING COUNTRIES

STUDIES IN THE ECONOMICS OF CENTRAL AMERICA

THE POLITICAL ECONOMY OF CENTRAL AMERICA
  SINCE 1920

Mexico and the North American Free Trade Agreement

Who Will Benefit?

Edited by

Victor Bulmer-Thomas
Director of the Institute of Latin American Studies
University of London

Nikki Craske
Department of Government
University of Manchester

and

Mónica Serrano
Academic Coordinator
Centre of International Studies
El Colegio de México

St. Martin's Press   New York

in association with
INSTITUTE OF LATIN AMERICAN STUDIES
UNIVERSITY OF LONDON

MAI 309 88051

First published in the United States of America in 1994

Printed in Great Britain

ISBN 0–312–12176–8

Library of Congress Cataloging-in-Publication Data
Mexico and the North American Free Trade Agreement : who will benefit?
/ edited by Victor Bulmer-Thomas, Nikki Craske, and Mónica Serrano.
p.   cm.
Includes bibliographical references and index.
ISBN 0–312–12176–8
1. Free trade—Mexico.   2. Free trade—North America.   3. Canada,
Treaties, etc.   1992 Oct. 7.   4. Mexico—Economic conditions—1982–
I. Bulmer-Thomas, V.   II. Craske, Nikki,   III. Serrano, Mónica.
HF1776.M49   1994
382'.917—dc20
                                                        94–5688
                                                          CIP

CONTENTS

382.917
M611

Preface   vii
Acknowledgements   viii
List of Contributors   ix
List of Abbreviations and Acronyms   xiii
List of Tables   xv
List of Figures   xvi
Map   xvii

Chapter 1   INTRODUCTION
             Jesús Silva Herzog   1

I. ECONOMIC DIMENSIONS

Chapter 2   Mexico and NAFTA: economic effects and
             the bargaining process
             Jaime Ros   11

Chapter 3   Is Mexico a back door to the US market or a
             niche in the world's largest free trade area?
             Adriaan Ten Kate   29

Chapter 4   The Mexican financial system and NAFTA
             Ignacio Trigueros   43

Chapter 5   Agriculture and farmers within NAFTA: a
             Mexican perspective
             Kirsten Appendini   59

II. SOCIO-POLITICAL DIMENSIONS

Chapter 6   NAFTA and labour migration to the United
             States
             Jorge Bustamante   79

Chapter 7   NAFTA and the environment
             Roberto Sánchez   95

Chapter 8   Is there an alternative? The political con-
             straints on NAFTA
             Adolfo Aguilar Zinser   119

III. INTERNATIONAL DIMENSIONS

Chapter 9   The impact of NAFTA on the Latin Ameri-
             can economies
             E.V.K. FitzGerald   133

Chater 10   The consequences of NAFTA for European
             and Japanese trade and investment in Mexico
             Gabriel Székely   149

Chapter 11   Canada's role in NAFTA: to what degree
             has it been defensive?
             Ronald Wonnacott   163

Chapter 12   Is NAFTA more than a free trade agree-
             ment? A view from the United States
             William C. Gruben and John Welch   177

IV. CONCLUSIONS

Chapter 13   Who will benefit?
             **Victor Bulmer-Thomas, Nikki Craske and
             Mónica Serrano**   203

Bibliography   233
Index   251

PREFACE

The North American Free Trade Agreement (NAFTA) symbolises the sweeping changes that have taken place in Mexico in recent years. Uniting Canada, Mexico and the United States in the largest free trade area in the world, NAFTA is also the first time that sovereign developing and developed countries have been joined together in an integration scheme.

NAFTA is a trade agreement, but the lengthy negotiations required to bring it to a successful conclusion led it to embrace much more than trade. Investment, the environment and the labour market all figure prominently in the final version of NAFTA while the agreement itself also carries major implications for Mexico's relations with the rest of the world as well as for political developments within Mexico itself.

There have been numerous studies on the expected impact of NAFTA on the three countries of North America. This book, however, concentrates on the gains and losses expected from NAFTA within Mexico. As the smallest country in economic terms, the impact of NAFTA is likely to be relatively greater for Mexico than for its partners and this can be expected to generate substantial costs as well as benefits. While supporters of NAFTA during its passage through the legislative bodies in the three countries focused almost exclusively on the benefits, and opponents on the costs, a true evaluation of the impact of NAFTA must take both into account.

This book arose from an international conference organised by the Institute of Latin American Studies, University of London, in May 1993. The contributors from Canada, Mexico and the United States, as well as Europe, were able to revise their chapters following the side agreements on the environment and labour reached in August. The manuscript was finally submitted to the publishers following the vote in favour of NAFTA in the US House of Representatives on 17 November 1993.

On 1 November 1993, the Treaty of Maastricht went into force and the name of the European Community was changed to the European Union. Throughout this book, however, it is referred to as the European Community (EC) as the change had not taken place when the authors submitted the final versions of their chapters.

vii

ACKNOWLEDGEMENTS

Acknowledgements are due to the following, whose generous support enabled the conference on which this book is based to take place: the British Council, the Foreign and Commonwealth Office, Gartmore Investments, Intermex Bank, the Mexican Lotería Nacional and the Nuffield Foundation.

The editors would also like to thank Tim Girven for his work on the index, Tony Bell for his help with the editing of the book, and Alison Loader de Rojo for preparing the text with skill, perseverance and good humour.

LIST OF CONTRIBUTORS

Adolfo Aguilar Zinser is a professor in the Universidad Nacional Autónoma de México (UNAM), where he teaches on US-Mexican relations. He is a leading commentator on current affairs. His articles include 'Authoritarianism and North American Free Trade: The Debate in Mexico', in *The Political Economy of North American Free Trade* (St. Martin's Press; Macmillan, 1993), edited by Ricardo Grinspun and Maxwell A. Cameron.

Kirsten Appendini is a professor at El Colegio de México and has been Visiting Fellow at the Center for US-Mexican Studies at the University of California, San Diego, and at El Colegio de la Frontera Norte, Tijuana. She teaches economics, agrarian studies and on the women studies programme. She has published widely in books and journals; her latest publication is *De la milpa a los tortibonos: La reestructuración de la política alimentaria en México* (México: El Colegio de México/-UNRISD, 1992).

Victor Bulmer-Thomas is Director of the Institute of Latin American Studies and Professor of Economics at Queen Mary and Westfield College, University of London. His research interests include international trade policy and regional integration in Latin America and he has worked as a consultant for the European Commission, the Inter-American Development Bank and the UN Economic Commission for Latin America and the Caribbean. He has been an editor of the *Journal of Latin American Studies* since 1986.

Jorge Bustamante is President of El Colegio de la Frontera Norte, Tijuana and Eugene Conley Professor of Sociology at the University of Notre Dame. He has taught at the University of Texas at Austin, the University of California, Riverside, as well as El Colegio de México. He is an acknowledged expert on US-Mexican migration and on the population of Mexican descent residing in the USA. In 1988 he was awarded the *Premio Nacional de Ciencias*, the first time the award has been given to a social scientist.

Nikki Craske is Lecturer in the Department of Government at the University of Manchester, where she teaches Latin American politics. She was a Research Fellow at the Institute of Latin American Studies in 1992-93, and was previously a Visiting Scholar at El Colegio de México. Her research interests include social mobilisation and regime change, and she has published in both English and Spanish on these subjects.

E. V. K. FitzGerald is Director of the Finance and Trade Policy Research Centre, Queen Elizabeth House, Oxford, Fellow of St Antony's College, Oxford, and Extraordinary Professor of Economics at the Institute of Social Studies (ISS), The Hague. He has held many academic posts including Assistant Director of Development Studies at Cambridge and Tinker Professor of Latin American Economics at the University of Texas, Austin. He is presently engaged in a joint research project with El Colegio de México on the macroeconomic impact of external capital flows.

William Gruben is Senior Economist and Policy Advisor in the Federal Reserve Bank of Dallas. His research interests have focused on the Mexican economy with particular reference to US-Mexican economic relations. Among his many publications is 'North American Free Trade: Opportunities and Pitfalls', *Contemporary Political Issues* (1993).

Jaime Ros is Associate Professor of Economics and Faculty Fellow of the Kellogg Institute for International Studies, University of Notre Dame. He has been Visiting Scholar at the Department of Applied Economics, Cambridge, St Antony's College, Oxford, and the World Institute for Development Economics Research (WIDER), Helsinki. He has also worked with the UN Economic Commission for Latin America and the Caribbean, the South Commission in Geneva, the International Labour Organisation and the United Nations University. His major research interests are the development, trade and macro-economic problems of developing countries.

Roberto Sánchez is Director of the Department of Urban and Environmental Studies at El Colegio de la Frontera Norte, Tijuana. His research has concentrated on US-Mexican border environmental issues, the management of transboundary water resources, and, more recently, the social and economic aspects of global environmental change. His articles on environmental issues have appeared in many journals.

Mónica Serrano is Academic Coordinator of the Centre for International al Studies at El Colegio de México. She was a Research Fellow at the Institute of Latin American Studies, London, in 1990-92. Her research has focused on Inter-American security issues, with publications including 'New non-proliferators: Brazil and Argentina', in Robert S. Litwak and Mitchell Reiss (eds.), *Nuclear Proliferation after the Cold War* (Washington, DC: The Woodrow Wilson Press, 1994), 'Shifts in Mexican Foreign Policy in the 1980s', in Neil Harvey (ed.), *Mexico: Dilemmas of Transition* (London: ILAS/British Academic Press, 1993) and 'Comercio internacional e integración: Las perspectivas mexicana y norteamericana', in Gustavo Vega (ed.), *México, Estados Unidos y Canadá, 1991-92* (México: El Colegio de México, 1994).

Jesús Silva Herzog was appointed Mexican Ambassador to Spain in 1991. After working for the Banco de México he became, in 1970, Director General of Public Credit at the Ministry of Finance and Public Credit. In 1979 he became Undersecretary of Finance and Public Credit. When the Third World debt crisis developed in 1982 he was Secretary of Finance and played a crucial role in the renegotiation of the Mexican debt.

Gabriel Székely is Associate Researcher at the University of California, San Diego, where he is Director of the Project on Japan-US-Latin American Relations and teaches in the Graduate School of International Relations and Pacific Studies. He is also professor in the Centre for Asian and African Studies at El Colegio de México. His latest book (co-edited with Barbara Stallings), *A New Trilateralism in the Western Hemisphere? The United States, Japan and Latin America,* is published by Macmillan. He has advised firms on NAFTA and MERCOSUR, and the Mexican Government on trade relations with Japan.

Adriaan Ten Kate is Adviser to the Mexican Ministry for Commerce and Industry (SECOFI). He was a member of the Mexican negotiating team for one chapter of NAFTA. He has taught at the Erasmus University in Rotterdam, the Universidad Autónoma Nacional de México, the Universidad de Guadalajara and in Costa Rica. His publications on trade issues include *La Política de Protección y Desarrollo Económico de México* (México: Fondo de Cultura Económica, 1979), published in English as *Protection and Economic Development in Mexico* (Aldershot: Gower, 1980).

Ignacio Trigueros is Professor of Economics at the Instituto Tecnólogico Autónomo de México (ITAM). He was Visiting Professor at Queen Mary College, London University, in 1989. He is a recognised expert on financial integration and international trade in services. His publications include 'Los servicios financieros y el Acuerdo de Libre Comercio: bancos y casas de bolsa' (co-authored), in *México y el Tratado Trilateral de Libre Comercio: Impacto Sectorial* (México: McGraw-Hill, 1992), edited by Eduardo Andere and Georgina Kessel.

John Welch is Senior Economist in the Federal Reserve Bank of Dallas. His areas of interest are monetary economics, international trade and finance, and economic development with special reference to Latin America. He has published extensively on the economies of Mexico, Brazil and Argentina. His book *Capital Markets in the Development Process: the case of Brazil* was published in 1992 by Macmillan.

Ronald Wonnacott is Professor of Economics at University of Western Ontario. He has taught at Harvard Law School, Harvard Economics Department and the University of Minnesota. He is the author of many books on economics which have been widely translated. These include *Free Trade Between the US and Canada* (Harvard University Press, 1967) and *The Economics of Overlapping Free Trade Areas and the Mexican Challenge* (Toronto: Canada-America Committee, 1991). He is a Fellow of the Royal Society of Canada, has been a member of the Board of Directors of the Social Sciences Federation of Canada and President of the Canadian Economics Association.

LIST OF ABBREVIATIONS AND ACRONYMS

ADRs	American Depository Receipts
AFTA	Asian Free Trade Agreement
APHIS	Animal and Plant Health Inspection Service
BANRURAL	Banco Nacional de Desarrollo Rural
CGE	Computable General Equilibrium
CONASUPO	Compañía Nacional de Subsistencias Populares
CUFTA	Canada-US Free Trade Agreement
EC	European Community
EMS	European Monetary System
FDI	Foreign Direct Investment
FIRA	Fideicomisos Instituidos en Relación con la Agricultura
FTA	Free Trade Agreement
G7	Group of Seven
GATT	General Agreement on Tariffs and Trade
GDP	Gross Domestic Product
GSP	Generalised System of Preferences
IDB	InterAmerican Development Bank
IIE	Institute for International Economics
IRCA	Immigration Reform and Control Act
IRS	Increasing Returns to Scale
ISI	Import-Substituting Industrialisation
LAC	Latin America and the Caribbean
LDCs	Less Developed Countries
LIBOR	London Inter-Bank Offer Rate
MERCOSUR	Mercado Común del Sur
MFN	Most-Favoured Nation
MNCs	Multinational Corporations
NACE	North American Commission on the Environment
NADBAF	North American Development Bank and Adjustment Fund
NADBANK	North American Development Bank
NAFTA	North American Free Trade Agreement
NICs	Newly Industrialised Countries
NRDC	National Resource Defence Council

NWF	National Wildlife Federation
OECD	Organisation for Economic Cooperation and Development
PAN	Partido de Acción Nacional
PEMEX	Petróleos Mexicanos
PRD	Partido de la Revolución Democrática
PRI	Partido Revolucionario Institucional
PRONASOL	Programa Nacional de Solidaridad
R & D	Research and Development
SEDESOL	Secretaría de Desarrollo Social
SEDUE	Secretaría de Desarrollo Urbano y Ecología
TELMEX	Teléfonos de México
TRQs	Tariff Rate Quotas
TRIMs	Trade Related Investment Measures
US	United States
USA	United States of America
USTR	United States Trade Representative

LIST OF TABLES

2.1	Summary of Recent Findings on the Economic Effects of NAFTA	13
4.1	Foreign Ownership Limits for Mexican Financial Institutions	49
5.1	Mexico-US-Canadian Agricultural Trade	61
5.2	Fruits and Vegetables: Area Planted and Production, 1980-90	65
5.3	Mexico's Access to the US Market: Tariff Elimination	71
6.1	Undocumented Migration by Source to the United States through Main Points of Entry, 1989-1993	87
6.2	Socio-Economic Profile of Mexican Undocumented Immigrants, 1988-1993	89
6.3	Destination of Mexican Undocumented Immigrants by Year of Border Crossing, 1988-1993	90
6.4	Undocumented Mexican Migrants that have Worked in the United States by Type of Employment, 1988-1993	91
9.1	Direction of Latin American Trade in Manufactures	135
9.2	Direction of total Latin American Merchandise Trade	136
9.3a	Net Transfer of Financial Resources to Latin America and the Caribbean, 1992	137
9.3b	Portfolio Investment in Latin America	137
9.4	Major Manufacturing Exports from Latin America and Mexico	139
9.5	Destination of Manufactured Exports from Latin America, 1990	140
9.6	Destination of Manufactured Exports from Mexico and Brazil, 1990	141
10.1	Mexico's Trade with OECD Countries	154
10.2	Foreign Direct Investment in Mexico	155
12.1	NAFTA: Schedule of Tariff Reductions	184

LIST OF FIGURES

10.1   Mexico's Trade with the World   152
10.2   Foreign Direct Investment by Sector   156

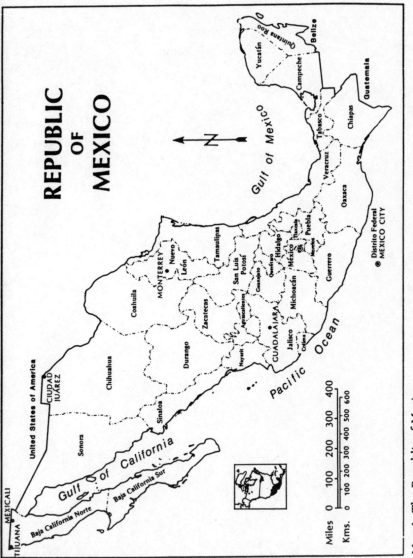

Map 1. The Republic of Mexico.

CHAPTER 1

INTRODUCTION*

Jesús Silva Herzog

The Mexican and the international press have transmitted to us almost on a daily basis the pros and cons of the NAFTA debate, drawing on the discussion in the United States. A group of senators expresses its support one day for the agreement, while the next a group of ecologists rejects the treaty and so on. The Mexican stock market reacts and people in Mexico become a little nervous. Under these circumstances, it is important to stand back from the daily events and reflect on the longer term implications of the whole process.

Let me state from the beginning that I am convinced that the Free Trade Agreement between the United States, Canada and Mexico will be approved by the legislative bodies and will come into effect. If it is delayed for a few months, it is not really that important. The key point, in my opinion, is that it is something that will happen sooner or later. And the basic reason for this is that the Free Trade Agreement is beneficial for all three countries.

Let us see why. The idea of a Free Trade Agreement between Mexico and the United States, not to mention a trilateral agreement to include Canada, was considered completely unrealistic just a few years ago. Asymmetry between the two countries was the essential element. In my public capacity** I was approached on several occasions to see if there was a possibility of starting negotiations for a Free Trade Agreement between the USA and Mexico. My negative position was immediate and reflected the majority view – I would say the unanimous view – expressed by all public officials in Mexico including the president. What has happened that today the perception in the three countries has changed so dramatically?

---

* Keynote speech delivered at the Conference 'Mexico and the NAFTA: who will benefit?' organised by the Institute of Latin American Studies, May 1993.

** [Editors' note] For details of the author's public career, see p. xi.

Several factors provide the explanation. First, the formation of economic regional blocs in different parts of the world has altered the situation. The European Community, the United States and Canada with the Free Trade Agreement (CUFTA) signed just a few years ago and, of course, the Japanese and the neighbouring southeastern countries of the Pacific all represent powerful trading blocs with a strong regional emphasis.

Secondly, the United States has a certain degree of backwardness in terms of technology, and it has been losing its competitiveness *vis-à-vis* Japan and Europe. The reasons for this are multiple and I am not going to explore them in depth.[1] However, the United States has the possibility of compensating for its deficiencies in competitiveness and in technological progress through the use of Mexican natural resources and cheap labour. This will permit the US economy to increase exports and to improve its international competitiveness.

In the case of Canada I would say that basically the same reasons apply, with the additional argument – a very important one – that Canada cannot afford to stay away from a bilateral agreement between Mexico and the United States.[2]

For Mexico, it would be impossible to think of a Free Trade Agreement with the United States without the transformation of the economy that has taken place in the last decade. That basic and profound transformation, I would say, has two essential elements. First, it is a redefinition of the role of the state and with that I imply basically a new attitude towards fiscal imbalances. The improvement that has taken place in Mexico in the fiscal accounts is really without precedent within our own economic history, and I do not know of any other country that in the space of a few years has gone from a fiscal deficit equal to 17 per cent of Gross Domestic Product to the surplus we now enjoy. Within that transformation the privatisation process, as well as the deregulation that was initiated just a few years ago, has played a major part.

The second basic element in this profound transformation is the change in trade policy. Until recently we were one of the most closed economies in the world and yet we are now probably one of the most open. We have changed from an import substitution model to an export-led growth model, in which Mexico is seeking a better insertion and integration into world markets.

What has happened as a consequence of this economic change? I would say that, in general terms, it has been quite favourable. We have resumed growth and the average rate of GDP increase in the last four years has been over three per cent (this is faster than the rate of population growth). We have been relatively successful in the control of inflation, coming down to 11 per cent in 1992, and the expectation is that we will end 1993 with a single-digit inflation rate. The foreign debt problem, which was at the centre of my concerns for many, many years (fortunately not any more), has not disappeared, but it is within much more manageable levels. We have also been able to attract very substantial amounts of money, through capital repatriation, portfolio investment and direct investment.

The Mexican basic economic strategy at this point, I think, can be encapsulated in the following points: (i) to foster exports as the most important vehicle to sustain economic growth in the coming decade; (ii) to attract investment, both domestic and foreign; (iii) not to be absent from the regional economic blocs; and (iv) to pursue the permanence of the present economic strategy.

If you look at those four points, I think it will be more clearly understood why we entered into Free Trade Agreement negotiations. A Free Trade Agreement with the United States and Canada will stimulate the fulfilment of those four basic objectives. So I think we can say that the negotiations for the Free Trade Agreement are not an invention; it is not something that came out of the sky, but it was a direct consequence of the basic economic strategy that the country has followed during the last decade.

The North American Free Trade Agreement (NAFTA) will create a market with 360 million people and a GDP of $6 trillion. This makes it a little bigger than the present European Community. Yet in interpreting these figures, we have to be careful, and we have to recognise the relative importance of the United States. Sometimes we tend to ignore that fact in our efforts to make the numbers look impressive, but we have to remember that they are very large because of the United States.

The objectives of NAFTA are to facilitate trade, expand investments and, in general, as an essential element, to improve the international competitiveness of Mexican, Canadian and US firms. The agreement does not establish a Common Market. This is a confusion that exists among many who tend to compare the European Community, which is a Common Market, with the Free Trade Agreement between Mexico, the USA and Canada. They are two different animals.[3] However, we have to recognise that the Free Trade Agreement between our three countries is more than the orthodox or traditional Free Trade Agreement, because it includes other elements that are usually not included. It has been claimed that the area is not going to become a fortress and that it will be open to multilateral trade. This has been reiterated again and again, but I am not completely sure. I think we have to put a question mark, with the final answer depending on what are the basic attitudes of the other regional economic blocs. Furthermore, I do not see anybody who can make a clear projection of what the basic attitude of those economic blocs is going to be in the next few years. Sometimes we see signals that appear to underline the commitment to multilateral trade, but the following day we see some decisions which suggest the opposite.

The asymmetry between the USA, Mexico and Canada – Mexico is one twentieth the size of the US economy – is quite clearly recognised and was the basic reason why we tended to reject the idea of a Free Trade Agreement some years ago. This asymmetry is recognised in several clauses of the agreement and is included in many of NAFTA's articles. There is an opinion in several quarters that, although this asymmetry is acknowledged, it is not properly recognised. There are some commentators who express the view that the asymmetry should have been more widely reflected in the agreement. It is true that NAFTA does contemplate a gradual approach with some safeguards in different sectors. There are, however, some opinions that consider that this gradualism is not enough and that in various sectors and regions of the Mexican economy the time span that is contemplated is too short.

In terms of market access the asymmetry is clearly recognised. The USA and Canada will eliminate tariffs in the first years on 84 per cent and 79 per cent of Mexican exports respectively and Mexico will do the same for 43 per cent of the US and 45 per cent of Canadian exports. Rules of origin have been a very controversial issue. There are many academics and trade experts who consider that the rules of origin in NAFTA are too complicated[4] and of an essentially restrictive character that tries to protect the firms within the region in an excessive manner. In general terms, NAFTA adopts a rule of origin that requires 50 per cent inputs in gross output to qualify for tariff-free treatment, and in certain sectors it goes above that.

Three sectors are particularly controversial. The first is textiles, which has been a very complicated trade issue all over the world and where we in Mexico have installations that are quite old and obsolete. It is estimated that about 850,000 workers are employed in the textile sector in Mexico and, even though there are some safeguards to protect certain branches, there is the perception that it is probably one of the sectors that will be most seriously affected. We have already seen in Mexico the closure of certain textile plants that were completely obsolete, lacking modern technology and using quite evidently the high protection that the former trade policy gave them.

The automobile sector is another controversial area. This is a highly sensitive issue in the United States, because it is considered that there is going to be a movement (as has already been happening in recent years) of automobile plants away from the United States into Mexico, which is already a significant exporter of automobiles, small trucks and automobile parts. It is worth remembering that the automobile sector is now the second most important export earner in the Mexican economy, just after oil. It would difficult to imagine this ten years ago.

The third sector is agriculture. In Mexico we still have approximately 25 per cent of the labour force in agriculture, although its contribution to Gross Domestic Product is less than 10 per cent. This differential between agriculture's contribution to employment and output demonstrates the need to improve productivity in the rural areas and this will necessarily mean a reduction in the number of farmers working the land. The liberalisation process here under NAFTA is much more cautious and in the case of maize, for instance, where half of the rural population is still engaged in production, fifteen years for full liberalisation is permitted. However, in my opinion, this is one sector where we have to be very careful, because it can produce important social and political impacts once trade barriers are eliminated, despite the fact that liberalisation is to be introduced in a long-term manner.

NAFTA also addresses the question of energy in various chapters. Mexico has maintained the sovereignty of its oil resources in very difficult negotiations with the United States, even though we have opened up the petrochemical sector in several areas to foreign trade and investment.

Land transportation and financial services – one of the sectors that is usually not included in a Free Trade Agreement – are also included, as is the problem of the environment. Nowadays, it is fashionable to talk about the environment. Ten years ago, or even five years ago, I think very few people would have been talking about it in trade negotiations and yet the environment is, for the first time as far as I know, included as a separate chapter in NAFTA. The real question is whether it is going to be complied with or not, but the fact that for the first time this question of the environment is included in a Free Trade Agreement makes NAFTA very pioneering.

Who will benefit from NAFTA? It is a very difficult question, but I think it is completely right to assume that in a process like this, involving a public policy change like the one we are talking about, there are going to be losers as well as winners. The basic issue is whether the net result between losers and winners will be positive for the three countries. I am one of those convinced that the gains will outweigh the losses.

For the United States I think the most important advantage is that it will permit an improvement in its export performance and increase exports to Mexico in a more dynamic manner than has already been happening in the last few years. In 1985 exports from the USA to Mexico were $13 billion. Last year (1992) they were $40 billion. We must also remember that each billion dollars of additional exports produces about 20,000 additional jobs in the United States. Carla Hills, the trade negotiator of the Bush Administration, has claimed that more than 600,000 workers in the USA owed their jobs to exports to Mexico. With the Free Trade Agreement, and I am quoting, this will increase to more than a million in a few years. So additional exports to Mexico will improve the employment rate in a significant manner. Sidney Weintraub, a professor of the University of Texas at Austin, has pointed out – and I think it is an interesting statement – that when Latin America sells to the United States, they spend the proceeds heavily on US goods and services. When the Asians sell to Latin America, they buy from Japan. And when the Europeans sell to Latin America, they buy among themselves. So, Weintraub concluded, Latin America – and Mexico in particular – is the best opportunity for the USA. It is a very important export market for US producers.[5]

The second advantage for the USA is in investment. NAFTA provides US firms with the possibility of combining skilled workers with semi-skilled workers and cheap labour, creating a kind of production-sharing scheme between the two countries. Let me mention that 35 per cent of Japanese firms use several countries in order to produce a final product. In the United States that number comes down to five per cent. I think, therefore, that we are going to see a tremendous expansion of activities of US firms within Mexican borders in order to achieve a combination of natural resources, high technology and – we have to recognise it – cheap labour. In 1990 the average industrial wage in Mexico was 12 per cent of the US equivalent. Even if the Mexican real wage increases seven points above the US rate, it will take ten years for it to reach 25 per cent of the US wage. And it will take 20 years to reach half of the US wage.

Another advantage, of course, is the US need to consider the stability of its southern neighbour, which is very important. One of the few advantages of the debt crisis of the early 1980s was that we were recognised for the first time as the southern neighbour. It sounds exaggerated, but it is not. Now, after the debt crisis, the US administration feels very clearly the importance of having a stable southern neighbour, and that means a growing southern neighbour – as well as the permanence of the new economic strategy that we have followed.

Without any doubt there is going to be a certain loss of jobs in the United States. However, the additional exports of the USA to Mexico and Canada will increase employment. Most experts coincide in the fact that the net effect will be positive. Net employment gains will also be positive in the other two countries. However, this does not ignore the fact that there are going to be dislocations by regions and by sectors. And there are going to be certain regions and certain sectors in the economy of the three countries that are going to be seriously affected.

In Mexico, we hear it said that the agreement will improve our export capacity and the possibility of the Mexican economy to attract additional flows of foreign and domestic capital; this, of course, will improve our competitiveness and improve employment conditions. The other advantages are better access to the US market, more certainty (which is a very important element), more credibility that what we plan to do today – to export to the United States – will be maintained as our policy and keeping the legal framework in place so that disputes can be resolved. There is no question that NAFTA is an investment attraction. It is an important factor that explains the flow of capital that has gone to Mexico in the last years.

The net change that is expected from 1990-1995 in the US trade balance with Mexico is an additional $9 billion surplus. The net change in the Mexican trade balance from 1990-1995 is an additional deficit of $12 billion. On the employment side the USA will gain 170,000 jobs net, taking both the ones that are lost and the ones that are created, and Mexico will gain over 600,000 new jobs from 1990-1995.[6]

What is the position of the other countries such as Japan? Mexico has become attractive to Japanese investors who consider the possibility of selling not only in the Mexican market, but also using their Mexican base to sell to the US and Canadian markets. Mexico can become a bridge, a door to the US and Canadian markets, as well as representing a huge market of 85 million people who are gradually improving their standard of living. Here we have to recognise some political considerations in the relationship between Japan and the United States. Is this relationship strong enough for Japanese investment to use Mexico as the bridge to enter the United States? We do not have a clear answer yet. With the European Community I think the relationship will depend on what degree of improvement in international competitiveness is obtained by the United States as well as the trade diversion and trade creation effects. Here, also, I think it is very difficult to make a final judgment.

There is a feeling in Latin America that Mexico has forgotten Latin America, has turned away from its southern neighbours, preferring to look north. Let us mention that, taking together all the trade that we have with Latin America, it amounts to less than five per cent of the total. Nevertheless, I would expect that the coming into effect of NAFTA will reinforce the traditional Mexican attitude towards making a closer economic and financial relationship with Latin America. In the last few years we have been playing a very active role in the region: the Free Trade Agreement with Chile, the Free Trade Agreement negotiations with Colombia and Venezuela, the framework agreement with Central America. These are just examples of a political recognition of our need to foster closer relations with a region with which we have political, cultural and historical relationships.

Now, what will be the final effects of NAFTA? We really do not know. It will take time for the effects to be felt and we have the erroneous tendency quite often to judge a measure like this by the results that will be seen in the first or second year. Instead, we will have to be very cautious and to give enough time for the real consequences to be felt in the three countries. In that respect I think we will have to keep our sense of proportion and not to reach hasty judgements. After twelve months we will not really be able to say that it is a failure or a success. It is a type of agreement that takes quite a considerable time for the full consequences to be felt.

Notes

1. [Editors' note] See chapter 3 for a discussion of this issue.
2. [Editors' note] See chapter 11 for a detailed analysis of this argument.
3. [Editors' note] A Common Market involves a Common External Tariff (CET) and full factor mobility (including labour). A Free Trade Agreement involves neither a CET nor factor mobility.
4. [Editors' note] The rules of origin represent some 200 pages of text in the Agreement.
5. [Editors' note] Although the USA runs a huge trade deficit, it has a surplus with Latin America – most of which is explained by trade with Mexico.
6. [Editors' note] These figures come from studies done by the Institute for International Economics in Washington, DC. See for example Hufbauer and Schott (1993).

PART I

ECONOMIC DIMENSIONS

CHAPTER 2

MEXICO AND NAFTA:
ECONOMIC EFFECTS AND THE BARGAINING PROCESS[*]

Jaime Ros

This chapter addresses some of the key issues involved in understanding recent trade negotiations between Mexico and the USA, as well as their significance for the process of economic integration in North America. Although the focus of attention will be the background of the negotiations for a North American Free Trade Agreement (NAFTA), these aspects are but the most visible manifestation of powerful regional and global trends: the end-of-century drive toward creating regional trading blocs in an increasingly competitive international economy, and the long process of 'silent integration' that has increasingly interwoven the economies and societies of Mexico and the United States for several decades.

Some of the more significant aspects of this process of integration are: (a) the increasing demographic and economic density along Mexico's northern border, where the main economic activity since the mid-1960s, the *maquiladora* export-processing plants, today accounts for around a fifth of Mexico's overall industrial employment and non-oil exports;[1] (b) the fast expansion, since the 1970s, of intra-firm and intra-industry trade in a number of industrial sectors including, most prominently, the automobile industry; and (c) Mexico's transformation, since the early 1980s, into the third largest trading partner of the United States. Moreover, the strengthening of economic ties has been accompanied by broader trends, which have increasingly brought the two societies closer together: since 1960, a growing population mobility has led more than two and a half million Mexicans to migrate legally to the

[*] This is an updated version of an article originally published in the *Journal of Interamerican Studies and World Affairs*, vol. 34, no. 2, Summer 1992. Parts of it have been presented in different versions at various conferences and workshops. I wish to acknowledge, in particular, comments by Roberto Bouzas, Guillermo O'Donnell and John Weiss.

USA, several million more to migrate illegally, and a much greater number to cross the border more than once. Not surprisingly, half of the Mexicans interviewed in 1986 – i.e., 40 million Mexicans if the poll was a representative one – admitted to having a family member in the United States.[2]

The chapter is divided into three sections. Using Mexico's experience with trade liberalisation as background, the first section examines the likely economic effects of NAFTA and reviews the large body of recent research on the subject. The findings of this research form the basis for a critique, in the second section, of the conventional analysis of Mexico-US trade negotiations. The third, and concluding, section summarises the main arguments.

Trade Gains and Capital Mobility: a Review of Recent Studies on the Effects of NAFTA

Table 2.1 summarises the research findings of some of the main quantitative studies on the likely effects of NAFTA.[3] The studies are classified in a 3 by 2 matrix. The two columns refer to (1) those studies (or scenarios within a study) that assess the size of income gains under the assumption that no additional investment will flow to Mexico as a result of NAFTA; and (2) those studies which aim to evaluate the income gains arising from both the effects of bilateral trade liberalisation and from additional capital flows.[4] The three rows refer to the type of model used. The first two rows represent computable general equilibrium (CGE) models that make different assumptions about technology: either (1) models with constant returns to scale (CRS); or (2) increasing returns to scale (IRS) and dynamic models. The third row refers to macro-economic models with a high degree of sectoral disaggregation.

Each entry in the matrix can then be seen as referring to different types of income gains. For example, in the first column the first entry focuses on classical gains from inter-industry trade and specialisation; the second entry focuses on 'new trade theory' effects from economies of scale and intra-industry trade (IRS models), as well as on investment effects arising from lower prices of capital goods (dynamic models); and the third entry refers to dynamic macro-economic effects.

There are two major *lacunae* to point out. The first is the absence of dynamic models with endogenous productivity growth effects; all we have are good theoretical reasons to expect that they can be very important (especially when interacting with capital flows), both from the findings of 'new growth theories' and the older insights of Allyn Young and Nicholas Kaldor among others.[5] The second is that no research has been conducted on macro-economic dynamics with endogenous capital inflows. The only macro-economic model in the matrix (that of INFORUM Report (1991)) assumes that no additional investment flows will result from NAFTA.

Table 2.1
Summary of Recent Findings on the Economic Effects of NAFTA[a]

	No capital mobility	Capital mobility
CGE-CRS[1]	< 0.5%	4.6%-6.4%
CGE-IRS and dynamic[2]	1.6%-2.6%	5%-8.1%
Macro-economic models[3]	small employment losses	

[a] As a percentage of Mexico's GDP except as otherwise indicated.

Sources:
[1] KPMG Peat Marwick (1991), Hinojosa and Robinson (1992), Roland-Holst, Reinert, and Shiells (1992, scenario with removal of tariffs only)
[2] Brown, Deardorff and Stern (1991a), Sobarzo (1991), Young and Romero (1992)
[3] INFORUM Report (1991)

By looking down the first column, one can draw the following conclusions about the income gains in the absence of increased flows of investment:[6]

1. Very small gains from trade as a result of resource reallocation and specialisation in foreign trade (first entry in first column). These welfare gains, resulting from further specialisation of the economy according to its current comparative advantage, turn out to be less than 0.5 per cent of GDP (approximately 0.3 per cent in the first two studies quoted and even less in the third).[7]

2. Larger but still small gains from economies of scale, industry rationalisation and lower prices of investment goods (1.6-2.6 per cent of GDP, in the scenarios without capital mobility of Brown et al (1991a), Sobarzo (1991), and Young and Romero (1992)).

3. Small but negative macro-economic adjustment effects.[8] In the INFORUM Report (1991), these are reflected in a fall of employment levels of less than one per cent over the base scenario and somewhat larger when the agreement includes a full liberalisation of agricultural trade.[9] Since the Report's methodology (unlike the rest of the studies) does not clearly separate the 'Ricardian' allocative gains from the macro-economic effects arising from 'Keynesian' processes of adjustment, which depend on initial absolute advantages, the interesting conclusion emerging from this study is that the latter (taking for granted that the former are positive) would, in the absence of additional flows of foreign investment, clearly be adverse for Mexico.

This set of results, which many have found disappointing, is in fact hardly surprising in the light of Mexico's recent experience with trade liberalisation – an experience which has involved even more drastic trade policy changes than those expected from NAFTA. As discussed elsewhere,[10] inter-sectoral resource reallocations in that experience have been remarkably smooth and, for this reason, have generated substantial allocative efficiency gains.[11] The effects on technical efficiency have been even more significant (though not always positive) as a result of processes of industry rationalisation in some manufacturing sectors. Finally, macro-economic effects have indeed been negative, though so far hardly visible, because they have been concealed, since 1989, by the turnaround of the capital account. It is worthwhile emphasising this point in the context of a free trade agreement. The presence of negative macro-economic effects arising from a NAFTA is, after all, highly plausible. As pointed out by the INFORUM Report (1991), Mexico's initial trade barriers, and thus its trade concessions, are larger than those of the United States, a factor which modifies the initial advantages determining the dynamics of adjustment in favour of the latter country. Moreover, the size of these negative effects is likely to be larger today than at the time of the INFORUM Report simulations, since the present real exchange rate is much less favourable than that in 1989 to mitigate the macro-economic adjustments resulting from greater integration.

Mexico's recent experience also tells us something about one of the major *lacunae* noted in recent research. This is, essentially, that endogenous productivity effects arising from virtuous circles between exports, investment and productivity growth have so far been largely absent. In fact, the only spectacular change that took place in Mexican industry in the 1980s was the export and investment boom in the auto industry which, however, had little to do with trade liberalisation and is likely to continue with or without a free trade agreement (see Ros, 1992b).

If the gains from trade are marginal, what are the real benefits that Mexico can expect from the agreement? The answer to this question can be found by looking across columns in Table 2.1. When the same models are simulated with additional capital flows, one can see the gains from NAFTA multiplied by at least a factor of four: in the IRS and dynamic models, for example, the move is from the 1.6-2.6 per cent to the 5-8.1 per cent range as a percentage of Mexico's GDP.[12]

Increased capital mobility is, of course, what both the public and the trade negotiators have in mind when talking about NAFTA. The difficulty here, however, is that one also moves onto shaky ground. The consequences of NAFTA in this area refer to those incremental capital flows that will result from two kind of effects: (1) those related to gaining more stable and preferential access to the US market causing investment diversion away from the rest of the world, and (2) those arising from reduced uncertainty about Mexico's trade and investment policies (the effects of locking in current policies) and the ensuing reduction of risk differentials between Mexico and the United States. These consequences are, by their very nature, very difficult to measure. A common difficulty is that they are both highly dependent on the assumed reference scenario which itself is very uncertain. In the first case, for example, the benefits to Mexico of preferential access to the US market may be eroded to a greater or lesser degree depending on whether similar preferences are extended to other countries in the Western Hemisphere and elsewhere, and on the effectiveness of the rules and institutions governing the multilateral trading system.[13] The gains from a more stable and predictable market access depend on how much 'insurance' NAFTA mechanisms will in fact provide against procedural protectionism by the United States (and, in this respect, it is known that Mexican, as well as Canadian, negotiators had to waive their original expectations).

With respect to the second type of effects, the uncertainties surrounding the reference scenario are compounded by the uncertainty about how investment will respond in a completely new situation for investors.[14] One way of addressing the problem is to speculate on the basis of the experiences of other countries as well as of Mexico's own recent experience with investment liberalisation (the 'historical method' favoured by Hufbauer and Schott, 1992b). Spain's experience of massive capital inflows has often been alluded to in this regard. Leaving aside the reservations that one could introduce after the crises of the European Monetary System (EMS) in 1992/3, I find this analogy unconvincing for at least two reasons. First, and despite the uncertainties, it seems implausible that Mexico's investment policies would be much different without NAFTA or that NAFTA will generate large investment diversion effects as a result of preferential market access.[15] In the words of the authors of the INFORUM Report:

> 'In Spain, the low wage country was soon to gain access to the well-protected markets of Europe. Moreover, with the prospect of "Fortress Europe" after 1992, many American firms were eager to get a toe-hold inside the Community. By contrast, Mexico has long had virtually unrestricted access to the US markets outside the apparel, textile, and steel industries. Foreign investment in Mexico for producing for export has been almost unrestricted since 1972. Further, there is no prospect of a "Fortress USA" looming ahead. An FTA would remove, at most, the prohibitions on majority foreign ownership for firms investing in Mexico to sell in Mexico. In fact, there seem to have been important exceptions to the present prohibitions. For example, all of the six major automobile companies operating in Mexico have over 90 percent foreign ownership. While an FTA would, we believe, improve the atmosphere for foreign capital in Mexico, there seems little reason to believe that the inflow would be massive.' (INFORUM Report, 1991).

It could be argued that, despite these differences, recent capital inflows into Mexico have been, after all, comparable in size to those of Spain some years ago. However, a substantial fraction of recent capital inflows into Mexico (repatriation of capital and foreign portfolio investment) appear to be of a one-time nature and mostly related to privatisations of public enterprises and state banks since 1989. The time pattern of capital inflows and privatisation revenues – increasing slowly in 1989-90, accelerating sharply in 1991-92 – clearly suggests this conclusion. Privatisation revenues began to decline in 1993 and, under current plans, will soon practically disappear.[16] While recent trends suggest that rising foreign direct investments may offset part of this decline, the point remains that most of the recent capital inflows have been determined by factors other than anticipations of NAFTA.

Even if a free trade agreement were to bring about substantial additional foreign investment, such a scenario raises a number of issues which have been neglected by recent research. What would be the time pattern of these flows and the associated macro-economic dynamics? Would these inflows come at a steady rate of, say, an additional $US 5 billion a year, or, even better, at a gradually increasing rate year after year? Or would foreign capital come in massively in the initial stages (say, an additional $30 billion in 3 years) only to be followed by a sharp slowdown? If that should be the case, would the capital inflows lead to a strong appreciation of the peso, causing severe damage to large parts of Mexican industry, followed by a period of acute balance of payments difficulties as capital inflows subsequently decline sharply? Or, on the contrary, would they put more gentle pressure on the exchange rate which, combined with the abundance of investment finance, would give an impetus to the technical modernisation of Mexican industry? The importance of these issues can hardly be exaggerated especially if, considering the recent EMS crises, the analogy with Spain is consistently pursued.

The lack of answers to these questions is closely related to the *lacunae* mentioned at the beginning of this section.[17] The uncertainty that surrounds them arises, primarily, from the fact that, while relaxing balance of payments constraints on economic activity but, simultaneously, enhancing vulnerability to external shocks and reducing autonomy in macro-economic policy, a higher degree of capital mobility is generally a mixed blessing, with the net balance of its effects depending on initial conditions. As a result, the interactions between endogenous productivity growth effects and macro-economic dynamics can cut both ways and broaden the range of possible outcomes enormously. This is likely to be the case especially when the process of economic integration involves two countries at such disparate levels of economic and technological development as Mexico and the United States. The possibility in such circumstances of unstable paths of either convergence or cumulative divergence in the technological and wage gaps is precisely the source of fears among public opinion in both countries: the fear in the USA that low wages give Mexico an absolute advantage in most industries, and the analogous fear in Mexico that the technological lead of US industry could have adverse consequences for Mexico's industrial development. To make reference again to the experience and future prospects of the southern European countries in the new European Community, it is worth quoting from the authors of a recent book on the subject:

'It was difficult to foresee which of the two divergent paths the new members would take. The double shock of accession and 1992 might drive their economies into depression or accelerate their modern-isation. Unfortunately, economic principles do not point to a pre-determined outcome. In fact, the degree of indeterminacy is so great that the outcomes may range between brilliant achievement and big difficulties' (Bliss and Macedo, CEPR Bulletin 1990, p. 7, quoted by Helleiner, 1991).

However, together with the mechanisms making for cumulative processes, there are stabilising forces that will operate with particular strength in the case of economies which are also very different in size: capital mobility will tend to stabilise any increases in technological and wage gaps that could occur if initial adjustments are detrimental to Mexico, while Mexico's limited capacity to absorb foreign capital (relative to the size of the US economy) would tend to slow down any processes of technological convergence that could take place in the opposite scenario. In any case, the set of forces operating is so complex, and the uncertainty about their potential interactions is so great, that economic analysis by itself is insufficient. This points to the need to give much more attention to problems of macro-economic dynamics and management during the transition and, more generally, to the role of the state and social institutions in the integration process.

The Bargaining Process and the Issue of Mexico's 'Side Payment'

Reaching an agreement involves a negotiation process when the parties face different sets of incentives. The analysis of this process has focused on the huge differences in economic size between the United States and Mexico, and has been inspired by the well-known neoclassical proposi-tion according to which, in the economic integration between a large and a small partner, the resulting gains from trade flow disproportionately to the small country. The reason is that the large country's domestic price structure will dominate in the determination of post-trade prices.

Thus, it is only in the small country that significant changes will take place in the structure of relative prices. Since the static gains from trade flow from the re-allocation of resources resulting from the expanded opportunities for specialisation associated with the new structure of relative prices, those benefits will accrue largely to the small economy. Adjustment costs (temporary unemployment of capital and labour in losing sectors) will also be greater in the small country; these are short-run costs, however, which should be more than offset by the long-term gains of the new, and more efficient, allocation of resources.

In any case, the large country has not much to gain since its price structure remains largely unaffected, and no new opportunities for specialisation arise from the opening of trade. The conclusion that follows, then, is that there is nothing significant for the large country in the agreement (Dixit, 1987). From this perspective, the next step would be to ask what concessions would Mexico have to make to reach an agreement, and examine the non-trade incentives, or even non-economic incentives, that could lead the United States into a free trade agreement. Some interesting analyses along these lines can be found in, for example, Helleiner (1991) and Cameron (1991).

The issue of 'side-payments' (or entry fees) – to 'bribe' the larger partner into an agreement – is an important one because it influences the likelihood and shapes the content of a final agreement. However, it is clear from our review of recent research on the effects of a NAFTA that this approach puts too much emphasis on the gains from trade that Mexico can derive from a greater integration with the United States. Ultimately, the basic reason why the premises of this approach, from which the issue of a 'side payment' by the small partner arises, are openly at variance with the findings of recent research is quite simple: the *status quo ante* involves two economies already deeply engaged in trade with another to the point that they are, respectively, the first and third trading partners of the other and, furthermore, have rather uniform tariff structures, low average tariffs (of the order of four per cent in the United States and nine per cent in Mexico), and non-tariff barriers for only a few products. Under these circumstances, the gains from additional trade opportunities are likely to be small – the price structure of the large country already dominates that of the small country – and need not necessarily flow disproportionately to the small economy. The latter's market is certainly smaller, but it is also more protected initially and, in a free trade agreement, its trade concessions will therefore be greater: its initial average tariff is higher, and quantitative restrictions affect a larger percentage of its tradable output.

As discussed in the first section, the most significant benefits that Mexico can expect from NAFTA arise from the higher degree of capital mobility that it is likely to produce. More precisely, the most important incentive is avoiding the costs which Mexico would otherwise have to suffer in the absence of the external capital inflows it needs to sustain its recent, and still fragile, economic recovery. Starting from this premise has, in turn, important implications for the analysis of the bargaining process. Contrary to the conventional approach, it means that NAFTA provides an important economic incentive for the United States. This is simply the counterpart of the inflows of additional capital Mexico is expecting: the relocation by US industry of some productive processes, especially in those sectors most seriously threatened by foreign competition in the domestic market, into a low-wage country with location advantages, in order to face the intensification of international competition that has taken place over the past two decades.[18]

Does this mean that there is a basic symmetry – rather than the asymmetry assumed by the conventional approach – in the bargaining position of the two parties? I believe the answer to this question is negative, but for reasons that are very different from the conventional ones.

The first reason concerns the distribution of benefits and costs within each country. In the United States, the benefits from a NAFTA are perceived to be very unevenly distributed: precisely because they have to do with mobility of capital rather than trade, the gains are seen to flow disproportionately to capital, up to the point where labour could actually lose from the agreement. Although it can be argued, as some studies have done, that labour would benefit in the long-run (compared to what would happen otherwise, which may be of cold comfort to those affected), the transitional adjustments introduce an element of conflict between the short-run and long-run interests of US labour. This factor is not present in Mexico where the distribution of gains is perceived to be more uniform. Labour benefits from the creation of new jobs and/or higher wages resulting from flows of additional investment, while local capital benefits indirectly from the faster pace of economic expansion that those investments make possible without, at the same time, being threatened by them, since they will flow primarily into activities that complement those of local capital.

These conclusions are violated in only a few, but important, areas which have been, precisely for this reason, points of conflict in the negotiations: (a) the agricultural sector that produces basic foodstuffs (particularly maize), where rapid liberalisation would have negative effects on rural employment and (b) financial services, where foreign investment would compete directly with local capital.[19]

The resulting asymmetry is, however, much more the consequence of perceptions than of reality and would not carry much weight without another factor that makes the eventual losers in Mexico structurally weaker in the political arena than their counterparts in the United States. This, to put it bluntly, can be stated as follows: in the United States, the eventual losers can put their case more loudly, have it taken more seriously, and have their votes counted more fairly than is true in Mexico.[20] This second difference carries paradoxical implications. The very strength of the executive and the lack of democracy in Mexico's political and social system have the effect of weakening its position at the bargaining table. The US negotiators have been, in fact, strengthened by a divided government and public opinion at home, as well as a more open and vigilant society. In facing a difficult issue, they can always reject the Mexican position as politically unviable and unacceptable to the US Congress. An analogous threat by Mexico's negotiators would totally lack credibility because, among other reasons, it is the Mexican Senate (whose members, with few exceptions, all belong to the government party) which had to ratify the agreement.

The conclusion that follows from analysing these asymmetries is that, after all, and as expected by the conventional approach to the bargaining process, Mexico may find itself in the position of having made additional trade or non-trade concessions in order to reach an agreement.[21] What then was this 'side-payment' likely to have been?[22]

One of the characteristics of NAFTA is that its agenda and coverage extend well beyond the realm of tariffs and other barriers on trade in goods. Since the early 1980s United States policy has tried to include in trade negotiations a set of (then) 'new issues' which included trade in services, foreign investment regulations and protection of intellectual property rights. The United States was successful in pushing these issues in bilateral agreements – such as the Free Trade Agreements with Israel and Canada – as well as into the negotiating agenda of the Uruguay Round in GATT, where they were seen, at the time, as the counterpart for opening developed countries' agricultural and textile markets in the global deal offered to the developing countries.

While the protracted state of multilateral trade negotiations makes these issues obvious candidates to extract 'side-payments' in exchange for enlarged access to the US market,[23] two factors turn them into 'not-so-new issues' in the context of US-Mexico relations and, therefore, reduce their value as 'side-payments' from the standpoint of the United States. First, the divergence of negotiating and policy objectives between the United States and Mexico has shrunk considerably in recent years, as a result of changes in Mexico's economic strategy (particularly the enhanced role of foreign investment in it), US 'aggressive unilateralism' (section 301 and 'super' 301), and international financial institutions' conditionality. Secondly, provided a pessimistic scenario as the final outcome of the Uruguay Round of trade negotiations does not prevail, it is likely that the preliminary agreements already the subject of bargaining in the multilateral arena will be eventually brought into operation. Any bilateral agreement with the United States is thus expected to go beyond what may emerge from a multilateral deal.

That the US policy stance weighs larger today is suggested by the new ground covered by NAFTA in these areas. The outcome of NAFTA has already gone beyond CUFTA[24] which, for instance, had left out intellectual property rights and 'grandfathered' many existing restrictions on foreign investment regulations and services. It is also likely to represent substantial 'incremental' departures from what may eventually emerge in GATT: a development which should be properly assessed against the background that, as a US concession, the opening of the textile and agricultural sectors has less significance for Mexico than for a typical developing country (in fact, as argued above, Mexico is likely to be a loser from agricultural trade liberalisation). It is also worth noting, however, that NAFTA covered less new ground in some areas than might originally have been expected. In the realm of foreign investment regulations, Mexico maintains restrictions in the energy sector and, to a lesser extent, in financial services.[25]

More fundamental perhaps, as an illustration of the asymmetrical relationship between the two bargaining parties, is the inclusion in the NAFTA negotiations of a set of 'brand-new issues' going beyond trade in services, investment regulations and intellectual property rights. A major ingredient in this agenda is the concern with environmental and labour standards, which have come to occupy a prominent role in negotiations and domestic debates.[26] The prominence acquired by these brand-new issues also reflects the concern for adjustment costs in the United States, which so far has attracted much more attention than the transitional problems in Mexico. Yet the latter, especially as a result of agricultural trade liberalisation, are likely to be far more difficult to tackle than the former. This 'political economy gap' between how costs are distributed and how they are being addressed is, as argued above, rooted in the asymmetries of the operation of domestic coalitions in the two countries.

Conclusions

The current drive towards greater economic integration in North America can only be fully understood in the context of powerful regional and global trends: (a) the long process of 'silent integration' which has increasingly interwoven the economies and societies of Mexico and the United States for several decades; (b) the shift in the ideological climate in the 1980s, with its broad repercussions for economic policy-making and the thinking on development strategies; and (c) the end-of-century trend towards creating regional trading blocs in an increasingly competitive international economy. With this background in mind, this discussion focused on the more proximate determinants of the NAFTA negotiations, as well as as on its likely economic consequences for Mexico.

In the first section it is argued that it is in the domain of capital movements, rather than trade, that one should look for the real levers behind the integration movement. The fact that traditional gains from trade are clearly of a second order should not lead, however, to an overestimation of the benefits to be derived from a higher degree of capital mobility in North America, and thus to neglect a number of important and difficult questions on this subject that much recent research has failed to ask. This discussion has not attempted to answer these questions, but has tried to identify the sources of our uncertainty. These have to do with the difficult issues of macro-economic dynamics in a context which has hardly any historical precedent, involving, as it does, two economies so different in size and in technological and economic development.

The second section examined the bargaining process, modifying the premises which have inspired previous analyses. Rather than emphasising the gains from trade and their appropriation by the smaller trading partner, as the conventional approach to the bargaining process does, the discussion focused on other important asymmetries between the two countries: the perceived distribution of gains within each country and their very different political systems. The resulting asymmetries in the operation of domestic coalitions in the two countries have determined, in particular, a 'political economy gap' between how costs are distributed and how they are being addressed, and contribute to explain why policies to deal with adjustment costs in the USA are receiving more attention than in Mexico. This analysis suggested then that the conclusions of the conventional approach are, after all, essentially valid: because the bargaining process involves asymmetrical players, its successful conclusion requires additional concessions by Mexico. Going one step further, one may explain, on this basis, the new ground covered by NAFTA in the areas of trade in services, foreign investment regulations and protection of intellectual property rights and why these 'not-so-new issues', which looked like privileged candidates to play the role of 'side-payments', are now being complemented by the 'brand-new' issues of environmental and labour standards.

Appendix

Consider the following game, in which each of the negotiating parties has the option of making, or not making, non-trade concessions. The different possible outcomes are described in the following schema:

MEXICO

		CONCESSIONS	NO CONCESSIONS
U S A	CONCESSIONS	Mutual concessions	US additional concessions
	NO CONCESSIONS	Mexican additional concessions	No concessions

Each entry in the table describes a different type of agreement. The second entry in the second row can be seen as the *status quo* or as an agreement without non-trade concessions (something similar to the 1987 bilateral agreement with some trade innovations).

The outcome of the bargaining process depends on each party's structure of preferences with respect to the different possible outcomes, and this structure, in turn, depends upon the nature of the concessions. To give an example, consider the case of 'minimum concessions', defined as follows. On the part of Mexico, this would amount to the inclusion in the agreement of GATT's new issues, i.e. the opening of the services sector, the alignment of intellectual property laws, and the liberalisation of trade-related investment measures (TRIMs), such as domestic content requirements, which are still present in a few Mexican industries. On the part of the United States, this would imply eliminating from the agenda such issues as those relating to environmental regulations and labour standards, which, if included, would tend to increase the costs of relocating plants or of shifting new investments to Mexico. Thus defined, and for the reasons given in the text, the most likely structure of preferences would be:

Mexico
Mutual concessions (4)
US additional concessions(3)
Mexican additional concessions(2)
No concessions (1)

United States
Mexican additional concessions (4)
No concessions (3)
Mutual concessions (2)
US additional concessions (1)

To simplify, we have assigned values of 1 to 4 to each of the possible outcomes. The payoff matrix corresponding to the preference orderings would then be as follows:

MEXICO

		CONCESSIONS	NO CONCESSIONS
U S A	CONCESSIONS	2,4	1,3
	NO CONCESSIONS	4,2	3,1

The United States has a dominant strategy (no concessions) – and Mexico does too (concessions!). The outcome of the bargaining process is clear: Mexico makes additional concessions. The assumed preference orderings are the reason behind this outcome:[27] the assumption, in particular, that Mexican negotiators value highly an agreement based on mutual concessions and very little the *status quo* (no concessions), an assumption which is related precisely to the non-trade nature of the benefits from NAFTA (arising from the investment liberalisation which negotiators would be willing to undertake in any case) and a powerful executive which does not face a strong domestic opposition to making additional concessions. This contrasts with the more traditional preference structure being assumed for US negotiators, yielding decreasing values as the outcomes involve higher net concessions and a relatively high value assigned to the *status quo* resulting from a stronger domestic opposition, the uneven distribution of the gains within the country and a divided government.

Notes

1. *Maquiladora* exports refer to exports net of imported inputs (i.e. equal, roughly, to the *maquiladoras'* value added). The gross exports from *maquiladoras* account for a fraction of total exports well beyond 20%.
2. Data on both migration and the results of the interviews (conducted by the New York Times in the Fall of 1986) are quoted by Pastor (1992).
3. The focus is on economy-wide studies, although some references in the text will be made to sector specific studies. For broader, more detailed surveys, on which Table 2.1 relies, see Brown (1992), Hinojosa and Robinson (1992), and Weintraub (1992).
4. The additional capital inflows may be either assumed exogenously (in which case the authors simply speculate on the likely path of these flows) or modelled endogenously and thus determined simultaneously with other economic variables.
5. One exception is the work of Kehoe (1991). However, the basic reference scenario (with which the free trade simulation is being compared) does not appear to be clearly defined.
6. In what follows, the discussion focuses on Mexico. In most studies, the gains for the USA are much smaller, roughly 10 times less than for Mexico as a percentage of the corresponding GDP.
7. The only exception is the scenario with elimination of tariffs *and* non-tariff barriers in the study by Roland-Holst, Reinert and Shiells (1992). In this case, income gains rise to around 2% of GDP. This suggests the reasonable conclusion – strengthened by the Trela and Whalley (1991) study of the textile and steel industries – that the removal of non-tariff barriers has a greater potential impact than the removal of tariffs; on the subject, see Lustig (1993).
8. More precisely, by adverse macro-economic effects I mean that, at the initial real exchange rate, the income and employment contraction in the losing sectors more than offsets the income and employment gains in the expanding activities, thus creating an aggregate contraction of output and employment compared to the base scenario. While this is to be generally expected from a unilateral trade liberalisation without compensating capital inflows (thus the need for a real devaluation to accompany it), this need not be the case in a

bilateral trade liberalisation or when liberalisation takes place in the presence of compensating capital inflows.

9. Levy and van Wijnbergen's (1991a) study of agricultural liberalisation also shows income and employment losses among the poorest segments of the Mexican population if agriculture (maize in particular) is fully liberalised.

10. See Ros (1992b).

11. This is even more so in reality than in the models' simulations. The latter tend to ignore the very different degrees of international capital mobility among industries (the old issue of the multinational corporations) and, thus, often fail to capture the actual direction of structural change. Very frequently, indeed, the processes of reallocation of resources in the post-liberalisation period have gone in the opposite direction to the one expected by traditional trade theory (see Ros 1992b).

12. In the CGE models with constant returns to scale the impact of additional investment inflows is much larger (15 to 20 times larger than the impact of removing trade barriers), but this is partly because the income gains, in the simulations in which no capital inflows are assumed, are so minute.

13. More effective multilateral arrangements are likely to erode the margin of preferences exchanged by NAFTA partners and thus reduce investment (as well as trade) diversion.

14. These difficulties, incidentally, exist quite independently of whether one models investment flows as exogenous or endogenous (see footnote 4), because, in the last case, one can only speculate about how much risk and interst rate differentials are likely to fall.

15. On this last subject, see Primo Braga (1992) and Bouzas and Ros (1993).

16. For this reason, it should not be surprising to see the conclusion of the NAFTA negotiations followed by a decline, rather than an increase, in Mexico's capital account surplus, even though NAFTA by itself is likely to improve Mexico's capital account surplus (compared with what would happen otherwise).

17. To be sure, the southeastern box in Table 2.1 is not completely empty. On the current stability of Mexico's present macroeconomic setting and the problems of macro-economic management created by the prospect of NAFTA, see Harberger (1991), McLeod and Welch (1992), Ros (1992a), Tornell (1990).

18. It can be argued that this option also exists without a free trade agreement. But the same can be said about Mexico: it is its wage and location advantages that, with or without a free trade agreement, make it attractive to foreign investors. By strengthening the guarantee of access to the US market and of stable rules for foreign investment, what NAFTA does, in essence, is to reinforce trends that have been present, on both sides of the border, for many years now.

19. See Hufbauer and Schott (1993), chapter 3, on the content of NAFTA in these two areas. On its implications for Mexico's maize producers and for the local banking system, see respectively chapters 5 and 4.

20. This 'political economy gap' (Bouzas and Ros, 1993) is probably reinforced by another asymmetry between small and large partners. As argued by Oye (1992), in the smaller partner, and in contrast to unilateral trade liberalisation, preferential agreements with a large trading partner will tend to stimulate coalitions in favour of liberalisation prompted by their interest in obtaining access to the larger country's market. These coalitions can balance the influence of those negatively affected by preferential trade liberalisation, therefore limiting the need to devise policies to compensate for the costs of adjustment. In the larger country, instead, sectors negatively affected are likely to be more vocal than those benefiting from market access to the small country's market.

21. As shown in the Appendix, the same conclusion follows from a rather more formal analysis of the bargaining process.

22. The remainder of this section relies on Bouzas and Ros (1993).

23. Helleiner (1991) mentions that, in the case of the Canada-United States free trade agreement (CUFTA), Canada's concessions had to do, precisely, with access for US foreign investors and an agreement on services.

24. On the subject, see Hufbauer and Schott (1993).

25. Thus, and not withstanding the convergence, differences in the USA and Mexico's negotiating positions did not disappear completely. In addition to selective restrictions on foreign investment, trade in some services of interest to Mexico (like labour services) remains also an area of divergent negotiating positions.

26. Pastor (1992) has argued – quite correctly – that the environmental and labour issues are not only part of the US agenda, but also of Mexican society. However, what is most relevant for the analysis of the bargaining process is that these issues are clearly not part of the agenda of the Mexican negotiators, who, on the contrary, tend to view them as external political pressures. Moreover, their inclusion in the bilateral agenda involves an explicit or implicit loss of national autonomy in policy design, which is unlikely to be equally shared by the two bargaining parties.

27. In turn, the preference orderings depend, of course, on the way in which 'concessions' have been defined. Depending on their exact content, the result could have been 'mutual concessions' or even 'no concessions'. If, for example, additional concessions had been defined as free labour mobility in one case, and a complete opening of the energy sector on the other, 'no concessions' would probably have been a dominant strategy for both parties with the *status quo* as the final outcome.

CHAPTER 3

IS MEXICO A BACK DOOR TO THE US MARKET OR A NICHE IN THE WORLD'S LARGEST FREE TRADE AREA?[*]

Adriaan Ten Kate

There is a general perception among US trade policy makers that the United States is surrounded by a world of unfair traders.[1] In the first place come the Japanese, supplying most of their manufactured products at unfair prices and disguising such dumping practices with a multilayered trading system at home, which makes it far more difficult to detect eventual price differentials between domestic and foreign sales.[2] Another way in which the Japanese often try to circumvent anti-dumping regulations, it is alleged, is by establishing subsidiaries in target markets which obliges trade officials in the importing countries to dig deep into the cost structures of the involved firms in order to prove that dumping has taken place.

In the second place there are the newly industrialising countries (NICs) of the Far East. From the US point of view those countries are full of engineers trained abroad, who do not respect intellectual property rights and who are thus in a position to offer a great variety of counterfeits at prices far below what would otherwise have been possible. They are considered the free-riders on the results of US research and development (R & D).[3]

Thirdly, there is the European Community which is blamed for its enormous subsidies to agriculture that give rise to exports at unfair prices of a great number of agricultural and agroindustrial goods, among which French wines have been an outstanding example in recent years. US trade officials seem to consider this issue so important that they have

[*] The author wishes to thank Fernando de Mateo for his comments on an earlier version of the chapter and Amarilis Morales Paredes for doing the typewriting. The opinions expressed are the author's own and do not necessarily coincide with those of the institution to which he is affiliated.

been ready to risk a trade war and the survival of the GATT system for it.

Last, but not least, there are the developing countries. Although many of these countries have recently been involved in a profound process of trade liberalisation, quite a few of them still keep tight trade barriers in force which contrast sharply with the preferential treatment accorded by the USA to imports from the developing world. Moreover, most developing countries strongly oppose the US insistence upon 'graduation' from preferential treatment as the level of development increases.[4]

It is beyond the scope of the present chapter to examine whether, or to what extent, this point of view is correct. Still, there is little doubt that this perception explains the main stream of US foreign trade policies during the last two decades. These policies are characterised by the following elements:

(a) an increasingly complex and sophisticated anti-dumping and anti-subsidy system, administered by the US International Trade Commission and the Department of Commerce

(b) retaliation against counterfeiters and against countries raising unjustified trade barriers to imports proceeding from the USA

(c) apart from countervailing duties imposed upon subsidised imports, an active policy to persuade foreign governments to withdraw export subsidies

(d) actions urging foreign governments to impose 'voluntary' export restraints under the threat of applying more severe measures against injuring imports (for example, under escape clause provisions)

(e) a strong insistence at both bilateral and multilateral levels not to limit trade negotiations regarding goods, but also to consider trade in services – such as banking, insurance, telecommunications, transport – foreign investment regulations and the protection of intellectual property rights.

In spite of all these actions – a number of them even quite successful – everything seems to indicate that the USA is losing the battle for international competitiveness and is quite aware of it. Although US labour productivity grows steadily, the increase does not keep pace with productivity growth in many other countries, particularly Japan and some European countries.[5] As a consequence, during the last fifteen years the United States has seen itself faced with enormous deficits on the commodity balance in spite of an almost continuous depreciation of the US dollar against the yen. Moreover, economic growth has been relatively weak and, after having been the richest country of the world for an extended period of time following the Second World War, US GDP *per capita* is now lagging behind that of Switzerland, Japan and some Scandinavian countries.[6] Add to the foregoing the general discomfort about the achievements of multilateral trade negotiations during the last two decades, and one approaches the context in which the US government decided to attempt closer trade relationships with its immediate neighbours, first in the form of a free trade agreement with Canada, which entered into force in 1989, later followed by the initiative to include Mexico in the scheme by means of a North American Free Trade Agreement (NAFTA).

For the USA the main objective of such an agreement is to come to a further division of labour between the three nations, to exploit the greater market size generated by NAFTA and to exploit to a greater extent the comparatively cheap labour abundantly available in Mexico. In particular, the latter element is distinct from the argument for free trade with Canada, where labour costs are comparable to those in the USA. In fact, it is hoped that access of US firms to cheap Mexican labour will contribute substantially to enhance US competitiveness *vis-à-vis* Japan and the European Community.

Although there are no indications that the NAFTA agreement will be used to raise protectionist walls against the rest of the world, care has been taken that the preferences derived from it are kept among the parties to the agreement and do not leak away to 'fourth' countries. Otherwise, Mexico might easily become a backdoor to the US market and, given the circumstances sketched above, it will be clear that that is not exactly what the US government had in mind with the agreement.

The purpose of the present chapter is to give a brief review of those provisions of the NAFTA agreement that are meant to keep NAFTA preferences exclusive. First, some attention is paid to rules of origin. Then, the regulations with respect to temporary imports and free trade zones are considered. In the third place, I examine to what extent rules for trade in services and foreign investment are designed to limit NAFTA privileges to the member countries. Fourthly, some general aspects are discussed regarding dispute settlement mechanisms and the degree of Mexico's autonomy to determine its future trade regime with respect to non-NAFTA countries independent of the other parties to the NAFTA agreement. To conclude the chapter, the argument is advanced that Mexico's attractiveness for foreign investments does not so much derive from an easy access to the US market under NAFTA, but rather from the possibility for Mexico to become a growth pole in the largest free trade area of the world.

Rules of Origin

Rules of origin are the instrument 'par excellence' to limit the privileges of preferential trade schemes to the eligible parties. Preferential tariffs, in general, and free trade agreements and customs unions in particular, always go together with rules making sure that the goods to receive preferential tariff treatment have origin in the region. Generally speaking, there are four criteria that are used to determine whether or not a good originates from a certain country. The first one is hardly controversial and applies to goods that are *wholly obtained or produced* in the country (region) under consideration. Problems arise, however, when the goods at stake contain inputs imported from outside the country (region). In that case the general rule is that the good must have undergone substantial transformation to be conferred origin. What is meant by 'substantial transformation' is usually governed by one of the following three criteria or by a combination of them:

  (i)   value added content,
  (ii) change in tariff classification,
  (iii) degree of processing.

Value added content rules require that at least a certain percentage of the value of the good is added in the country (region) of origin. Value added rules have been applied in practically all economic integration schemes and systems of tariff preferences around the world. However, they suffer from a number of serious shortcomings from an administrative point of view. To mention a few, there is no single generally accepted way of product-wise cost accounting: what concepts are allowed to form part of the cost of a product and how are they to be valued? Then, there is the problem of chaining: what to do about inputs acquired in the country which themselves have an imported content? Moreover, such information is not readily available to customs officials so that thorough company auditing may be necessary to solve conflicts about origin.

In the US-Canada Free Trade Agreement (CUFTA) there was an important shift of emphasis towards the change in tariff classification criterion. According to such a criterion, a good originates in a country if the processing of imported inputs causes a change in tariff heading qualified to that end by the agreement. In that case, the agreement must define exactly which changes confer origin and which do not.

The enormous advantage of the latter sort of rule is that they are easy to administer and that the information necessary for their application is readily available with customs authorities. An inconvenience is that tariff classification schemes, such as the harmonised system, are usually not designed for the purpose of origin rules. In specific cases a single tariff position may cover both inputs and the final product even when substantial transformation is required to turn the former into the latter. In such cases, change of tariff classification rules have to be supplemented by other criteria.

To give an example of the criterion, it may be established that the weaving of yarns into fabrics by itself confers origin, or the fabrication of apparel from fabrics, or only both of these processes together. Conversely, certain processes may be qualified as insufficient to confer origin. Such is usually the case with processes such as simple packaging or combining and the mere dilution of materials with water or other substances.

Origin rules in the NAFTA agreement are a combination of the four criteria mentioned above with a heavy predominance of the change in tariff classification criterion. During the negotiations everything was done to establish the NAFTA origin rules as much as possible upon changes in tariff classification and to limit the use of the other criteria to exceptional cases where the change in tariff classification rule obviously does not work. The result is a set of fairly detailed origin rules mainly based upon changes in tariff classification. For chemicals, machinery and equipment, transport equipment and some durable consumption goods these rules are occasionally complemented with value added requirements. For textiles and garments, some minimal processing is needed to confer origin to the goods.

Generally speaking, NAFTA rules of origin are designed in such a way as to preclude the circumvention of US tariff barriers by bringing in products through Mexico. In fact, a fair amount of processing in Mexico is necessary to make the goods eligible for reduced or zero tariff treatment in the USA under NAFTA. Moreover, it should be borne in mind that, on average, Mexican Most-Favoured-Nation (MFN) tariffs –i.e. tariffs applicable to imports from 'fourth' countries – are higher than US tariffs, which makes it even less likely that triangulation of goods *via* Mexico would result in a net tariff gain.

Still, one might think that triangulation of goods *via* Mexico could be rendered profitable by making use of temporary import provisions exempting them from import duties in Mexico, in the case that those goods were exported to the USA after some transformation conferring origin. This possibility is discussed in the following section.

Temporary Import Schemes

Most countries of the world have temporary import provisions granting duty-free entry to products that are exported afterwards, or to products that are incorporated into other products to be exported afterwards. Mexico has several such schemes in force. In the first place there is a drawback provision granting tariff refunds to occasional exporters. Second, there is the PITEX programme providing for duty-free importation of parts and equipment to firms selling the major part of their output abroad. Then, there is the well-known *maquila* programme which is mainly used by US and Japanese-owned assembling plants taking advantage of cheap Mexican labour and exporting the assembled products to the USA. In terms of tariff treatment the *maquila* programme grants roughly the same privileges as the PITEX schemes, but there are some additional advantages regarding accounting requirements. Finally, there are a number of free trade zones which are essentially different from the so-called foreign-trade zones in the USA. In fact, Mexico's free trade zones comprise extended areas, often with a resident population, enjoying preferential tariff treatment for a great number of goods, not all of them to be re-exported later. The foreign trade zones in the USA, on the other hand, are legally rather than spatially separated from the customs territory and are not allowed to have a resident population; i.e. no private consumption is allowed within the zones.

If such temporary import schemes should be kept in force under NAFTA, fourth countries would be able to bring their goods duty-free into Mexico, then apply a transformation conferring origin and finally export the transformed good under the NAFTA reduced rate to the USA. This would imply, however, an unfair competition against US manufacturers performing the same transformation in the USA, because the latter have to pay US import duties on non-NAFTA imported inputs.

That is the reason why the NAFTA agreement eliminates the

temporary import schemes,[7] at least as far as duty-free importation of inputs for export of the final product to one of the other members of the agreement is concerned.[8] That is to say, if the final product is exported to the USA or Canada, whether or not under NAFTA reduced tariffs, the import of inputs to Mexico proceeding from fourth countries can no longer be duty-free and will pay Mexican tariffs. Thus, if final products enter duty-free in the USA or Canada, full Mexican tariffs must be paid on inputs.

Regarding the *maquila* programme, the NAFTA agreement is not explicit. However, according to what has been agreed concerning the elimination of temporary import schemes, which is to become effective by the year 2001, the *maquila* programme would lose its *raison d'être* by that time, given the fact that duty-free importation of intermediate inputs is its main pillar. With regard to US-based *maquila* plants, there is no reason for concern because the privileges they are enjoying at present form part of the privileges NAFTA will eventually grant to all Mexican industries. Thus, the distinction between *maquila* and normal industries will gradually disappear. Japanese-owned *maquila* industries, on the other hand, will lose their duty-free import rights by the year 2001.

It is interesting to observe that under the present *maquila* regime Mexico is, to a certain extent, a backdoor to the US market for Japanese firms, particularly in those cases where the final products are eligible for preferential treatment under the Generalised System of Preferences in the USA. In that respect, NAFTA, rather than opening new back-doors, closes existing ones.

Services and Direct Foreign Investment

In spite of the fact that the USA has insisted upon the inclusion of services and foreign investment in multilateral trade negotiations since the early 1980s, liberalisation of trade in services and, to a lesser extent, in Direct Foreign Investment is still in its infancy. This is hardly surprising when one considers the fact that impediments to trade in services and to Direct Investment are usually less explicit than impediments to trade in goods and are also often even difficult to identify. Whereas most obstacles to trade in goods are in the form of tariffs and outright licences, barriers to trade in services are usually embedded in a framework of domestic regulations which is completely different from one service industry to another. That makes it difficult to establish general – i.e. non-sector-specific – criteria that go beyond declarations of good intentions. To give an example, for trans-border trade in services NAFTA establishes, as a general principle, national treatment (or MFN treatment if this should be better) to service providers from parties to the agreement, but in order for Mexico to become an important exporter of, for example, health services to the USA,[9] the main impediments are to be found in US domestic medical and social insurance regulations. Such problems are not touched upon by the NAFTA agreement, but are crucial to a further liberalisation of trade in services.

Also the NAFTA rules of origin for trade in services are of a very general nature and comparable to a 'substantial transformation' criterion for trade in goods with no further specification of what is meant by substantial transformation. For trade in services, origin is not conferred on the services traded, but on the providers of those services. The official phrasing (Article 1211.2) is that '[...] a Party may deny the benefits (of the agreement) to a service provider of another Party where the Party establishes that the service is being provided by an enterprise that is owned or controlled by persons of a non-Party and that has no substantial business activities in the territory of any Party [...]'.[10] There is a similar rule of origin for Direct Foreign Investment (Article 1113).

Dispute Settlement

Another way in which companies of fourth countries might try to take advantage of NAFTA privileges in the USA or in Canada is by establishing themselves in (or by shipping their goods through) Mexico: such an establishment may provide access to dispute settlement procedures that are supposedly superior to the existing dispute settlement mechanisms of the international trading system. To give an example, in conflicts about countervailing duties and anti-dumping actions the Mexican government may appeal under NAFTA to a binational panel for a review of final resolutions, whereas fourth country governments would have to go through the cumbersome and time-consuming dispute settlement procedures of the GATT system. However, access to NAFTA procedures for the settlement of conflicts about unfair trade practices is limited to goods for which the competent authority of the importing Party determines whether they are from another Party (Article 1901.1). That is to say, NAFTA rules of origin do not apply in such cases, rather it is the importing country that decides. Evidently, the importing country is supposed to be bound by GATT rules in this respect.

In spite of the fact that it is still far from clear how the dispute settlement mechanisms of the NAFTA agreement are going to work out in practice, there is hardly any reason to believe that fourth country companies could take an easy advantage of the supposed superiority of NAFTA dispute settlement regulations over those prevailing in the multilateral trading system.

Trade Barriers vis-à-vis 'Fourth' Countries

Another important consideration coming to the minds of potential 'fourth country' investors in Mexico is the question of what will happen to the Mexican foreign trade regime *vis-à-vis* fourth countries once NAFTA is fully operational. Will it be liberalised further? Will NAFTA privileges be fully or partly extended to non-members to the agreement? Or will trade barriers become tighter?

In principle NAFTA does not limit the autonomy of its member countries to determine future foreign trade policies with respect to non-member countries. It is implicity understood, however, that no member country can liberalise its MFN treatment ahead of, or at the same pace as, the agreement. If one of the member countries should do so, the other members would lose their preferential margins and their incentives to remain party to the agreement would no longer be so strong. Generally speaking, further liberalisation by a member country of its MFN treatment erodes the preferential margins of the other members. If, and to the extent to which, Mexico should incorporate NAFTA privileges in its new general Law on Foreign Investments, 'fourth country' investors would have the same rights as US and Canadian investors, by which the latter would lose preferential margin.[11] Likewise, if the Multi-Fibre Agreement should come to an end in the near future, Mexico's preferential margins as an exporter of textiles and textile products to the USA would be reduced significantly.

On the other hand, MFN tariff reductions by a member country, particularly for intermediate and capital goods, improves the competitive position of its industries with respect to that of the other member countries. As mentioned earlier, the fact that Mexican manufacturers pay tariffs on imported intermediates and capital goods that are, on the average, higher than tariffs paid by their US and Canadian competitors places them in an unfavourable competitive position. In fact, in any free trade agreement there is an implicit incentive for the higher tariff countries to reduce their tariffs to the levels prevailing in countries with lower tariffs. In other words, there is an implicit incentive to become a Customs Union with tariff levels lower than those prevailing at the moment the free trade agreement became effective. [12]

There is, however, another argument favouring the point of view that the NAFTA agreement will lead to more liberal MFN treatment in general. The argument is that, for administrative reasons, it is often impractical to confine NAFTA treatment to member countries. For example, more flexible customs procedures negotiated under NAFTA that require a reorganisation of the customs system come automatically to the benefit of fourth countries; and so does further homogenisation of standards etc.

Altogether, there are hardly any reasons to believe that the NAFTA agreement would convert the North American region into a closed trading block. On the contrary, there are a number of indications pointing in the direction of a further liberalisation of trade with the rest of the world. This is particularly likely to happen to Mexico which, in terms of average MFN tariffs, is still more protected than the other members to the agreement.

Conclusions

Summarising the above discussion, it is unlikely that Mexico will become a backdoor to the US market with the entry into force of the NAFTA agreement. On the one hand, it is not among the aims of the agreement to convert Mexico into an easy export platform to the USA and Canada, and on the other, it is definitely not in the interest of the USA to allow such a thing. Therefore, it is not surprising that there are a number of clauses in the agreement intended to keep NAFTA preferences exclusive to the parties. In the sphere of trade in goods, they are explicitly expressed in the form of rules of origin and the elimination of temporary import provisions. As far as trade in services and in foreign investment are concerned, there is a kind of equivalence to an origin rule – albeit of a more general nature.

This does not imply that Mexico would lose its attractiveness as a target for foreign investment. In the first place, whenever foreign investors establish subsidiaries in Mexico and perform substantial transformations which confer origin, their products will be allowed to move freely around in the NAFTA region under NAFTA preferential treatment. In the second place, and perhaps more importantly, the Mexican domestic market in itself forms an interesting target for foreign investment.

Even though the growth rate of Mexico's GDP has remained modest and has not yet responded fully to expectations, there are a number of formidable achievements to be mentioned both in the macroeconomic environment and at the microeconomic level. In the macroeconomic sphere inflation, which reached an annual rate of 159 per cent in 1987, has been reduced dramatically and has now reached levels below 10 per cent on a yearly basis. Likewise, the financial deficit of the public sector, which reached levels of over 15 per cent of GDP in 1982 and 1986, was subsequently reduced continuously until it turned into a surplus (estimated at 0.5 per cent of GDP for 1992), even without taking into account the once-and-for-all benefits from privatisation of public enterprises. As a consequence, the debt position of the government has been brought back to reasonable proportions and, at present, compares favourably with that of the USA and Japan.[13]

Also, interest rates on the domestic financial markets have shown a steady decline both in nominal and real terms since 1987. Nontheless, domestic interest rates – not only the interest rates for depositors but also, and even more so, the rates for borrowers – remain much higher than in the USA, Europe and Japan and form an important obstacle to an acceleration of economic growth. In particular, the small and medium-size enterprises that have no easy access to dollar financing are suffering from this situation.

Another important point of concern in the macroeconomic environment is the high deficit on the current account of the balance of payments, which reached 6.5 per cent of GDP in 1992. This deficit is to a great extent attributed to capital inflows and could easily be financed by them. In view of the high level of international reserves held by the Central Bank and of the continuing capital inflows, this deficit does not seem to pose a serious problem in the short-run. In fact, leaving the exchange system to market forces, there is a trend towards peso *appreciation* rather than *depreciation*. In the medium-term, however, certain adjustments might become necessary particularly if the response of exports to the structural reforms should turn out to be slower than expected.

In the microeconomic environment there has been a pervasive trade liberalisation since 1985, converting the Mexican economy from a very closed one in the early 1980s to one of the most open regimes of the developing world at present.[14] Moreover, privatisation of public enterprises and attempts to deregulate sectors, such as the trucking and the financial sector among others, have introduced a hitherto unknown element of competition in the economy. The role of competition as a motor of economic progess will be further enhanced by the anti-trust law, which became effective in June 1993.

Since 1988 the Mexican economy has been involved in a profound process of structural adjustment, of which the transition costs are felt at present and the fruits are to be reaped in the future. This is appropriately recognised by the international financial community which continues to direct significant capital flows to the Mexican economy. Under those circumstances, everything seems to indicate that, with or without NAFTA and with or without a peso devaluation during the present administration, the president entering into power in December 1994 will inherit a better starting position than any of his predecessors.

Notes

1. An exhaustive description of the objections of US trade politicians against foreign-trade practices of other countries can be found in the annual reports of the United States Trade Representative (USTR) on Foreign Trade Barriers. See, for example, USTR (1992c).
2. See, for example, Finger and Murray (1990).
3. For a review of the intellectual property issue in the Uruguay Round, see Stern (1987).
4. The graduation issue is discussed by Hindley (1987).
5. According to the OECD, annual labour productivity growth in the USA over the period 1960-1973 was 2.2% as compared to 8.6% in Japan and 4.1% in European OECD countries. Over the period 1973-1979 these figures were 0.0, 3.0 and 2.6% respectively and from 1979-1988 0.8, 3.2 and 2.0% respectively. See OECD (1990), Table 46.
6. See World Bank (1992b), Table 1.
7. The elimination of temporary import provisions does not become effective until the year 2001. Thus, there is a transition period of seven years during which duty-free imports under those schemes remain possible.
8. Evidently, the temporary import provisions remain in force for exports to fourth countries.
9. One may think particularly of labour-intensive health services such as the care of elderly or of permanently disabled people.
10. The idea is to avoid operations through so-called 'mail-box companies'.
11. Evidently, the USA would be the main country affected, being by far the most important source of foreign investments in Mexico.

12. Effectively, for the reasons set out here, individual member countries would benefit from lowering their MFN tariffs whereas tariff increases would require joint action. Apart from that, since MFN tariffs are bound under GATT, they cannot be increased at will.

13. According to preliminary estimates by the Bank of Mexico for 1992, net public debt amounted to 29.0% of GDP of which 20.3% corresponded to foreign debt. See Bank of Mexico (1993), Table 6.

14. For a review of the trade liberalisation process, see Ten Kate (1992).

CHAPTER 4

THE MEXICAN FINANCIAL SYSTEM AND NAFTA

Ignacio Trigueros

One outstanding characteristic of the Mexican financial system is the prevalence of high financial margins, especially in the retail segment of the market. Average 'implicit' protection for Mexican banks ranges between 33 per cent and 90 per cent compared to the USA and Canada, and for retail services it is close to 200 per cent.[1] The combination of a very restrictive regulatory framework until the end of the 1980s and the lack of competition between intermediaries appears as the most logical explanation of this feature.

These factors have also contributed to the rather weak development of the Mexican financial system, which in principle has a considerable potential for growth. However, this potential is to a certain extent at risk, since with the present trend towards the globalisation of financial services, there is the possibility that an increasing fraction of financial services will migrate from Mexico to the markets in which financial margins are smaller.

During the last few years some steps have been undertaken to remove restrictions affecting the operations of banks and other financial intermediaries. The continuous progress in terms of macroeconomic stability-reflected, for instance, in the achievement of a 10 per cent annual inflation rate by May 1993 – should also strengthen the performance of the financial system. However, the movement towards the promotion of a more competitive environment has been mixed. Thus, the lifting of various restrictions regarding the determination of interest rates, service fees and the allocation of funds, as well as the privatisation of the banking system, in principle promote more competition in the financial system. However, with the constitution of financial groups, the merging of stock brokerage firms with banks has increased the degree of concentration.[2] Additionally, regulation still imposes high entry barriers in the form of minimum capital requirements, discretional ruling in the authorisation of new intermediaries or restrictions on the establishment of foreign financial firms, which discourage competition.[3]

The negotiation of the financial services chapter of NAFTA was especially important in this context. The elimination of restrictions on the operation of foreign financial firms in Mexico could contribute to increase the degree of competition, widen the variety of products offered in the market and improve the technology utilised in the provision of financial services in the country. At the same time, the trend to locate financial activities in the markets which offered more advantages would be reinforced by the closer commercial and financial links between the countries of North America that would emerge from the Agreement. Considering the complementarity between financial services and other productive activities, the effect of these processes on the cost of credit would be a key factor in determining the fate of many Mexican firms facing increased foreign competition as a result of the Agreement.

On the other hand, some of the recent reforms to the Mexican financial system suggest caution with regard to the promotion of increased foreign competition. A distinctive feature of financial services is that the displacement of domestic firms by foreign competition might have adverse effects on other productive activities. The failure of specific financial firms often undermines the public's confidence in the financial system as a whole, impairing the performance of the economy and exerting pressure on the government's budget. In general, this type of situation does not necessarily call for direct restrictions on competition. However, given that Mexican banks have been under the control of the private sector for only a short period, after being controlled by the government for almost ten years, they are probably still vulnerable to foreign competition and this justifies a certain degree of protection.

To what extent the section on financial services in NAFTA deals with each of these issues is the subject of this chapter. The first section provides a brief discussion of the implications of trade in financial services in general. This discussion establishes that the specific effects of the liberalisation of trade in financial services are, from a conceptual point of view, to some extent uncertain, while the available empirical evidence does not allow any sharper judgement in this respect. However, from the analysis of the nature of trade in financial services it is possible to identify both how different features of the liberalisation scheme could affect the operation of the financial system and the way the processes of deregulation and liberalisation interact with each other to determine the effects of the latter. The second section presents a summary description of the financial services chapter, emphasising the modalities, timing and structure of the liberalisation package negotiated by Mexico, and the third section presents an assessment and analysis of its implications. The conclusions of the chapter are presented in the final section.

Trade in Financial Services: Some General Features

International trade in financial services takes place in either of the following forms: (a) a resident of country X utilises financial services offered by an intermediary located in country Y (which gives rise to the so-called cross-border transactions); or (b) an intermediary of country Y establishes operations in the financial markets of country X. Each of these forms of trade, and the interactions between the two, gives rise to a different set of issues regarding its effects on the operation of the financial system.

For instance, given Mexico's geographical situation, and the technology utilised in financial transactions, the restrictions on cross-border trade are in general absent or ineffective and, therefore, the outcome of the negotiations in this area would appear to be of limited importance. However, the increased presence of foreign financial intermediaries, and the development of deeper commercial relations as a result of NAFTA, will probably open new opportunities in this area and the trend towards the globalisation of financial services may therefore be strengthened.[4]

The economic consequences of this trend will be determined by whether the relocation of financial activities responds to cost advantages or to regulatory arbitrage. Under the former, comparative advantage is being exploited and gains from trade are being attained. However, regulatory arbitrage could result in efficiency losses and, under certain circumstances, to strong distortions in the functioning of the financial systems.[5] A certain degree of harmonisation in the way financial activities are regulated in the countries involved is necessary to avoid this problem.

Besides this feature, because of the way in which financial activities are organised, it is difficult to assess any other consequences of increased liberalisation of trade in financial services. A key factor in this respect is the fact that in financial services transactions, and especially in those that pertain to the retail segment of the market, the presence of a network of branches, or the relationship between intermediaries and its clients, constrains the entrance of new firms. Additionally, price competition may act against the profits of new entrants, because of problems of adverse selection. Given these barriers to entry, foreign intermediaries might limit their participation, at least in the short-run, to serve clients of their home country, or to operate in the wholesale segment of the market, where those barriers are lower.

In the case of Mexico, the service of domestic banks to clients in the USA or Canada has been relatively unimportant, while the participation of foreign intermediaries in the wholesale segment of the market (through cross-border transactions) has been intense, especially in the last few years. From this perspective, the effects on the functioning of the domestic financial system of allowing the establishment of foreign financial firms in Mexico could be marginal. For foreign financial intermediaries it would be costly and risky to enter the most profitable segments of the market, limiting their efforts either to activities that would be hardly considered by Mexican financial intermediaries or to types of operation in which they already have a significant participation through cross-border transactions.

However, it should be recommended that wholesale and retail operations are not perfectly segmented. In fact, with the trend towards securitisation that is observed in the major financial centres, the dividing line between wholesale and retail activities has become increasingly thin. The development of mutual funds has increased the access of small investors to the securities markets, while the standardisation and packaging of loans has, as a matter of fact, widened the access of small creditors to that same market.

Additionally, considering the economic policy reforms implemented in Mexico during the last few years, previous relations between clients and intermediaries probably do not constitute an insurmountable barrier for new entrants. The development of new industrial and commercial firms (some of them with the participation of foreign capital) as a response to the trade liberalisation and deregulation programmes, opens opportunities that in principle could be exploited by either domestic or foreign financial intermediaries. Finally, joint ventures (which are a form of establishment for foreign financial intermediaries) constitute another means of overcoming the entry barriers derived from the network of branches and the relations between the intermediaries and its clients.

In this way, there are factors acting against each other in terms of assessing the effects of the liberalisation of trade in financial services over the performance of the financial systems. Sometimes, the importance of each of them can be ascertained according to the characteristics of the adopted liberalisation scheme. However, on other occasions their importance depends on some characteristics of the financial systems which are hardly identifiable, at least from a conceptual point of view.

The available empirical evidence does not allow clear judgements in this respect. Contrary to what happens with merchandise trade, the instances in which foreign financial intermediaries cover an important fraction of the domestic markets are exceptionally rare, except in the wholesale segment. Similarly, the trend towards price equalisation in financial services is less clear. Situations in which, in spite of liberalisation, financial margins tend to remain relatively high for a number of years are often encountered. However, it is hard to establish whether price differences are attributable to the nature of trade in financial services or are the result of trade restrictions. The fact that financial services are often regarded as a strategic sector, reserved to domestic firms, may have something to do with the absence of widespread trade in financial services, especially in the retail segment of the market.

Even if one accepts that it is the presence of legal barriers that explains the absence of widespread trade in financial services, the elimination of those barriers does not guarantee the materialisation of gains from trade. Financial services tend to be more strictly regulated than other economic activities. The use of minimum capital requirements, the close scrutiny of financial statements, and the presence of compulsory deposit insurance schemes are to a certain extent necessary to correct market failures pertaining to the financial sector. However, they also discourage competition between intermediaries. For instance, minimum capital requirements constitute an entry barrier, whereas government supervision of financial intermediaries can give rise to captured regulation that enhances the exercise of market power.

Under these conditions, the liberalisation of trade in financial services might lead only to the transfer abroad of monopolistic rents and therefore to a reduction in domestic economic welfare. This does not necessarily imply that entry of foreign intermediaries should be restrained, but rather that the form in which financial activities are regulated might be crucial to determine whether or not gains from trade would be attained.

Summing up, given the characteristics of trade in financial services, and the way in which it interacts with regulation, in the assessment of a liberalisation scheme the following factors seem to be of crucial importance: a) to what extent the adopted liberalisation scheme, and the differences in regulation between the countries involved, can give rise to regulatory arbitrage; b) to what extent the liberalisation scheme eliminates entry barriers for foreign financial firms; c) to what extent the interaction between different segments of the market can guarantee an increased degree of competition, even if foreign firms limit their participation to just a few of them; and d) to what extent the degree of competition that prevails in the domestic market is consistent with the fact that the gains derived from lower costs and prices as a result of the liberalisation outweigh the transfer abroad of monopolistic rents.

A comprehensive answer to these questions demands either evidence that is not yet available (for instance, because the deregulation process of the Mexican financial system is too recent to establish in a clear-cut way the degree of competition that would prevail among intermediaries, or to identify the strengths and weaknesses of them), or a deep analysis of the current situation (for instance, in terms of identifying the type of competitive strategy followed by different financial firms) that would lie beyond the objectives of the present chapter. However, in most cases, the comparison of regulatory frameworks, an analysis of the way in which financial activities are organised and the contents of NAFTA allow for substantial progress towards that end. This is the approach followed below. Thus, in the next section the contents of the chapter on financial services are summarised, and later an analysis of its implications in terms of the above mentioned questions is undertaken.

Financial Services in NAFTA

NAFTA focuses on types of financial intermediaries rather than on financial products, an approach that is more congruent with Mexico's regulatory and supervisory practices. It includes rulings related to: (a) the form of establishment of foreign financial firms in Mexico; (b) cross-border transactions; (c) the jurisdiction of the different regulatory frameworks; and (d) the operation of the agreement. In what follows, we summarise the contents of the agreement in each of these aspects.

Establishment: NAFTA prescribes liberalisation in almost every segment of financial intermediation in Mexico, including non-bank banks, that have had an important development in the US market. Each of the parts of the agreement grants national treatment to the financial firms of the others. Only public pensions plans (the *Sistema de Ahorro para el Retiro*, for instance) remain reserved to Mexican intermediaries. Foreign financial firms can establish operations in Mexico only through subsidiaries, that is, through firms constituted in Mexico according to current laws.

For the major segments of financial intermediation (banks, stockbrokerage houses, leasing and factoring) a gradual liberalisation scheme was adopted.[6] In most cases, gradualism takes the form of limiting – until the year 2000 – the participation of Canadian and US financial firms in the Mexican market, both individually and globally. The limits are established in terms of maximum capital values for foreign financial firms. In some cases the operations of these firms are also temporarily restricted. The limits – individual and global – for different segments of the market are presented in Table 4.1.

Table 4.1
Foreign Ownership Limits for Mexican Financial Institutions

	Individual limit (%)		*Global limit (%)*	
	1994-2000	*≥ 2000*	*1994-2000*[b]	*2000-2004*[d]
Banks[a]	1.5	NA	8 to 15[b]	25
Stockbrokers	4	NA	10 to 20[b]	30
Factoring and leasing	NA	NA	10 to 20[b]	NA
Non-bank banks	NA	NA	3[c]	NA

[a] refers to the aggregate net capital of domestic banks.
[b] increases linearly within the referred period of time.
[c] refers to the sum of banks' and non-bank banks' assets.
[d] refers to safeguards that could be applied (just for one time, and for a maximum of three years) if the participation of foreign firms reaches those percentages.

NA = not applicable

In the case of banks, establishment is also restricted, even after the year 2000, if it takes the form of the acquisition of more than 30 per cent of the capital of a Mexican bank. Under this option, the net capital of the resulting institution cannot exceed four per cent of the net capital of existing banks. Additionally, the issue of subordinated debt by foreign banks is forbidden during the first six years of the operation of the Agreement, and there is the possibility of restricting the issuance of foreign banks' stocks in the Mexican market. However, these restrictions are rather mild considering that the differential cost of loanable funds acts against the Mexican market. In the case of stockbrokerage houses, there is the possibility that the Mexican authorities might allow the establishment of this type of firm, even if they are specialised in some specific segment of the market – a situation that is currently discouraged by existing regulatory practices.

Cross-border transactions: In this area Mexico imposes various restrictions, designed to promote activity inside the Mexican territory. The financial firms of the other parties can offer their services only through subsidiaries according to the above-mentioned restrictions. Thus, foreign financial firms cannot supply cross-border financial services inside Mexican territory. Mexicans could acquire this type of services only by moving abroad or through the use of telecommunications. The agreement also establishes the right to limit the transfer of funds abroad, if the transfer is made with the purpose of avoiding capital restrictions.

Some other restrictions on cross-border transactions are directed to enhance monetary policy management in Mexico (for instance, when the agreement prescribes that Mexican residents will not acquire cross-border financial services if they are denominated in pesos). Through this measure the Mexican government has tried to restrict the development of a foreign market in Mexican pesos that could impair the effects of different monetary policy actions.

Jurisdiction of the regulatory frameworks: Mexico maintains complete freedom to implement prudential measures, as well as those oriented to preserve the integrity of the financial institutions operating in the country, or to promote the usual tasks of monetary, exchange rate and credit policies. There is even the possibility of restricting trade in financial services in order to protect the balance of payments.

Operation of the Agreement: In this area the establishment of consultation and dispute settlement mechanisms deserves to be mentioned. These mechanisms enhance the legal security of the prescriptions of the agreement.

Implications of the Negotiated Scheme

Forms of liberalisation: The liberalisation scheme negotiated by Mexico favours trade through the establishment of local subsidiaries, as opposed to cross-border trade which is intended to be discouraged. Additionally, the form of establishment demands a certain degree of commitment towards the domestic market on the part of foreign financial firms to the extent that it has to take place through the constitution of subsidiaries. It is also worth mentioning that certain types of financial services remain reserved for Mexican intermediaries. The issues arising from this form of liberalisation might be reduced to the following: (a) to what extent the restrictions on cross-border trade preclude the possibility of regulatory arbitrage, in the case that the risk for such an event is real; and (b) to what extent the restrictions on establishment imposed by the constitution of subsidiaries, and the exclusion of foreign firms from the provision of certain services, have any counterpart in terms of strengthening the performance of the Mexican financial system. We shall comment about each of these issues in what follows.

Cross-border trade and regulatory arbitrage: As was mentioned above, Mexico's geographical situation and the technology utilised in the provision of financial services, render the restrictions on cross-border financial trade almost ineffective. The prohibition on foreign intermediaries offering cross-border services in Mexico is difficult to enforce,[7] whereas the possibility of acquiring cross-border financial services abroad remains open. This type of trade would not be problematic if it were motivated by differences in prices or quality, backed by technological or factor endowment advantages. However, if it were motivated by distortions in the resource allocation process, it might lead to efficiency losses.

Such distortions could emerge from basic differences in the way financial services are regulated in Mexico, and in the other members of NAFTA. In order to promote the stability of the system and to protect small investors, the regulation of financial services in Mexico relies heavily upon the imposition of various restrictions on the operation of financial intermediaries, while the rules prevailing in the USA and Canada make more use of information disclosure and supervision practices. Thus, certain types of operations (such as holding open foreign exchange positions, making repurchase agreements with some securities, or offering some specific financial instruments) are entirely banned, or strongly restricted, in Mexico, with the objective of avoiding situations of insolvency (even in those institutions that do not take deposits from the public), or to limit interest conflicts between the intermediaries and its clients. Because of these restrictions, Mexican financial firms are at a disadvantage compared to those operating abroad, with regard to the variety of products that they can offer. This situation might become more stringent as a result of the establishment of subsidiaries of foreign firms on Mexican territory.

Based on the premise that such disadvantages would hardly be attenuated by restrictions on cross-border trade, the challenge for Mexico is to implement an increased harmonisation of its regulatory framework with that prevailing in the USA and Canada.[8] The risk of not undertaking this task is that an increasing fraction of the financial services demanded by Mexican firms and investors will be undertaken abroad, resulting in efficiency losses (to the extent that the possibility of attaining economies of scope is substantially reduced), that could harm the type of services demanded by small firms and investors that in general face a more restricted access to cross-border transactions.

Restrictions on the form of establishment, competition and regulation: By limiting the form of establishment to the constitution of subsidiaries, the access of foreign firms becomes more restricted, and therefore there are fewer possibilities for improving prices and quality of financial services in Mexico. Something similar occurs by limiting the offering of certain financial services to Mexican firms.

As a counterpart to the reduction of the degree of competition derived from the subsidiaries regime, there are some gains; these include simplifications in defining the jurisdiction of different regulatory frameworks, the adoption of a stronger commitment to the domestic market on the part of foreign financial firms, and the leveling of the competitive positions of domestic and foreign intermediaries, regarding capital requirements, constitution of reserves or access to funds of the home country.

Of these three factors the one related to the jurisdiction of the regulatory framework seems to be the most important. With the subsidiaries regime the financial firms operating in Mexico are subject to the regulation prevailing in the country, a feature that could lead to the avoidance of interest conflicts arising when a foreign financial firm finds itself in a situation of insolvency. The stability of the financial system remains a responsibility of the authorities of the receiving country, independently of the degree of participation of foreign intermediaries.

Considering that the process of deregulation of the Mexican financial system is quite recent, and under the assumption that the regulation of financial activities in Mexico is still in a relatively primitive stage, subject to a process of learning that may take several years, it seems reasonable to maintain all financial intermediaries operating in Mexico under a common regulatory framework, even if it results in a lower degree of competition.

Regarding the exclusivity granted by NAFTA to Mexican financial intermediaries in the offering of some services, it is more difficult to identify any factors that counteract the adverse effects on competition. The restrictions imposed on foreign financial firms during the first years of the agreement seem to be enough to justify any infant industry argument. Thus, this exclusivity looks more like a concession to Mexican financial firms.

Timing of the liberalisation: For the main segments of financial intermediation the agreement prescribes a gradual liberalisation scheme, in which the participation of foreign firms is limited during a period of six years. For several reasons these limitations reduce the degree of competition that will be faced by Mexican financial firms during that period. By themselves, limits on market share favour the use of oligopolistic practices. To the extent that the gains from an aggressive competitive strategy on the part of foreign financial firms are restricted by the market participation limits, those strategies become less attractive. Additionally, in the case of wholesale operations, the limits to the participation of foreign firms on an individual basis could constitute an obstacle to their attaining a reasonable degree of risk diversification, and therefore to their active participation in the domestic market. The possibilities of diversification are reduced if services are directed only to large clients.

However, a gradual liberalisation scheme could be justified in terms of both strengthening the competitive position of Mexican intermediaries, which is especially important in the case of the recently privatised banks, and in terms of generating some margin for the implementation of changes to the regulatory framework. Consequently, it would be more congruent with the financial system in which there is more competition, and the risk of regulatory arbitrage is greater. Additionally, the fact that the participation of foreign financial firms is going to be widened until it is practically free generates incentives for the modernisation of Mexican intermediaries, so that some of the benefits of the liberalisation are attained immediately.

Nonetheless, a balance between the necessity of consolidating the Mexican intermediaries, against the possibility of increasing the degree of competition in the Mexican financial system, indicates that the timing of liberalisation is too slow. Even if it is difficult to assess the time that would be required by Mexican banks to attain the conditions for international competitiveness, the restructuring of major financial firms usually does not involve a period of more than three years. Additionally, as was mentioned above, the participation of foreign financial firms in the wholesale segment of the market is already strong and, therefore, disregarding the problems derived from regulatory arbitrage, the risks for domestic financial firms of increased liberalisation in this area are marginal.

On the other hand, domestic financial firms enjoy a considerable advantage in the retail segment of the market, because they already have a wide network of branches, and the information about their clients would not be easily obtained by foreign intermediaries in a short period of time. With a faster liberalisation process, the risk that Mexican financial firms would have been absorbed by those from abroad was minimal, while there was more certainty about the gains from trade, in terms of increased competition, better technology and wider variety of products available in Mexico.

Structure of the liberalisation: According to the terms negotiated in the agreement, the speed and extent of liberalisation are different between groups of financial intermediaries. In general, these aspects favour Mexican banks, to the extent that liberalisation in this area is slower, and there are limitations of a more permanent character on the entrance of foreign banks in the retail segment of the market. The possibility that foreign financial firms may count on a wide network of branches, that allows them to compete effectively in the offering of these type of services, is limited by the restrictions that the agreement imposes on the association of Mexican and foreign banks, or to the acquisitions on the part of the latter of established banks. In this sense, the restriction prescribed by the agreement that these type of operations could be undertaken only once the transition process is concluded, and if the participation of the resulting institution does not exceed four per cent of the domestic market, appears to be quite stringent: foreign banks would be able to exercise these options only by setting up a rather small bank.

With this measure the retail segment of the Mexican financial system remains openly protected, even after the transition period, without there being any easily identifiable element that counteracts the efficiency loss derived from that. Once it has been decided that foreign banks are going to participate in the Mexican financial system, through the constitution of subsidiaries, subject to the minimum capital requirements and supervisory norms dictated by the Mexican authorities, the nationality of banks' stockholders seems to be of secondary importance. Even accepting the idea that, for the case of big banks, minimum capital requirements are not enough to discourage excessive risk-taking (because of the 'too big to fail' argument), there does not seem to be any reason to favour domestic over foreign capital on this matter, since in either case the capital and the reputation of the stockholders is at risk. Probably, the only justification to discriminate against foreign capital through the protection of the retail segment of the market is that, to the extent that foreign ownership is more widespread, the moral persuasion often used by the financial authorities on various countries lose its effectiveness. In any case, the lack of transparency of such methods to regulate financial activities, or to conduct monetary policy, makes this argument highly questionable.

The protection of retail banking services might be counteracted by the development of other segments of the market. The increased securitisation of financial operations that has been observed in the major financial centres is a clear example in this respect. However, with the exception of short-term Treasury notes, the Mexican securities market lacks the depth and liquidity needed to constitute a serious challenge to retail banking. Additionally, some other segments of the market that could in principle compete with retail banking – e.g., leasing activities – are too regulated to perform that task effectively. Finally, it is possible for banks to extend their market power to other segments of the market through bundling or tied sales. Therefore, a doubt remains, at least regarding NAFTA, about the degree of efficiency to be attained by retail financial services in Mexico.

Conclusion

The liberalisation package negotiated by Mexico under NAFTA constitutes an important step in terms of promoting (a much needed) greater efficiency in the Mexican financial system to the extent that it allows the entrance of foreign financial firms. However, there remain some questions regarding the thrust of this effort. The timing of liberalisation seems to be too long; even if one considers seriously the need to consolidate the recently privatised banks, the presence of individual and global limits on the participation of foreign financial firms casts some doubt on whether any of the gains associated with the liberalisation would materialise during the transition period. Additionally, those segments in which the presence of foreign competition could have the most dramatic effects are the ones that remain more protected. A long tradition in which control and restrictions ruled over competition in the organisation of financial activities seems to be still present in spite of the recent reforms. There is also the challenge of going further with the deregulation process, especially in those areas in which the variety of products that could be offered by domestic firms is restricted. The margin granted by the transition period may well be utilised to undertake such reforms.

A further reduction in legal entry barriers would also be welcome, especially those related to minimum capital requirements. Minimum capital requirements in Mexico seem to be out of proportion considering what would be necessary to discourage excessive risk-taking, and therefore may constitute an effective limit to competition. In the absence of a competitive environment the possible gains associated with the liberalisation process might never be attained, because foreign financial firms may limit their efforts to collect monopolistic rents, instead of promoting increased efficiency in the Mexican financial system. These are important issues that will have to be addressed shortly, considering the adverse influence that an expensive financial system can exert on other productive activities.

Notes

1. See Gavito, Sánchez and Trigueros (1992) for more details about these comparisons.
2. This higher degree of concentration is probably already resulting in reduced competition, as banks' financial margins have been increasing during the last few months.
3. Furthermore, in the case of banks, minimum capital requirements become more restrictive through time, to the extent that they are determined as a fixed proportion (0.5%) of the sum of the capital of the banks already in operation.
4. The degree of globalisation of financial services in Mexico is already high. Almost any major Mexican firm finances an important fraction of its liabilities through the issue of securities in foreign markets. Additionally, about 50 per cent of the daily operation of the Mexican stock exchange is undertaken between foreign investors.
5. For instance, when commercial banks transfer their deposit operations to the country in which the deposit insurance programme is softer, encouraging excessive risk-taking at the expense of this country's taxpayers.
6. However, this is not the case for mutual funds and bonding operations, in which the liberalisation is immediate.

7. This type of restriction has been present for a long time in the Mexican legislation on life insurance. However, it is frequently heard that a Mexican insurance agent has been rewarded for his performance in the sale of US companies' policies.

8. Contrary to what is agreed in the unification of financial services in the European Community, NAFTA does not exhibit any direction in this respect. This situation is somewhat unfortunate because the harmonisation of financial services regulation removes a source of regulatory capture, and therefore a source of market power. NAFTA, to some extent, favours this type of behaviour, because it leaves open the possibility of erecting barriers to trade in financial services in the event of balance of payments problems.

CHAPTER 5

AGRICULTURE AND FARMERS WITHIN NAFTA: A MEXICAN PERSPECTIVE

Kirsten Appendini

The issues concerning free trade and agriculture are always complex, even more so when considering economies with such different levels of development as those of Mexico, the USA and Canada. In the case of Mexico, the issues are further complicated by the fact that agriculture is still a major source of employment, accounting for over twenty per cent of all jobs and nearly ten percent of GDP.

Mexico has a comparative advantage in growing certain crops, such as fruits and vegetables, due mainly to its geographical location, climate and low labour costs, but the majority of Mexican farmers, growing basic food and feed-grains for the domestic market, are not competitive internationally. Consequently, agriculture is a vulnerable sector in a free trade context. Most agriculture is particularly disadvantaged since it has stagnated for many decades and, during the 1980s economic crisis, infrastructure was eroded, investment fell and, in general, the resource base of farmers and peasants deteriorated. The debate concerning agriculture and NAFTA has therefore focused not only on trade issues, but even more so on the consequences of free trade on the rural sector in general and the fate of its population.

These issues underlie the trade negotiations and the current debate on future sectoral policy. Mexico is as much concerned with trade as it is with the possibility of transforming a stagnated and crisis ridden agricultural sector into an internationally competitive industry. This is particularly the case for activities involving food production catering to the domestic market. In addition, the government is seeking to diminish the economic and social costs of transition.

The fact that most Mexican farmers are poor peasants on dry rain-fed land, who survive by making constant choices about growing basic food crops (maize) and/or seeking wage-work, poses a serious challenge to the labour market, including migration north of the border. Due to the interlinking between agricultural policy, its impact on production and labour markets, changes in the agricultural sector

concern the economy as a whole as well as key social and political
issues. Mexico therefore confronts issues that are much more complex
than those facing its partners. Like the USA and Canada, Mexico aims
at increasing trade; however, unlike its partners, Mexico also expects
that the impact of liberalisation will allow the country to transform, that
is modernise, agriculture and livestock activities. This double objective
is clearly set out in the statement of purpose of the agreement which, on
the one hand, aims to gain access to the US market, do away with non-
tariff trade barriers, and obtain reciprocity and equity on trade; on the
other, it states that the agreement should, among other things, favour
capitalisation in the countryside, promote crop restructuring and develop
agro-industry (SARH, 1992b).

In order to realise these goals, Mexico relies on the impact of free
trade on different sub-sectors, regions and producers within the clauses
negotiated in NAFTA – namely the time-periods for lowering tariffs and
access to the northern markets, as well as the margins set for sectoral
policy implementation within the NAFTA rules. But the cost of
restructuring and transition accrues only to Mexico.[1]

The real challenge for Mexico's agricultural and livestock sectors
is to become competitive. This has been promoted in the last three years
through a complete restructuring of agricultural policy based on
deregulating markets and diminishing state intervention, including
changing the legal framework regulating land tenure and investment in
the *ejido*[2] sector. However, this has completely changed the framework
in which farmers operate, since subsidies and access to markets through
state agencies have been severed. Farmers and peasants must become
more efficient and competitive while at the same time facing severe
constraints on resources which were formerly subsidised by the State.[3]

In this chapter I will try to set down the main trends in the debate on
agriculture within NAFTA, focusing on the main issues. What is the
situation of Mexican agriculture in the face of trade liberalisation?
Where are the advantages/disadvantage for the main groups of crops?
What are the perspectives considering the agreements negotiated? What
are the current policy changes and its impact on transforming agriculture
towards higher levels of productivity? What is the impact on farmers
and peasants?

Agricultural Trade

Trade between Mexico and the USA in agricultural commodities has
always been important, and it increased at an annual rate of 11.6 per

cent from 1982 to 1988 in dollar value terms. The USA is Mexico's major trading partner; in 1991 Mexico exported $2.5 billion worth of agricultural and livestock goods to the USA (see Tables 5.1 and 5.2) (11 per cent of US imports of these goods).[4] Mexico's imports of agricultural commodities coming from the USA amounted to $2.9 billion (69 per cent of total agricultural imports).[5] Mexico is the third largest single country market for US agricultural exports, and the second largest supplier for the USA (see Table 5.1).

Table 5.1
Mexico-US-Canadian Agricultural Trade (millions of dollars)

	Mexico-US Trade		Mexico-Canada Trade	
	Mexican imports	US imports	Mexican imports	Canadian imports
1980	2468	1059	89	83
1981	2432	1102	183	90
1982	1156	1158	86	73
1983	1942	1280	81	74
1984	1993	1279	79	69
1985	1439	1446	81	73
1986	1080	2080	73	83
1987	1202	1867	113	83
1988	2234	1820	128	97
1989	2731	2280	127	104
1990	NA	NA	NA	NA
1991	2918	2517	116	115

SOURCES:
1980-1989, GAO (1991, p. 19-20); 1991 (USDA, 1991, p. 34)

Trade between Canada and Mexico, on the other hand, has been of little importance (see Table 5.1); Canadian exports to Mexico only account for 3 per cent of total agricultural imports, whilst Mexican agricultural exports to Canada are 15 per cent of its total agricultural imports.[6]

Trade liberalisation on the Mexican side has already taken substantial steps forward in the past few years. In 1986 (the year Mexico applied to join GATT), Mexico's maximum applied tariff rate was reduced to 20 per cent from 100 per cent. In 1991 the average tariff was 12 per cent (Banamex, 1991). Since 1989, import licenses on most agricultural products have been abolished; exceptions are food staples, maize and beans, powdered milk, eggs and poultry meat which are duty-free. Thus, in 1990 only 57 commodities were subject to licenses in comparison with 317 in 1985 (GAO, 1991). However, seasonal tariffs have been established for some crops (soybeans, for example).

In sum, Mexico has liberalised its imports unilaterally in recent years and expects NAFTA to ensure reciprocity with its northern neighbours. Mexico expects to increase its exports substantially as trade and non-trade barriers are reduced for Mexican goods. Mexican exporters have been particularly concerned with restrictions involving non-tariff barriers such as sanitary and phyto-sanitary requirements, and quality standards that have hampered entry into the USA. As pointed out below, some mechanisms have been negotiated to deal with these problems. Mexican small farmers and peasants, however, have been concerned with competition from US grain. They argued for keeping maize and beans out of the negotiations and demanded agricultural policies to support the technical transformation of basic crop farming.

It is clear that there are losers and gainers in the process of liberalising trade and there will continue to be once the free trade agreement becomes effective. In the debate about agriculture and free trade there is a consensus that fruit and vegetable crops will gain from the agreement while basic food-crops and feed-crops will lose.[7] However, whilst promoters of free trade argue that losers can be absorbed into more productive occupations than growing maize with low yields (Levy and van Wijnbergen, 1991b), the opponents point to dangers of food dependency and social disarticulation within the countryside, resulting in even more poverty as well as migration to cities and to the northern border (Barraclough, 1991; Calva, 1991).

A number of econometric models developed over the last years, dealing with the impact of freeing trade in crops, confirm the trends of losers and gainers. As Josling points out in a review of these studies, they:

> 'generally bear out the qualitative assessments of gains to grain, oilseed and livestock producers and losses to those that compete with Mexico in fruits and vegetables...all these studies agree that the impact on fruit and vegetable producers is small and likely to be offset by additional sales to Mexico as income rises and barriers fall...The overall picture then is one of rather modest developments in agricultural markets stemming directly from NAFTA, and some

quite dramatic changes in Mexico (to the benefit of exporters) if Mexico continues to liberalise internal markets for agricultural products ...' (Josling, 1992, p. 168).

For example, according to the model advanced by Burfisher, Robinson and Thierfelder (see Josling, 1992), agricultural trade liberalisation would mean gains of 8.0 to 10.5 per cent for the USA, versus 4.2 to 5.4 per cent for Mexico, depending on different scenarios. US grain and corn exports to Mexico may increase in the range of 80 to 140 per cent, and corn from 118 to 222 per cent. Increases in feed-grain exports may vary from 52 to 74 per cent. Estimates for Mexico's gains in fruit and vegetable exports are 25 per cent (with a corresponding 15 per cent for US exports to Mexico).[8] Partial equilibrium models show that the welfare impact on farmers is negative since the majority of Mexico's farmers/peasants grow crops for the domestic market, but consumers' welfare increases as goods become cheaper.[9]

The Winners: Fruits and Vegetables

Fruits and vegetables account for about 40 per cent of the total value of Mexico's agricultural exports, but they account for less than six per cent of cultivated land in Mexico; most vegetables are grown on irrigated land. Export crops are specialised in specific regions where irrigation is available, such as the large districts of the North Pacific coast (Sinaloa, Sonora and Baja California Norte), the irrigated valleys of El Bajío (in Querétaro, Guanajuato, Michoacán), and in subtropical and tropical regions appropriate for export fruits such as the lowlands of Michoacán, Guerrero and the coastline along the Gulf of Mexico.

These crops are generally grown on large farms or by firms controlling vast amounts of land either by leasing (often *ejido* land, the leasing of which was illegal until 1992) or contract farming, mostly with medium-sized privately owned farms. Farmers contract with brokers, who market crops for export, or with agro-industry processing plants for the Mexican market (for example in the regions of El Bajío, Guanajuato and Querétaro).

NAFTA is expected to increase investment in growing fruits and vegetables as well as developing agro-industry. Agro-industry should provide an increasingly important source of foreign exchange and investment. Furthermore, these crops would also mean an important source of labour demand, thus helping to solve Mexico's ever pressing problems of rural unemployment.

A number of policy measures have favoured export agriculture in recent years. First, during the 1980s, overall macro-economic policy helped to decrease costs in dollar terms and enhance competitiveness through the under-valuation of the Mexican currency (until the stabilisation policy implemented a virtually fixed exchange rate at the end of 1987), through the liberalisation of trade on inputs and equipment following entrance to the GATT in 1986, and through a wages policy which has kept rural labour costs low.

Since 1989, agricultural policy has been completely restructured following the general trends of privatisation and market deregulation, with the goal of attracting investment into agro-industry. For example, abolishing state intervention in marketing a number of basic crops (some of which compete for irrigated land), was expected to 'set prices right' and attract investment in high value crops.[10]

Lowering the costs of imported inputs and equipment and following a policy of fixed wages has continued to benefit fruit and vegetable growers. However, some policies have been contradictory; reducing the public deficit has lowered subsidies to farmers (the loss of water and energy subsidies particularly affect these growers), and the exchange rate policy has overvalued the peso in detriment to exporters.

One of the most important policy measures which is expected to attract investment to agriculture, and particularly to agro-industry, is the reform of article 27 of the Constitution regarding land tenure, which was approved in early 1992. This has legally abolished restrictions on private ownership of land and on joint ventures between private capital and *ejidatarios*, which had been a constraint on investment in agriculture for decades. Under the new agrarian law, although private property is still limited, shareholding firms may own up to 2,500 hectares. Leasing of *ejido* land is now legal, and there are a number of ways in which private capital and *ejidatarios* can now associate. Furthermore, *ejidatarios* are now also allowed to use their land as credit collateral. With these changes, private capital is expected to become the main agent in pushing Mexico's stagnant agriculture towards higher levels of productivity and competitiveness (SARH, 1990).

Two years on from the constitutional changes, the trend in agriculture is still uncertain. Although output has surpassed the 1985 levels, there is no evidence of important investments in the fruit and vegetable sector (Table 5.2). Rather, farmers face a number of current problems with rising costs of operation, scarce credit and, also, high interest

Farmers on irrigated land, who could switch from basic crops to fruits and vegetables, have, since 1990, turned to cultivating maize as a substitute for sorghum, soya and rice; there has been an increase of 1.6 million hectares from 1989-1991. Maize, still a protected crop, guarantees secure profitability for high yielding producers with little investment, while reconverting to export crops requires high investment and high transaction costs such as technology and marketing (Runsten, 1992).

The prospect of increasing land available for growing export crops – through, for example, extending irrigated areas – still seems to depend on public investment in infrastructure. However, there are also physical limits on the possibility of increasing water resources in the next decades, complicated by predictions of a warmer and drier climate.[12] The kind of crops which Mexico exports demand water and the use of agro-chemicals. Crop restructuring affects water use, both soil and ground water depletion; these are problems which have not seriously been taken into account within official discussions on NAFTA.

Another trend for increasing fruit and vegetable production is through foreign investment in agro-industry which is expected to move into Mexico and perhaps associate with larger farmers. Also it is expected that smaller producers - *ejidatarios* - may embark on joint ventures with private capital (domestic or foreign).

Runsten (1992) and Runsten and Wilcox (1992) discuss some of the problems concerning foreign investment and joint ventures (*asociaciones en participación*) between *ejiditarios* and private capital, based on their research experience in El Bajío. Although the state is promoting the associations through finance institutions such as FIRA, private capital access to subsidised credit is being used as a way of paying former debts held with the public agricultural bank, rather than for new investment. It is also a way of giving private capital access to earlier investments made by the Mexican government in the *ejidos*: land, irrigation, machinery, animal structures, packing sheds, etc. There are few examples from these new joint ventures where infrastructure is initiated alongside investment in established programmes.

Another problem is that contracts are short-term; this allows small producers to complement larger concerns when demand increases, but they are then excluded when it contracts. There is little or no transfer of technology and research efforts, both private and public, are non-existent. Consequently, in some crops, technological dependency has widened the gap between US and Mexican growers (Runsten and Wilcox, 1992). Soil and water deterioration from intensive cropping and chemical inputs is also an issue. Currently, firms move to other regions when these resources are depleted.

Other problems arise directly from trade and competition. Whilst US farmers in these crops fear competition from low cost and lax environmental regulations in Mexico, several authors point to the fact that Mexico's competitiveness is neither assured nor permanent (Runsten and Wilcox, 1992; Runsten, 1992; Josling, 1992).

US and Mexican fruit and vegetable markets are complementary rather than competitive. Many horticultural products are subject to 25 per cent tariffs upon entering the USA, and to tariffs varying on a seasonal basis to coincide with the marketing period for domestic US production. Some crops are subject to phyto-sanitary regulations and market standards, causing problems which have not been resolved (for example avocados are still banned due to disease problems).[13]

The cost advantage of Mexican products is not necessarily large in a number of crops, particularly tomatoes, green peppers, squash and cucumbers, and the advantage that does exist is vulnerable to marginal changes in costs and exchange rates. Also productivity in Mexico is lower than competing crops in the USA. The cost advantage in terms of average wages in export crop regions is 6:1 (with fringe benefits the ratio is in the range of 7:1 or 8:1), but if productivity is considered the ratio is much lower; for example, comparing tomatoes in Baja California and California the difference in wage rates is nine to one. However, this is reduced to 2.5:1 if the difference in productivity factors is taken into account (Runsten and Wilcox, 1992).

To date, there is no sign of definite trends in significant expansion of fruit and vegetable production in Mexico. Besides some of the problems noted above, there are other possible explanations for the lack of expansion: the reform of agrarian legislation is too recent, the policy framework for agriculture is still uncertain, since resolutions on new mechanisms for subsidies have not been decided, and NAFTA itself was not signed until the end of 1992, so Mexican producers have still faced trade barriers to the US and Canadian markets.

In sum, the expansion of fruit and vegetable production requires substantial investments in cropping, storing, packing, processing and marketing facilities. It also requires research and environmental regulations in order to attain a sustainable level of activity. Access to the markets north of the border is the main incentive for investment and this is only possible after NAFTA goes into operation.

Finally, sugar is another crop which is expected to gain on a medium- and long-term basis as Mexico gains preferential access to the

US market. However, the recently privatised sugar industry is in a profound crisis,[14] both in cropping as well as in the refining industry and output is insufficient to satisfy domestic demand. In order to grow and export, a complete restructuring of the agro-industry is required. Thus, the gains from trade liberalisation in sugar are expected to be realised only in the longer term.

The Losers: Maize and Peasants

The main debate concerning the NAFTA negotiations on agriculture has been on maize – Mexico's main crop and food staple. Maize represents 20 per cent of total value of agricultural output, and accounts for 48 per cent of acreage (59 per cent of rain-fed and 28 per cent of irrigated land); it also involves the majority of peasant producers. Average yields for maize are about two tons per hectare (compared with 7.4 in the USA); 38.6 per cent of producers do not cover costs at current support prices and only 7.9 per cent would be profitable at world prices (SARH, 1992a). Free access of imported corn to the Mexican market, where current domestic prices are double international prices, is considered an important threat to the livelihood of about 2.4 million peasant producers plus their families.

Most of the peasants farmers who grow maize do so on poor rain-fed land with low yields and little investment in inputs and equipment. For the farmer on rain-fed land, investment in maize cultivation has traditionally been linked to access to resources such as credit (to buy equipment and inputs), to support prices when selling to the marketing agency Conasupo, and to opportunities for wage work. The relationship between maize prices and wages has been a crucial factor in the choice peasant families make regarding how much to grow (the 'ideal' minimum being the family's consumption needs), and how to cultivate. This requires making choices about resource and labour allocation.

The majority of peasants have little chance of ever becoming competitive, and have in fact been excluded from agricultural policy programmes (credit, extension, etc.) that support only economically viable farmers (SAHR, 1990, 1992a; Appendini, 1992). The future of these peasants, and their families, is more related to the labour market and thus to the growth of the overall economy (Cornelius and Martin, 1993). At present rural labour markets are in a precarious situation, as is the employment situation in general. According to recent surveys, 20 to 30 per cent of the population engaged in agriculture and livestock receive no payment at all (being mostly family labour), 68 per cent of the economically active population in the sector and 40 per cent of household units with agriculture and livestock as the main activities have an income equal to or less than one minimum salary.[15] An impoverishment of peasants will only add to a worsening of the situation of Mexico's poor (50 per cent of the population lives below the poverty line according to some estimates). Social and political costs of transition in restructuring of agriculture through free trade have made policy-makers more sensitive to the demands of peasant producers (Encinas et al, 1992; Calva, 1991). The response has been the slow, gradual liberalisation of maize and the current debate on how to operationalise direct subsidies for agricultural producers. However, maize is not the only crop that is problematic; the majority of Mexico's food-grains and feed-grains are not competitive at international prices, either due to lower levels of productivity or to the fact that the USA, as well as the EC, subsidises grains heavily – or to both factors together. Soya and sorghum farmers, for example, have been seriously affected by the free access of feed-grains to Mexico and the government had to reimpose temporary tariffs and subsidising schemes to compensate producers' income both in 1991 and 1992.

Livestock activities are also having difficulties competing with imported products, although the situation varies in the different areas. In general, livestock activities have suffered a severe crisis, first due to demand contraction during the economic stagnation of the 1980s, and then to a productivity crisis resulting from the lack of investment which led to an increasing technological gap with the USA, particularly severe for beef and pork products (Chauvet, 1993).

NAFTA Negotiations and Perspectives for Agriculture

Within NAFTA, Mexico has been given the status of a less developed country which entitles it to a long period of transition to free trade, and allows it to give a certain level of support to agriculture, which will not be considered as subsidies and therefore not subject to compensatory tariffs. Mexico has obtained an average period of ten years for trade liberalisation in agricultural products; the longest period is for maize and beans (15 years). Import quotas with zero tariffs have also been agreed during the transition period.

On trade issues, Mexico's aim was to eliminate all non-tariff barriers; the USA has agreed to eliminate all quantitative restrictions and establish tariff-rate quotas. Both countries will retain safe-guards for commodities which may be sensitive to competition from imports.[16] Canada and Mexico have agreed to eliminate the most important quantitative restrictions, but some will be retained. Agricultural inputs will be immediately liberalised.[17]

The USA will immediately free 61 per cent of agro-industrial goods from Mexico, including the most important items traded, such as cattle, and a number of fruits and vegetables. Table 5.3 shows the items under the immediate and long phasing-out periods; some of the most important items, such as cucumbers and cantaloupe melons, are only liberalised on a seasonal basis, and consequently retain a 15-year protection during the US production season. The most important export vegetable, tomatoes, has a 10 year phasing-out period. The USA also maintains safeguards on some of the most important imports for Mexico such as tomatoes, aubergines, chili peppers, squash, watermelons and onions.

Through import quotas, Mexico gains market access for concentrated and frozen orange juice, but this item has a long transition period for abolishing tariffs. Although the USA has negotiated a 15 year transition period for sugar, Mexico will be allowed to export a maximum of 25,000 tons of sugar for the first six years, and 150,000 tons from the seventh year onwards (SARH, 1993).

In sum, the USA retains tariffs for some of the commodities most vulnerable to competition from Mexico, and strongly defended by Florida and California growers (Avery, 1993). On sanitary and phyto-sanitary barriers, the agreement gives each country the right 'to establish sanitary and phyto-sanitary measures that are based on scientific principle and a risk assessment' (SARH, 1993). Agreement has been reached on recognising 'pest free or disease free areas' and 'areas of low pest or disease prevalence'. Furthermore, mechanisms to avoid unfair practices and to solve disputes have been established.

Mexico is obliged to free only 35 per cent of its imports from the USA. The latter country has subjected 33 per cent of its commodities to a long period of liberalisation, whilst Mexico has 60 per cent of its commodities under a regime of long liberalisation. Mexico holds safeguard mechanisms mainly for livestock products, such as pork meat, and also for apples and processed potatoes. Gradual liberalisation will be on the basis of a slow decrease in tariffs plus a fixed tariff-free import quota.[18] Canada will immediately liberalise 88 per cent of its agricultural commodity imports from Mexico (including orange juice, which is important), while Mexico will liberalise 40.3 per cent.

Mexico has established a 15-year transition period for maize, with a tariff of 250 per cent at the beginning, which gradually decreases until the seventh year, after which it drops sharply. The long period of transition is expected to allow Mexican farmers to adjust productivity levels and become competitive, and for marginal farmers to enter into other activities.

Both the response to the opportunities offered by NAFTA for export agriculture and the challenge to the survival of basic crop farmers and peasants depend more on Mexico's ability to transform its agricultural sector than to trade liberalisation alone. Mexican agriculture is profoundly in need of a clear medium- and long-term agricultural policy, as well as specific mechanisms of support after a decade of resource contraction during the 1980s debt crisis and the uncertainty resulting from economic restructuring. Private capital does not seem to be responding rapidly to the privatisation of rural institutions, and has not been a substitute for former public resources. This is true for the private agricultural sector, and even more so for the so-called 'social sector' including *ejidatarios*, which were under state tutelage for decades.

Policy-makers are indeed very concerned about the need for a policy that will support the transformation of Mexico's agricultural sector, while at the same time promoting privatisation and capital investment in the countryside. In the last two years, public expenditure for the countryside has increased slightly, responding to demands mainly from peasant organisations. These funds have generally been channelled through the official credit institutions, and through President Salinas's poverty assistance programme, PRONASOL (*Programa Nacional de Solidaridad*), which has increased expenditure on productive projects in the last three years. However, these resources are not well planned and do not respond to a specific strategy of developing agriculture. Today the main issue in policy discussion concerns subsidy mechanisms for producers such as direct payments to farmers in order to support income, mainly to compensate for decreasing market prices for food-grain and feed-grain producers.[19] These mechanisms will be the main instrument of support for farmers and peasants, but they are more a way of helping farmers through the transition period than an instrument for pushing agriculture towards higher levels of productivity and competitiveness; this, it would seem, has been left to the market.

Who will benefit and who will lose does not have a straightforward answer. The expansion of certain activities and the contraction of others will have differential impacts on different crops, types of producers and regions of the countryside. Certainly the regions best equipped with natural resources and capital infrastructure will be the ones favoured by the more dynamic export activities, while marginal rain-fed lands in central and southern Mexico may be even more abandoned since they are less attractive to investors. However, the consequence of expanding trade, which I have focused on in this chapter, is one aspect of the future dynamics of the Mexican countryside. Integrating agriculture into a North American free trade area means a profound change for the role of agriculture in the Mexican economy, which will need to be subject to a national development project and adjust to the dynamics of the North American market. Mexico's role will probably be limited to supplying specific crops, which will be determined by investment decisions not necessarily confined to the national boundaries. The integration or exclusion of certain production branches, agro-industries, groups of producers, marketing agencies, etc., will have a great impact on the productive and spatial reorganisation of the Mexican countryside.

Notes

1. Unlike the European Community (EC), the NAFTA partners have no special provisions for compensation and adjustment funds for less developed partners (Conroy and Glasmeier, 1992/93).
2. *Ejido* is state-owned land distributed to peasants through agrarian reform. The *ejidos* account for half of cultivated land in Mexico.
3. For a review of the recent restructuring of agricultural policy, see Appendini (1992a).
4. The most important items are cattle, coffee, tomatoes, pepper, onions, and other vegetables. In the statistics of the US Department of Commerce, beer is included as the fourth most important agricultural import to the USA from Mexico (SARH, 1993: p. 8).
5. Mexico imports sorghum, soya, beef and pork meat, pork fat and offals. Also agro-industrial products such as vegetable oils and powdered milk (USDA, 1991).
6. Canada imports coffee, mangoes, bananas and tomatoes from Mexico and exports wheat, dairy cows, powdered milk, pork meat and offals (SARH, 1992b, pp. 16-17).
7. See Appendini (1992), Barraclough (1991), Conroy and Glasmeier (1992/93), Cornelius and Martin (1993), GAO (1991), Josling (1992), Levy and van Wijnbergen (1991b), Runsten and Wilcox (1992).
8. Scenarios vary from trade liberalisation to considering different degrees of subsidies to domestic agriculture. See Burfisher, Robinson and Thierfelder model (cited by Josling, 1992, p. 153).

9. Levy and van Wijnbergen (1991b); Krisdoff and others, cited by Josling (1992). Levy and van Wijnbergen, advocates of free trade in maize in order to reduce public expenditure on crop subsidies, estimate that those most hurt would be peasants cultivating for the market (330,000 or 15% of all producers), whilst the majority of the 1.9 million subsistence producers would be little affected. Cornelius and Martin (1993), citing several econometric models, mention estimates ranging from 800,000 to 2 million (30% of the rural labour force) being in danger of losing jobs. However, Cornelius and Martin point to the fact that models based on employment coefficient by crop do not consider the diversity of income generating activities in rural families, which may diminish the impact of liberalisation on the labour market and migration.

10. Until 1989, basic crops had support prices and could be sold to the state marketing agency Conasupo (Compañía Nacional de Subsistencias Populares). Support prices for all crops except maize and beans were abolished in 1989. This led to a fall in profitability of wheat, soya and sorghum, which are cultivated on irrigated land (sorghum is also grown on rain-fed land). However, as is shown below, these crops were substituted by maize rather than vegetables and fruits.

11. Banrural is the Banco Nacional de Desarrollo Rural, and FIRA is Fideicomisos Instituidos en Relación con la Agricultura of the Banco de México. Commercial banks increased lending to agro-industry up to 1986, while they were nationalised. There is no disaggregated data on private banks' lending for recent years (Myhre, 1993).

12. For example, models concerned with the impact of global warming on Mexico predict temperature increases of 1 to 5° C in coming decades (some models predict increase in rainfall, others decreases). Even so, with temperature increases, evaporation will also increase and so water deficits may rise (Liverman, 1991).

13. Zones that are free of fruit fly have been established in the states of Sonora and Sinaloa, so that apples, grapefruits, oranges, peaches and tangerines may be exported from specific areas of Sonora to the USA without quarantine treatment. Mangoes have to undergo a hot water dip treatment for fruit fly. Citrus must be treated under the APHIS programme (USDA's Animal and Plant Health Inspection Service). A disease affecting citrus, mainly limes, is still under investigation. Avocados are prohibited because of various pests that attack the fruit. There are proposals to establish pest-free areas, but this problem has not been resolved. Potatoes are also prohibited because of pests. There is a special rule, Section 608e of the Agricultural Marketing Agreements Act of 1937, which says that US imports of specified fruits and vegetables are required to meet the same grade and quality standards as US products that are regulated by marketing orders.

14. Indeed, a prediction of a short-run fall in output is cited by Conroy and Glasmeier (1992/93, p. 18). It is surprising that in Mexico there has been no debate on the sugar industry within the NAFTA framework.

15. Data from Encuesta Nacional de Empleo (1988) and Encuesta Ingreso-Gasto (1989), both carried out by INEGI; see Appendini (1992a).
16. Examples are tomatoes, aubergines, chilies, pumpkins, watermelons, onions.
17. The most important are tractors (new and used), machinery, tools, fertilizers, agro-chemicals, vaccines, insecticides.
18. The quota is established for each commodity on the basis of the average amount imported during the three preceding years. This is the case of maize, rye, beans, potatoes, poultry, animal fats, milk and eggs.
19. This scheme, known as PROCAMPO, was finally announced by President Salinas in October 1993.

PART II

SOCIO-POLITICAL DIMENSIONS

CHAPTER 6

NAFTA AND LABOUR MIGRATION TO THE UNITED STATES

Jorge A. Bustamante

A Mexican saying claims that politics is the art of doing what is possible. The balance of power between Mexico and the United States is asymmetrical and, from a political perspective, it seems impossible that Mexico can correct this imbalance by decree. The asymmetry is very dynamic, however, and political and economic conditions in the different regions within the two countries play increasingly important roles in the US-Mexican relationship. We are no longer able to speak about Mexico as a homogeneous entity nor to make generalisations about economic development without identifying distinctions between different regions and different sectors of the economy.

When examining Mexico, an underlying assumption should be that it is a nation of enormous contrasts. Recent developments have allowed the country's industrial sector to compete with some of the most advanced sectors in other parts of the world. At the same time, other sectors resemble some of the poorest, most underdeveloped countries of the world. This contrast must be taken into account in order to understand what is occurring in Mexico with regard to NAFTA. A generalisation leaning towards one extreme or the other is going to be problematic, if not mistaken.

This chapter discusses the question of international labour migration from Mexico to the United States, beginning with some basic assumptions. First, NAFTA was a political strategy that was the best option in the absence of other feasible options for Mexican economic development. Economic development is primarily a strategy to create a massive number of permanent jobs, under the assumption that the creation of these industrial jobs will improve income distribution in Mexico. This is an important dimension of economic development because, within the western hemisphere, income inequality in Mexico is second only to Brazil. It was assumed that an improvement in income distribution would in turn improve the standard of living. Obviously, this logic cannot be applied in a uniform way in all regions of the country. It

79

applies only under certain conditions and this will affect the ability of Mexicans to benefit from the opportunities under the free trade agreement.

NAFTA was originally proposed by President Salinas. This must be emphasised to combat the negative impression that NAFTA is somehow a result of the asymmetry of power between Mexico and the USA, or an imposition of the United States upon the less powerful nation of Mexico. In fact, the proposal of NAFTA took the United States government by surprise. In Mexico, regional free trade was an option which had been carefully studied prior to any public announcement, although it was only made precise in the context of a very difficult process of negotiation.

The social dimension of free trade arose very early in the negotiating process. In fact, before the formal process of negotiations started, the US government established one very clear basic premise: labour migration was not on the negotiating agenda. Again, if politics is the art of the possible, then Mexico had two options: to insist on including the labour migration question on a take it or leave it basis or to accept exclusions with the hope of securing concessions within the negotiations on trade liberalisation. Once the negotiations of NAFTA had culminated with an agreed draft, President Salinas informally proposed the initiation of separate negotiations on the labour migration question to the US government.

Political and economic conditions changed greatly during the two years of negotiations. From the beginning, the Mexican government decided to open the process of consultation to representatives of different sectors of the economy. An advisory committee on the free trade agreement negotiations was organised, consisting of representatives of business, organised labour, agriculture and academic sectors of Mexican society.

It could be argued that this is far from a complete representation of all parts of the Mexican economy. Many groups, however, spoke openly in favour of their own interests, demonstrating considerable disagreement among the different sectors. Regardless of what might happen with NAFTA, the debate generated real progress in the coordination of the business community in Mexico. Organisation in the private sector had no historical precedent; never before had such diverse segments of the Mexican economy united in such an effort. This new network, connected through state-of-the-art communications technology, became involved in the creation of the 'next-room' negotiating context. Private sector representatives were always present with the Mexican negotiators, ensuring that whatever was negotiated had their backing.

To say that these negotiations were conducted in secrecy, without the knowledge of the Mexican people, is simply not true. Obviously, however, an essential element of any negotiating process is that the various sides do not show all their cards to the public. Negotiations proceed through a mechanism agreed upon by the governments and selected groups of the countries involved, not through the mass media, political parties, or other institutions – each country is then assured that its best interests are being advanced.

The negotiations were in some ways a reflection of the asymmetry of power between Mexico and the United States. Canada played an integral part in the process – sometimes leaning towards one country, sometimes to the other. During these negotiations, it was understood that the question of asymmetry had to be dealt with in terms of the gradual implementation of the agreement. Although this was an explicit way to address the asymmetry, it may not have been sufficient.

The results of the November 1992 election in the United States created a difficult problem for NAFTA. President Clinton was not willing to take the agreement reached with his opponent as a *fait accompli*. Partisan politics forced him to demand an input from his administration into the final product to be known as the 'parallel agreements'. These focus on two main questions: a) environment and b) labour standards.

In terms of environmental issues, there was little disagreement. The two sides shared basically the same definitions at the governmental and grassroots level, and neither country wanted to do anything that could be interpreted as hurting the environment. Some in the United States mistakenly believed that the Mexican people would allow the Mexican government to settle NAFTA on the basis of lower standards of environmental regulation. The fallacy of this impression is demonstrated by the grassroots environmental movements that have arisen in Mexico at various points along the border with the United States.

Bilateral commissions have dealt actively and intensively with the question of the environment. Agreements have been reached and legislation has been introduced. These agreements are not perfect, nor will all groups be happy with them, but their very existence represents the important difference between the environmental question and the question of labour. On the two sides of the US-Mexican border there are still significant differences on the question of labour. In the United States, undocumented immigration is defined as a crime-related phenomenon, which requires a law enforcement solution. In Mexico, undocumented immigration is considered an economic, labour-related phenomenon. The two governments bypass each other with definitions that are entirely unconnected, leaving little hope for common ground.

Labour Migration

President Salinas suggested that the discussion of immigration with the Clinton administration should be a priority for the Mexican government. Immigration negotiations in this case would have to overcome from the outset disagreement about the definition of the problem, and also over the right figures to be used to define quantitatively its impact on society and economy respectively. Hoping that an agreement can be reached regardless of these fundamental differences, the Mexican government has initiated a strategy in which the first premise is to verify the credibility of data and scientific information about the costs and benefits of immigration. President Salinas and others have made it clear that both sides must agree upon information that will not become a political issue between the two countries, and must utilise the data in a reasonable way to rationalise the question of immigration.

One project, conducted by the author, has been counting, observing and interviewing a systematic random sample of undocumented immigrants as they cross the border between Mexico and the United States at the most intensive crossing point on the 2,000 mile border, Tijuana. The survey began in September, 1987. Interviews were conducted on Fridays, Saturdays and Sundays, when the most intensive crossing occurs.

According to this study,[1] 60 per cent of the total number of undocumented immigrants have destinations in the state of California. This number varies during the year, with the highest number in the summer months and the lowest in December. In the peak summer month of 1991, for example, approximately 1.75 million undocumented immigrants crossed into the United States. In December, that number declined to approximately 800,000, a difference of almost one-half.

Illegal immigration is difficult to calculate accurately, but studies like this one can generate some estimates about remittances, which are extremely important for the Mexican economy. In 1991, Mexican workers in the United States remitted approximately $3.5 billion to Mexico. The origin of migrants is highly concentrated (80 per cent come from 10 states in central, western and northern Mexico), so remittances have a significant impact on the local Mexican economies.

The study estimates that no significant impact will be felt on the phenomenon of undocumented immigration in the first five years after the signing of NAFTA. In six to ten years, the impact will be no more than a 25 per cent reduction in the volume observable today. In 11 to 15 years, the study predicts a maximum reduction of 50 per cent. This figure will increase as time goes on.

NAFTA's impact over the next five years will be minimal because most of the jobs created in Mexico will require a different skill level than that possessed by the average migrant. The psychological impact of NAFTA will register first, as people hear that jobs are opening. Although they may not benefit directly from these new jobs, they will hear about them and will tend to stay in Mexico. The direct economic impact will register when the creation of jobs begins to create additional labour demand in Mexico. These conclusions are based on the assumption that nothing else changes from the present situation.

Undocumented immigration and its related conditions are sensitive issues on both sides of the border. There is a general misconception about undocumented immigration. Many seem to believe that surreptitious movement across the border is a unilateral desire of Mexican citizens in that region. It is not well known, however, that the United States was the only country in the world where, until recently, immigration legislation allowed employers to hire foreigners even if they had entered in violation of immigration laws. This juridical aberration was corrected in 1986 with the passage of the Immigration Reform and Control Act (IRCA). However, IRCA has a loophole, one that makes a mockery of sanctions on employers of illegal aliens. US firms that hire foreigners must prove, with certain documents, that their workers are in the country legally and have the right to be employed. Yet US employers are not legally obliged to keep copies of these documents. That is the loophole. Thus, questionable situations place the word of the employer against the word of the immigration official or anyone challenging the employer's decision. The most important effect of the IRCA has been the rapid growth of the trade in forged immigration documents. At the inception of the IRCA in 1987, the cost of a forged document in San Diego, California, was about $500. Today that price has fallen to around $10.

This unnatural phenomenon was created by forces that have made undocumented immigration part of a *de facto* international labour market, one that responds to the interaction of a demand for cheap labour in the United States and a willing supply in Mexico. Mexico and the United States have not established official communication regarding the definition of this phenomenon. Obviously, if the United States were to accept the definition of undocumented immigration as a labour-related phenomenon rather than a crime-related phenomenon, the cost of labour would increase. As a result of the asymmetry of power between the two nations, however, the United States does not have to do that.

This asymmetry remains one of the most complicated elements in the integration aspirations that have already been realised at the border, where a vital free trade area has operated for many decades. In Tijuana, for instance, consumers already enjoy the options that are expected to result from NAFTA. Producers at the border have already seen changes take place in the labour force; certain parts of the labour force are already operating under conditions such as 'just-in-time' production formulas and other practices common in the United States.

The question of labour migration could become more complex and difficult than the negotiations for NAFTA itself. Economics, social inequality, human rights, politics and a multitude of other sensitive issues are all related to the question of labour migration between the two countries. Unless the parties find a way to utilise the experience of NAFTA and view this question in a manner that seeks to establish a rational solution, irrational conditions will continue to prevail. At the same time, border relations will continue to demonstrate the extent to which the Mexican people of this region will take advantage of conditions of free trade.

It is well known that many of the workers involved in immigration flows into the United States return to their country of origin. In the case of migration from Mexico to the United States, which has persisted for over a hundred years, not only has there been a return flow, but it has also included the majority of migrants. These workers return to Mexico after a migratory 'career' that involves alternating stays in the receiving areas in the United States and in their home communities in Mexico. Such a migratory 'career' can continue for several years, but it generally ends with an ageing worker's definitive return to Mexico. Obviously this is not true in every case. A growing proportion of migrants is choosing to remain permanently in the United States. Perhaps the decision to remain in the United States or to return definitively to the home community is a function of the intensity of the interaction between the sending community and the receiving community, reflected in the number of family members that the first-time migrant has in the United States. That is, the fewer family members a migrant has in the United States, the more likely it is that he or she will return definitively to Mexico.

Data obtained from a study carried out by the author reveal a process of circular migration from Mexico to the United States, which is clearly related to the geographical proximity of these two countries.[2] Circular migration is understood as the process by which an individual alternates stays of more than six months in Mexico and in the United States, between his or her family residence and job residence. This continues until either age, success or failure allows him or her to permanently establish family residence at some point on the circular route, either in Mexico or the United States.

The notion of circular migration holds two methodological implications. Because length of stays in the United States might be increasingly long, returns to Mexico become increasingly short and job residence becomes permanent as a result of family reunification. Then, new entries to the United States from Mexico might increase the volume of the migratory flow, giving to the observer the impression of an increase in immigration to the United States, when in fact what is being observed is an increase in the intensity of a circular movement, including Mexican citizens who might have moved on a permanent basis to the United States. Secondly, when measured properly, circular migration might become an indicator of the intensity of the interactions between 'structural conditions' and 'factors' located on the two sides of the border, which are associated with the phenomenon of international migration between the two countries. There are also two theoretical implications. First, the definition of a migrant should no longer depend on his or her position on the map, but on his or her engagement in an international labour market. Traditional definitions of a migrant require the crossing of a geographical boundary for a certain period of time. The notion of a circular migration should be operationalised from the theoretical assumption that a migrant is a person who is no longer a permanent resident of his or her home town because of a decision to join the international labour market in response to a perceived labour demand in another country. This means that a person is a migrant from the moment he or she has left home with the intention of looking for a job in another country.

The other reason is that, as a consequence of the above, for the purpose of an estimate of the number of international migrants, the count should begin when they join the migratory circle, regardless of whether the person has crossed an international border or not. The migratory circle includes the geographical space between the last permanent residence and the place of migratory destination. The latter could be of various types from a desired to a realised destination. The researcher's selection of the type of migratory destination might depend on the scope of the analysis. The important implication here is that all persons who are in the international migratory circle should be included in the enumeration of international migrants, whether or not they have left the country of origin or reached the country of destination.

Table 6.1 shows the Mexican states with the highest proportion of actual undocumented migrants as detected in the last five years. It is worth noting the appearance of the United States in the list of origins of those who crossed through the cities of Tijuana (see Column 1), where they represented 7.1 per cent of the total for that city; Mexicali (see Column 2), where they represented 2.2 per cent and Ciudad Juárez (see Column 3) where they represented 1.6 per cent. The inclusion of the United States in this table was due to the question that asked for the actual 'state of residence'. There were persons interviewed who stated that they no longer had a residence in Mexico, but instead permanently resided in the United States. These data suggest a paradoxical situation of an undocumented immigrant who claims no residence in his or her country of origin.

The circular nature of international migration between Mexico and the United States can best be measured when we are able to identify migratory flows in spatial, temporal and numerical terms. The fact that most undocumented migrants cross at some point along Mexico's northern border, where they can be interviewed, has enabled the author's research team to identify principal flows in terms of their origin and destination. The measurement of migratory flows has been the surest means devised thus far for calculating variations in the volume of undocumented migration; this is the case because efforts to measure the total numbers of undocumented migrants are hindered by the fact that the undocumented status of these individuals forces them into a covert existence in the United States. Measurements of migration flows are even more valuable when we can determine the socioeconomic characteristics of the migrants.

Despite advances made towards calculating the total number of undocumented Mexican migrants in the United States, including the recent work of David Heer,[3] these calculations are still necessarily indirect. A number of factors have made it impossible to get direct counts of the population of undocumented Mexican migrants in the United States at any specific moment. Thanks to studies done at the end of the 1970s, we know that the number of undocumented Mexican migants may fluctuate by over 50 per cent in a given year.

Table 6.1
Undocumented Migration by Source to the United States through Main Points of Entry, 1989-1993

Tijuana	%	Mexicali	%	Ciudad Juárez	%	Nuevo Laredo	%	Matamoros	%
Michoacán	13.5	Sinaloa	12.6	Chihuahua	31.5	Nuevo León	17.7	Tamaulipas	31.3
Jalisco	12.5	Michoacán	9.7	Durango	16.6	Guanajuato	15.6	San Luis Potosí	13.2
Mexico City	9.1	Jalisco	9.3	Coahuila	16.2	Mexico City	11.7	Veracruz	11.1
USA	7.1	Guanajuato	8.8	Zacatecas	9.0	San Luis Potosí	11.1	Centro América	7.0
Oaxaca	6.8	Sonora	7.7	Mexico City	6.6	Coahuila	7.9	Est. México	5.7
Guerrero	6.5	Mexico City	5.8	Guanajuato	2.3	Zacatecas	5.3	Nuevo León	4.0
Guanajuato	5.4	Nayarit	5.4	Jalisco	1.6	Est. México	5.1	Mexico City	4.0
Sinaloa	5.0	Oaxaca	5.0	USA	1.6	Centro América	3.0	Michoacán	3.1
Puebla	4.9	Zacatecas	4.9	Aguascalientes	1.5	Querétaro	2.8	Guanajuato	2.7
Morelos	4.3	Guerrero	4.3	Est. México	1.5	Veracruz	2.8	Hidalgo	2.3
Est. México	3.5	Est. México	3.5	Puebla	1.3	Michoacán	2.7	Querétaro	2.3
Zacatecas	3.5	USA	3.5	Veracruz	1.0	Jalisco	2.3	Guerrero	1.5
Nayarit	3.2	Veracruz	3.2	Michoacán	1.0	Tamaulipas	1.8	Jalisco	1.4
Colima	2.1	Hidalgo	2.1	San Luis Potosí	1.0	Durango	1.6	Zacatecas	1.1
Sonora	1.7	Chihuahua	1.7	Sonora	0.9	Guerrero	1.4	Chiapas	1.0
Others	10.9	Others	18.9	Others	6.4	Others	18.3	Others	8.3

SOURCE: Bustamante et al (1993).

We also know that the lowest numbers regularly occur in December and the highest in July and August. Unfortunately, the count of how many undocumented migrants there are in the United States has become highly politicised. On occasion, political interests in the United States inflate these numbers to their highest credible levels, a phenomenon the author reported as early as 1979.[4]

International Migration as a Process of Interaction

Data presented in the following tables are drawn from a selection of basic socio-economic characteristics of undocumented migrants from Mexico.[5] Table 6.2 shows a selection of socio-economic characteristics of Mexican undocumented migrants over the last six years. With regard to gender, the table shows a relative stability in the proportion of women. It should be noted, however, that there are significant variations when data are broken down by state of origin. Migrants from the metropolitan area of Mexico City show the highest proportion of women (24 per cent), whereas in more rural states such as Guerrero that proportion drops to less than 10 per cent.

With regard to age, Table 6.2 suggests there is a tendency towards a higher concentration in the most productive age cohorts (between twenty and thirty). This could indicate increasing competition in the labour market in the United States and/or a shorter 'migratory career', meaning the time through which an individual keeps him/herself in the circular process of migration between the two countries. As far as education (years of school attended) is concerned, it is interesting to note a decrease in the percentage for the least educated, which suggests an increase in the 'human capital' value of the undocumented immigrants.

One of the most important findings reported in Table 6.2 is the relatively rapid increase of the urban origin of undocumented migrants from Mexico (12 per cent in less than 6 years). A hypothesis could be drawn from this, which posits that there is a higher opportunity cost for the migrant's home economy since the migrating labour force appears to be of an increasingly high 'human capital' value. Finally, data taken from the question, 'have you ever had a job in the United States?' at the bottom of Table 6.2, provide some empirical foundation for the notion of 'circular migration' put forward here. The rise in the proportion of affirmative responses suggests an increasingly intense circular movement of migrants between the two countries.

Table 6.2
**Socio-Economic Profile of Mexican Undocumented Immigrants,
1988-1993**

	1988	1989	1990	1991	1992	1993*
Gender						
Female	16.3	16.5	14.6	21.4	19.2	16.6
Male	83.7	83.5	85.4	78.6	80.8	83.4
Age						
Under 20	18.0	13.8	14.7	17.0	17.3	14.6
20 to 24	31.2	31.7	30.9	29.9	33.7	33.8
25 to 29	22.3	26.0	30.4	26.6	25.3	28.9
Older than 30	28.5	28.5	24.0	26.5	23.7	22.7
Education						
Elementary (incomplete)	37.8	29.4	23.9	19.6	17.3	12.8
Elementary (complete)	26.5	39.5	39.0	30.8	33.4	35.8
Secondary (complete)	22.7	22.4	27.0	33.2	35.9	39.2
More than secondary	13.0	8.7	10.1	16.4	13.3	12.2
Occupation in Mexico						
Farm work	31.4	32.1	32.3	26.0	24.6	27.4
Urban	48.1	50.4	52.3	54.4	58.1	60.3
Unemployed	20.0	17.3	14.8	19.2	16.7	11.9
Unspecified	0.4	0.2	0.6	0.3	0.7	0.4
Have you had a job in the USA?						
Yes	46.2	43.3	42.9	49.4	54.1	55.6
No	53.2	56.6	56.7	50.4	45.3	43.7
Unspecified	0.5	0.2	0.4	0.2	0.6	0.7

* From January to April only

SOURCE: see Table 6.1

Table 6.3 shows the US destination of undocumented migrants from
Mexico. It confirms previous findings about the increasing preference
for California in general and Los Angeles in particular. Indeed, almost
sixty per cent of the total number of undocumented Mexican migrants
to the United States are now heading towards California. This pattern of

concentration is mirrored by the relative decline in the preference for other regions of the United States or Canada in addition to the decline in the percentages of migrants who responded that they did not know where they were heading at the time of the interview.

Table 6.3
Destination of Mexican Undocumented Migrants by Year of Border Crossing, 1988-1993

Destination	1988	1989	1990	1991	1992	1993*
California:						
Los Angeles	22.7	23.8	30.4	29.3	29.1	29.8
Rest of California	22.2	26.7	25.2	26.7	27.9	29.4
Texas:						
Houston/Dallas/San Antonio/El Paso	21.4	20.6	21.6	23.5	21.8	20.3
Rest of Texas	1.4	0.8	1.1	1.4	1.3	0.6
Chicago	1.7	2.7	1.8	0.9	0.9	1.0
Rest of USA	13.2	8.7	6.2	7.0	7.7	7.8
Canada	0.3	0.1	0.0	0.1	0.1	0.0
Unknown	17.1	16.7	13.8	11.1	11.2	11.1
Total	100	100	100	100	100	100

* From January to April only

SOURCE: See Table 6.1

Finally, Table 6.4 provides empirical support for the claim about the persistence of a US demand for undocumented Mexican immigrant labour. This table indicates the reported previous job experience in the United States of individuals preparing to enter the United States again. The trend for farmworking, where a clear decline seems to be taking place, is noteworthy. This seems to be consistent with the patterns of increased educational levels among undocumented immigrants noted above.

Table 6.4
Undocumented Mexican Migrants that have Worked in the USA, by Type of Employment, 1988-1993

Activity	1988	1989	1990	1991	1992	1993[*]
Tourism	8.3	8.2	7.6	9.1	8.5	9.4
Domestic Service	16.6	21.7	22.3	23.8	21.4	17.8
Other Service	6.6	6.2	8.5	5.8	6.9	6.7
Agricultural	40.5	38.9	39.4	29.9	29.5	33.4
Manufacturing	9.4	9.0	6.4	6.4	6.8	6.9
Construction	14.0	12.5	12.7	20.8	22.9	22.4
Self-Employed	1.7	1.9	1.5	0.9	0.2	0.1
Other	2.9	1.6	1.7	3.3	3.8	3.3
Total	100.0	100.0	100.0	100.0	100.0	100.0

[*] From January to April only
SOURCE: see Table 6.1

Towards a Pragmatic Approach to Labour Migration from Mexico

In early 1992 there was an important meeting in Washington DC, at which representatives of the Mexican and US federal governments discussed the problems of violence on their common border. On the eve of that meeting, a high-level US functionary, who asked not to be identified, told the author, 'there are no official proposals from the Mexican side on what to do about undocumented immigration; they only have proposals to talk about the problem, but not about how to resolve it'. Meanwhile, of course, it is painfully clear that the US government does have proposals. These proposals share a common characteristic: all adopt the law enforcement focus that the US government consistently places on undocumented migration. The US government never wavers from defining this phenomenon as a crime problem requiring police-type solutions. The persistence of this view of migration from Mexico led the US government to reject categorically the idea of considering labour migration within the NAFTA negotiations. The US government will only agree to deal bilaterally with the problem of undocumented migration if it is in relation to law enforcement policies. Its refusal to view the issue as a labour issue has been inflexible. However, this inflexibility has not been expressed openly and hence it has not appeared in the mass media.

In my view, it is a political miscalculation on the part of the Mexican government to allow the US government to acknowledge its inflexibility only within internal diplomatic circles. At the opening of the free trade negotiations in Mazatlán in 1990, a spokesperson for the United States refused to include the migration issue and this went unchallenged. The rationale put forward since that time has been that labour migration would only be included in negotiations for a common market.[6] This rationale masks the fact that the United States prefers to continue addressing the migration issue unilaterally as a crime issue, since undocumented migration provides an inexhaustible source of cheap labour that the United States can regulate, and has regulated, according to its economic needs. It also has an additional advantage: these migrants serve politically as scapegoats every time the US government wants to hide from the US public the true causes of some hardship such as high rates of unemployment, drug trafficking or social unrest such as the 1992 disturbances in Los Angeles. To address the migration issue as an economic phenomenon would mean bringing it to the bilateral negotiating table and that, in turn, would increase the costs of this labour force that is kept cheap by virtue of the fact that it is kept undocumented and hence criminal. The US refusal to focus on undocumented migration as a labour issue saves the US economy several billion dollars every year. This is the chief reason for the current US position, and it is what lies behind US inflexibility on dealing with the migration issue as anything other than a law enforcement matter. This inflexibility is nothing other than a flagrant expression of the power asymmetry characterising the US-Mexican relationship across all dimensions. In this light, the United States is unjustified in saying that 'there are no official proposals from the Mexican side'.

The situation suggests that the Mexican government should formulate a proposal detailing what has been voiced by a series of Mexican presidents, government ministers and high-ranking members of Congress: (a) that Mexico wants to export products, not people; (b) that undocumented migration is an economic issue and a human rights issue; (c) that these issues should be negotiated bilaterally in depth and over the long-term. This has been the position of the Mexican government during the last four administrations, ever since President Echeverría decided over twenty years ago not to seek renewal of the *bracero* agreements which had lapsed in 1965.[7] The US government has never officially accepted points (b) and (c) since the US view does not accept that migration is a trans-border issue demanding 'international cooperation'. It continues to hold that migration is a domestic national security issue or a law enforcement issue. In order to correct this lack of a precise definition of Mexico's national interests in the issue of undocumented workers, the author proposes a strategy that includes the agreement by the two national governments to form a bilateral commission with three objectives: (1) to produce a bilateral report that defines and describes legal and undocumented migration, both of Mexican citizens to the United States and US citizens to Mexico; (2) to discuss and defend this report before representatives of the respective legislatures and before representatives of the major media networks, of key associations from the private sector, and of organised labour from each country; (3) to act as consultants to the official negotiators of a Migration Treaty between the two countries with commission members filling this role in their respective countries. Negotiating such a treaty would be the next step, which could only be attempted once the set of objectives outlined above had been accomplished.

The irrationality that permeates the mythology of Mexican-US migration leads us to assume that a necessary precondition for reaching agreement on a Migration Treaty would be to de-mythologise undocumented immigration. This could be accomplished through a scientific analysis that would be produced and supported bilaterally, making it acceptable and credible on both sides of the border. Under current conditions, it is impossible to reach any agreement that would be acceptable to the respective political institutions and civil societies of Mexico and the United States. It is imperative that these conditions change. This would be the primary objective of the proposed bilateral commission. This commission would be made up of one member from each country's respective government sector, and two members each per country from the business sector, organised labour and academic institutions. It would have a budget with which to finance independent studies on the condition that they be bilaterally directed. Its secretariat or permanent staff would include members from both countries; these individuals would be charged with implementing the decisions of the commission. Once the research efforts had produced their results and the negotiations of the Migration Treaty had begun, commission members would act as consultants to their respective country's team of negotiators, except in the case of government representatives on the commission, who could serve as members of their country's negotiating team. The complexity of the issue of migration between these two countries is so great that we should not expect its negotiation to be any less intricate than the NAFTA negotiations. What the United States has to gain from a Migration Treaty is not substantially different from what it expects to gain from NAFTA: a neighbouring country economically capable of buying more US-made products and with sufficient political stability to institutionalise similar rules of the game to those of Canada and the United States so that all three countries can adopt strategies on a regional basis in order to compete successfully with the European Community and the Asian countries.

Notes

1. Full details are available from the author on request.
2. This study focused on Cañón Zapata, a frequently used point of entry to the USA. See Bustamante et al (1993).
3. See Heer (1990). This book includes the most serious and complete effort that I have seen so far to calculate the number of undocumented Mexicans residing permanently in the United States.
4. See Bustamante and Martínez (1979).
5. The data are drawn from the Cañón Zapata project. See note 2.
6. Since a common market, unlike a free trade area, implies free movement of all factors of production, it could only be established if free movement of labour was permitted.
7. The *bracero* agreement provided quotas for Mexican migration to the United States. It was designed primarily to provide cheap labour for low-cost agriculture in the USA.

CHAPTER 7

NAFTA AND THE ENVIRONMENT

Roberto A. Sánchez

Before the proposal of NAFTA, few national environmental organisations had tried broadly to influence environmental conditions along the US-Mexico border, or to engage in the linkages between international trade and the environment. The prospect of an imminent North American free trade zone has evoked environmental concerns to an unprecedented degree, enhancing government attention to environmental problems in Mexico.[1] The environmentalist agenda now aims for a comprehensive North American environmental regime. Environmentalists fear that free trade would undermine existing national environmental regulations, creating inequalities arising from differences in national environmental regulations and their enforcement.[2] Some groups have also been concerned that growth arising from intensified trade and investment will aggravate environmental abuses, particularly in Mexico. The absence of a reliable environmental impact assessment of NAFTA's potential environmental risks encouraged these fears.[3] Environmentalists also blamed NAFTA for limiting public participation in the rule-making and dispute settlement procedures.

These arguments are a clear example of the rising importance of environmental issues in the discussion of the economy, the wide diversity of opinions on how to deal with them, and the lack of consensus on the role they should play in planning economic growth and social well-being in each of these three countries and between them.

Central to these problems are the expectations and demands of the environmental community. For the first time, environmentalist groups have made a serious attempt to influence international trade policy. Environmental mobilisation generated new levels of intergroup cooperation in policy-making, information sharing and networking, as well as setting the stage for the creation of a new North American alliance of environmental organisations. Yet disagreement on the results of the parallel negotiations on the environment sparked profound division among the groups.

95

NAFTA and the Environment

Among the structural changes Mexico has experienced during the last decade, the management of the environment has been gaining attention. Mexico is upgrading its environmental protection system.[4] This is a process that former President De La Madrid began ten years ago, on a modest scale due to Mexico's economic crisis, but with visible results only during the last four years.[5] A milestone in this process is Mexico's new environmental legislation and its 83 *normas técnicas* (environmental standards). Although the new legislation provides a broader support for environmental protection, its environmental standards are still being developed. Mexico's environmental agency, SEDESOL, announced it will publish 80 more *normas técnicas* by the end of 1993, and it expects to publish 70 more in 1994.[6] This compares to hundreds of environmental standards in the USA and Canada developed in the last two decades.

A key problem for Mexico is environmental enforcement. Lack of adequate economic, human, material and technical resources, as well as economic constraints in the public sector, limit significantly Mexico's possibilities to reinforce environmental protection. This situation is aggravated by years of neglecting the environment, the absence of a comprehensive environmental policy, and the concentration of environmental enforcement only in federal agencies until this year. Hence it is no surprise to find Mexico immersed in an environmental crisis.[7]

Although far from perfect, the USA and Canada have followed a more comprehensive approach to environmental protection in the last 20 years. Their 'end of the pipe policy' has yielded higher levels of environmental protection than in Mexico. They also have the resources to enforce environmental management at a federal, state and local level.[8] Based on these differences in environmental protection, opponents of NAFTA argue that lax enforcement in Mexico creates effects similar to those of subsidies, attracting production and jobs, and distorting trade.

The pressure by environmental groups, unions and other groups resulted in environmental provisions being written into the NAFTA preamble. NAFTA also included the recognition of the primacy of a specific list of environmental accords and provision for adding new treaties and agreements to the list (Article 104 and Annex 104.1).[9] NAFTA also guarantees state and provincial governments the ability to impose their own higher environmental standards.[10] Chapter 7 of NAFTA, on sanitary and phytosanitary measures, defines appropriate levels of protection to mean 'the level of protection of human, animal or plant life or health in the territory of a party that the party considers appropriate'.[11] This chapter outlines some objectives that could lead to the eventual harmonisation of pesticide standards between Mexico and the USA. It calls the three countries to base their sanitary and phyto-sanitary measures on scientific evidences that are outlined in accordance with risk assessment methodologies agreed by all parties (Article 765(2)).[12] Article 756(3) urges each exporting country to make its testing and inspection facilities easily available to importing countries and make available information on relevant procedures. Chapter 9 states that no unnecessary obstacle to trade has been created if 'the demonstra-ble purpose of such measures is to achieve a legitimate objective and such measure does not operate to exclude goods of another party that meet their legitimate objective'.[13] Articles 906(1), 906(2), and 906(3) commit the parties to work together to enhance environmental measures and seek compatibility. Annex 913-A and Annex 913-C establish subcommittees which, among other functions, would set emissions and environmental pollution levels that affect land transportation in North America. Article 1114(2) commits the NAFTA countries to avoid lowering environmental standards or failing to enforce environmental standards, as a means of attracting or maintaining investment. Article 2101.1 incorporates GATT Articles XX(b) and XX (g). Article XX (b) includes 'environmental measures necessary to protect human, animal or plant life or health'. Article XX (g) includes 'measures relating to the conservation of living and non-living exhaustible natural resources'. Article 2005.4 provides that in the event of a disagreement raising 'factual issues concerning the environment, health, safety or conserv-ation', the party having adopted a measure 'to protect its human, animal or plant life or health, or to protect its environment' would have the option of electing to have the dispute considered exclusively according to the NAFTA dispute settlement mechanism.

Absent from NAFTA are mechanisms such as the withdrawal of trade benefits that would compel strict enforcement of Mexico's environmental laws. NAFTA administrative and institutional shortfalls are also apparent. There is no additional provision for public participa-tion, particularly by state, local representatives or NGOs. NAFTA fails to guarantee citizen knowledge rights, and does not enhance opportuni-ties for environmentalists to participate in dispute resolution boards. It does not provide for an environmental commission to monitor and enforce the environmental conditions of the agreement. All of these are mechanisms strongly advocated by the environmental community. Environmentalists complain also about the poor definitions of key environmental issues in NAFTA and the absence of a timetable to harmonise environmental standards.

Although environmental provisions in NAFTA go beyond the environmental considerations in any other trade agreement, it falls short of the environmental objectives envisioned by the environmental community.[14] Feeling they have failed to achieve their core objective of transforming NAFTA into a strong instrument for advancing an agenda of environmental protection in North America, environmental groups gathered further support from the US Congress to maintain their pressure on the Clinton administration. President Clinton's commitment to address environmental concerns without reopening NAFTA drove the three countries into a new round of supplementary negotiations.

The Actors

Prior to the conclusion of the supplementary negotiations, the environmental groups in the USA were divided in three: those in favour of the agreement (National Wild Life Federation and National Wildlife Fund); those seeking higher safeguards in the supplementary negotiations (Natural Resources Defense Council, Environmental Defense Fund, Audubon Society and other regional groups at the US-Mexico border, such as the Border Ecology Project, Texas Center for Policy Studies, and the Arizona Toxics Information); those opposing NAFTA (Sierra Club, Public Citizens, Friends of the Earth). Greenpeace, another of the major national groups in the USA, did not have a clear position regarding NAFTA. Environmental groups in Canada and Mexico could be divided in the same way. Canada Pollution Probe, Grupo de los Cien, Asociación de Grupos Ambientalistas (a network of Mexican environmental groups), and Red Fronteriza de Salud Ambiental (a network of border environmental groups) had a similar position to those in the USA seeking higher safeguards in the supplementary negotiations; El Pacto de Grupos Ecologistas, part of the Red Mexicana de Acción Frente al Tratado de Libre Comercio, opposed NAFTA.

While specific assessments varied from group to group, most environmental organisations shared a set of common concerns with respect to NAFTA. These groups insisted on an 'explicit commitment on the part of the signatories to ensure that trade rules and trade activities would contribute to sustainable development'.[15] Their concerns included minimal safeguards that include the following five components:

(i) Environmentalists demanded secure resources for environmental infrastructure, environmental clean up, and for the administration of the agreement to assist public participation; they also wanted to secure funding for a North American Commission on the Environment. Possible sources for funding mentioned were compensatory, green tax or tariff measures, perhaps in combination with effective bond mechanisms, and a strict application of the 'polluter pays' principle.

(ii) To improve compliance and enforcement of domestic environmental laws through the judicial process and the possible use of trade sanctions against governments and individual companies.

(iii) A higher public participation in the administrative and dispute process of NAFTA and in the North American Commission on the Environment as advisers and including an active involvement in decisions. The groups also seek to establish community right to observe laws in all three countries consistent with principle 10 of the Rio declaration.

(iv) Environmentalists also required that the supplementary agreements should address language problems on product and process standards of the NAFTA text (chapter 7 and chapter 9). They also demanded an explicit guarantee for the preservation of the state's rights (higher standards not to be restricted).

(v) With regard to the North American Commission on the Environment (NACE), environmentalists seek a clear guarantee that the commission will be able to carry out independent research and to prepare annual reports on the state of the environment. Environmentalists also required that the NACE acts as a policy forum empowered to follow up on the recommendations of its reports.[16]

The environmental community demanded also the 'grandfathering' of other international environmental agreements (Article 104), and the creation of a Border Environmental Commission to decentralise authority in the management of the border environment. Some additional differences arose in the position of some groups seeking a clear definition of what should be considered a minimal base for product standards before they are considered unfair trade subsidies. Although all groups agreed there should be an upgrade harmonisation, some groups seek to move from product standards to process standards, and to best available technology standards as basic criteria for harmonisation.

Almost all of the groups supported the creation of a North American Commission on the Environment (NACE). Originally a proposal by the Natural Resources Defense Council (NRDC), the three governments approved the creation of the commission in September 1992 without a clear definition of its jurisdiction and functions. As proposed by NRDC the commission would work to 'raise environmental standards and enforcement practices to the highest levels within the free trade area', complementing, but not superseding, the work of the US Environment Protection Agency and its national counterpart agencies in Mexico and Canada.[17] The National Wildlife Federation (NWF) proposal on NACE called for a participation of the commission in three phases of the NAFTA dispute resolution process: consultation between parties; meeting of the NAFTA trade Commission in cases where consultation fails to resolve a dispute, and convening of the NAFTA panel.[18] In its original proposal NWF sought NACE jurisdiction to include the right to provide recommendations as part of the NAFTA Trade Commission deliberations. A similar proposal was also presented by the Asociación de Grupos Ambientalistas.

Most of the major environmental groups in the USA signed a letter (4 May 1993) to Ambassador Michael Kantor supporting NAFTA if the supplementary agreements included most of the provisions mentioned above.[19] The letter implies a recognition among these groups of Mexico's political and economic need for NAFTA. It also showed a disposition in favour of flexibility and cooperation.[20] Reaching a middle point between the demands of the environmental groups, Congressional opposition to NAFTA and the positions of Canada and Mexico, proved to be a difficult task for the US trade negotiators.

The Supplementary Negotiations

A core issue in the supplementary negotiations was the debate over the introduction of supranational functions in the NACE to impose trade-related sanctions. Canada and Mexico stressed at all times their opposition to a commission with supranational functions, arguing the defence of sovereignty. Business groups in the USA also showed concern over a supranational commission. This is one reason why the supplementary negotiations extended beyond their initial target date (June 1993). A final version of the supplementary agreements was available by the end of August 1993, and the Presidents of Mexico, the

United States and the Prime Minister of Canada signed them simultaneously two weeks later. The negotiations went through periods of strong disagreements between the three parties. A middle ground was finally reached in which the original US proposal was modified in several ways.[21]

Trade-related sanctions were maintained as an environmental enforcement tool, but the standard of lax enforcement that must be met in order for a panel to find a government violating the accord was modified from 'a persistent and unjustifiable pattern of non-enforcement of a domestic law' to 'a persistent pattern of failure to effectively enforce a domestic law'.[22] NAFTA benefits can be suspended (Article 36 and Annex 36B) if a country fails to comply with dispute panel decisions on sanctions through a process that mirrors Chapter 20 of NAFTA. Repeated enforcement failures relate to 'workplaces, firms, companies, or sectors that produce goods or provide services traded between the parties or that compete with goods produced and services provided by another party'. The accord could not be applied retroactively, so that only patterns of non-enforcement that occur after 1 January 1994 would be subject to its provisions. However, Annex 36A states that if Canada is the Party complained against, the procedures set out in Article 36 shall not apply. Instead, the Commission for Environmental Cooperation, at the request of a complaining Party, may file in court of competent jurisdiction a certified copy of a panel determination (Annex 36A).[23] This was the compromise that the parties reached, given the strong opposition of Canada to accept trade-related sanctions.

Another important modification to the original US position is that, under the definition of environmental law that the US, Mexican and Canadian negotiators have crafted, domestic measures aimed at preventing pollution, controlling hazardous materials and protecting wild flora and fauna and their habitat would be covered under the environmental pact's dispute settlement provisions. Largely at Canada's insistence, however, the public cannot complain and no government can bring a challenge on provisions governing the management of the 'commercial harvest or exploitation, or subsistence or aboriginal harvesting, of natural resources' (Article 45).[24] Canada insisted on this exception so that challenges could not be brought against timber or fishery management programmes.[25]

The final text of the supplementary agreement has also further curtailed the relatively independent investigative powers of the secretariat of the North American Commission on the Environment originally proposed by the USA.[26] While the secretariat can still receive complaints of lax enforcement directly from the public if they meet certain criteria, it can no longer propose to environment ministers that one of its investigations be pursued further by a dispute settlement panel, and it is limited to establishing a 'factual record' on the allegations that does not include any recommendations (Articles 13, 14 and 15). The council may also object to making public the report of the secretariat. The provision of information by the Parties is also restricted: 'if a Party considers that a request for information from the secretariat is excessive or otherwise unduly burdensome, it may so notify the council. The secretariat shall revise the scope of its request to comply with the limitations established by the Council by a two-thirds vote' (Article 21). Furthermore, any Party may argue in writing that the information requested would impede 'its environmental law enforcement' or 'is protected from disclosure by its law governing business or proprietary information, personal privacy or the confidentiality of governmental decision making' (Article 39).

The consultation and resolution of disputes procedures follows a process similar to the one established by Chapter 20 of NAFTA. After consultations, the Council shall convene an arbitration panel (Article 24). If there is a persistent pattern of failure by the Party complained against effectively to enforce its environmental law, the panel may impose a monetary enforcement assessment (Article 34).[27] When a Party fails to pay a monetary enforcement assessment within 180 days after it is imposed by a panel, NAFTA benefits are suspended in an amount no greater than that sufficient to collect the monetary enforcement assessment (Article 36).

A recent study by the Texas Center for Policy Studies shows that the final text of the agreement did not incorporate important provisions requested by the environmental groups as a condition for their endorsement of NAFTA and its side agreements.[28] These provisions are: a strong and effective public participation in the commission operations; a commission secretariat with independent power to prepare reports and conduct investigations; access to specific reports from the commission (evaluation of environmental law enforcement in all three countries, implementation of NAFTA and its side agreements, border environmental issues, trade and natural resources, status of upward harmonisation of environmental laws); flexible procedure for citizen complaints; right-to-know laws; clarification of procedures of Chapter 20 for dispute resolution procedures in NAFTA; clear definition on the effects of NAFTA on federal, state and local environmental laws and standards, and the incorporation of additional international agreements to Annex

104.1 of NAFTA. The final draft of the agreement shows the strength of Canada's objections to trade-related sanctions and its opposition to include the management of natural resources within the agreement. In contrast, Mexico did agree to trade-related sanctions, although it opposed them for months in all public statements.[29] Nevertheless, Mexico succeeded in establishing a long process before a Party can reach the stage of trade-related sanctions. The opposition of Mexico and Canada to citizen participation in the operation of the commission also prevailed, as well as the restriction on the flow of information outside the commission. The final version of the supplementary environment agreement is a middle point between the original position of the three Parties.

The supplementary agreements have had a political impact in the USA. A strong dispute among US environmentalists has exposed the ideological rift among some groups over support for the White House and the business community behind NAFTA. Those national groups supporting the pact (National Wildlife Federation, Conservation International, Natural Resources Defense Council, World Wildlife Fund, National Audubon Society, and Environmental Defence Fund) have voiced their support for NAFTA, calling the groups attacking the pact misinformed.[30] The groups opposing the pact (Public Citizen, Sierra Club, Friends of the Earth, Greenpeace, Earth Island Institute, Public Interest Research Group, Rainforest Action Network, American Human Society) formed a new coalition, The Citizens Trade Campaign, to campaign to prevent its passage.[31] Deep in the division among environmentalists is their social conception of the environment. Although this division is not new, environmentalists in the USA and in other parts of the world had successfully concealed their ideological differences under one common objective – the protection of the environment. The environmental movement has been a very peculiar phenomenon during the last 20 years due to its ability to recruit people from very different ideological and social backgrounds. It seems that NAFTA has shattered the fragile unity among US environmentalists. The new divisions are likely to be permanent and will also shape the public's support for environmental groups according to ideology rather than a common goal. In the USA, where environmental groups count their membership by the hundred thousands, and millions of dollars, this is not a trivial question.

The financial question for environmental management and clean-up under NAFTA is important because it is one of the concrete benefits that can be obtained in the short-term to solve current environmental problems and to prevent the potential negative effects on the environment of the trade agreement. Three proposals to finance the NAFTA package have been made public: one presented by the National Wildlife Federation and the Environment Defense Fund, another one by The Sierra Club, and the third by The US Council of the Mexico-US Business Committee. The three proposals are similar in many ways. The first proposal estimates funding needs for the NACE at $29 million annual operating costs, and $7.6 billion dollars for the environmental infrastructure, such as sewage treatment plants and drinking water supply on both sides of the US-Mexico border during the first decade of NAFTA (1994-2003). It estimates also that basic conservation needs throughout Mexico, i.e., preservation of natural areas and biodiversity, could be addressed through a 'Green Fund' that would generate $5 million annually out of an initial endowment of $75 million. The US Council of the Mexico-US Business Committee estimates (July 1993) that $6.5 billion is required for water, sewage and solid and hazardous waste services and facilities along the border until 2003. The proposal estimates also that over the same ten-year period, approximately $4.6 billion in projected financing from public financial resources on both sides of the border will be available for the US-Mexico border region. This proposal does not include any financing provisions for NACE.

The Sierra Club proposal (July 1993) is more comprehensive than the other two. It includes a wide range of issues to improve environmental management and clean-up along the US-Mexico border and throughout Mexico. The Sierra Club estimated total costs for NAFTA-related environmental needs at $21 billion through 2003. Within that $21 billion figure, environmental needs (air, water, hazardous wastes, solid wastes, habitat and wildlife protection) would cost $13.5 billion. Multiple purpose investment with significant environmental benefits would cost $7.5 billion. This proposal includes financing for water supply (infrastructure and regulation), sanitation (treatment, infrastructure and regulation), solid wastes (future needs and clean up, including collection and landfills), hazardous wastes (clean up, future needs and regulation), air quality (regulations, public infrastructure, private sector), conservation, NACE and environmental management. $10.2 billion would be allocated to Mexico and close to $3.3 billion to the USA. The multiple purpose needs include border roads, border crossing, public transportation, worker and community health, and pollution prevention and technology transfer.

The three proposals do have differences in their suggested funding mechanisms. The National Wildlife Fund and Environment Defence

Fund proposals rely on three alternatives: a fee on imports (crossing one or both borders); earmarking a portion of tariffs prior to their phase out; an earmarked increase in corporate taxes. The US Council proposal assumes that funds provided through the Border Integrated Environmental Plan ($460 million from Mexico and $406 million from the USA), World Bank loans to Mexico for water supply and sanitation, Inter-American Development Bank (IDB) loans, as well as the potential participation of the International Finance Corporation, the Inter-American Finance Corporation and the Eximbank, would secure $4.57 billion dollars in a ten year period (1993-2003). To finance the $1.89 billion gap the proposal suggests a user fee concept and a real state expansion concept. The user fee concept would transfer the cost of new facilities to the users. This fee would also target the *maquiladora* industry, making it 'bear its fair share of the costs, through property taxes and user fees, to finance new environmental facilities'.

The Sierra Club recommends a funding mechanism consisting of an Environmental Fund to guarantee bonds and loans and to provide grants for environmental investments. To ensure that the beneficiaries of NAFTA pay for the costs generated by expanded economic activity, the Sierra Club proposes to capitalise the fund through a broad-based transaction fee on goods and services and investment crossing both the US-Mexico border and the US-Canada border. According to this proposal, leveraging would allow the fee needed to generate the capital to cover environmental needs on the US-Mexico border to be less than one per cent on all border transactions between the USA and Mexico over the next ten years.

The Clinton administration has unveiled plans for a $5 billion fund to pay for environmental clean-up along the US-Mexico border. The fund is to provide seed money for a development bank. As part of this strategy, the United States and Mexico will also create a Border Environmental Administration to coordinate and oversee the programme to reduce air and water pollution and manage the disposal of solid waste.[32] Preliminary reports suggest that the Border Environmental Administration would coordinate a regional plan on environmental infrastructure, incorporating the views of local communities and non-governmental organisations. The plan includes also the creation of a Border Environmental Finance Bank, which could be housed in the IDB and would provide loans and partial guarantees as required for each project. The Border Environmental Administration could coordinate financing of the projects through private sector sources and government support (grants, credits, the Brady Bond arrangement, etc.). The proposal estimates that $150 million in US appropriations per year for five years could support financing at least $5 billion in credits and guarantees over five years ($1 billion per year could be leveraged with two-thirds of the appropriation), and it would still provide $304 million in grants from the USA alone ($61 million per year). The financial structure for infrastructure projects would be supported through a special purpose corporation created by the US and Mexican municipalities affected to own and construct the proposed project. Equity would be shared between the states and localities benefiting from the projects in Mexico and the USA (it is expected that Mexico's federal government would guarantee these resources through credits from international organisations). In the capital structure of the Border Environmental Finance Bank, 85 percent of the shareholders would be in the USA and 15 percent in Mexico.[33]

Financing is a critical issue in all of these proposals. Mexico and Canada have opposed any fee on imports, arguing that it is against the spirit of free trade. Without this new source of revenue it is difficult to imagine how any of these proposals could be feasible. Finding new financing sources in Mexico and in the USA is a very difficult task. Transferring money already allocated to the states and municipalities to finance border environmental infrastructure would impose a heavy political price in the USA. Mexico would probably depend on credit from international agencies, but this would increase even more its already large foreign debt. If Mexico decides to finance its share of the border environmental infrastructure and clean up through an increase in its foreign debt, it will subsidise even more polluters and heavy users of that infrastructure.

For Mexico, it is important to make sound decisions without transferring the economic cost of those decisions to the rest of society and future generations (an increase in foreign debt). It is unwise to rely too heavily on future economic growth through NAFTA. This argument would lead Mexicans to believe that the increase in their foreign debt is the price they have to pay now to give NAFTA a chance to improve their economic and social well-being in the future. At the same time environmental problems in Mexico must have a solution with or without NAFTA. What is questionable is not the solution of these problems, but how this solution is achieved and what the distribution of its cost is among social groups. Mexico may therefore need to explore new sources of finance including those which have been resisted so far (e.g. import fees).

In that sense, it is worth noting that the proposal from the Sierra

Club is intended to transfer the cost of environmental protection to polluters and infrastructure users. The proposal tries also to avoid any increase in Mexico's foreign debt. One final advantage of this proposal is its comprehensive approach to environmental problems. It is the only proposal that seeks funds to improve environmental management in the rest of Mexico. This is also a critical issue because the environmental crisis in Mexico is not restricted only to its northern border area, but is also manifest in the rest of the country. Potential negative environmental effects from the trade agreement will not be restricted to the border area either. Nevertheless, binational attention to the environment and NAFTA has been concentrated on the US-Mexico border region. This might create a significant imbalance in Mexico with the northern border area being able to solve its environmental problems, but with the rest of the country unable to do the same. Regional imbalances will likely increase social disparities in Mexico.

This leads me to what I consider a key question. What else could Mexico have obtained from the supplementary negotiations? It is clear Mexico tried to compromise as little as possible on labour and environmental issues, but at the same time was willing to provide enough arguments to increase the chances of the agreement passing through the US Congress (to a certain extent, Canada and even the USA had a similar position). Mexico was also the weak party in the negotiations in the sense that it was more likely to be exposed to trade-related sanctions due to its lax environmental enforcement and its still incomplete environmental protection system. Nevertheless, Mexico could have tried to obtain time and resources to expand and improve its environmental protection and management system. This is a task that Mexico has to do as soon as possible, with or without the free trade agreement. It is also a structural issue that has severely affected the management of the environment and natural resources, affecting the development possibilities of the country. Any improvement in this area will also enhance Mexico's resources to prevent the emergence of new environmental problems and to control the potential negative environmental effects of NAFTA. Mexico could have reversed the pressure exerted by environmental groups and members of the US Congress before and during the supplementary negotiations by providing alternatives to expand and improve its environmental enforcement capabilities in the short and medium-term. If successful, Mexico could have provided a middle ground for compromise between the three countries with major benefits for itself while at the same time improving the opportunities to pass NAFTA through the US Congress.

Mexico's strategy could have been based on a detailed programme for environmental enforcement with specific goals to be achieved periodically during the next 15 years. An important component in this alternative would be a domestic plan to develop human resources in Mexico in cooperation with its trade partners.[34] Collaborative programmes to develop professional environmental managers, inspectors, technicians, and planners could provide the required human resources at a state and local level for environmental enforcement and environmental management to control environmental pollution and to achieve a sound management of natural resources. The programme could begin on a short-term (one year) basis, depending on the financial resources available, to create regional teams of environmental managers and environmental inspectors. These teams would provide additional support to the state and local governments in their new role as enforcement agencies for environmental quality control and environmental management following the decentralisation programme already implemented by SEDESOL. Priority would be given to those areas already facing critical environmental problems, or those expected to suffer a higher negative impact under NAFTA. A second phase (three to ten years) would assist state and local communities to develop progressively their own human resources. This would complete a national network for environmental management and enforcement. The follow up to this programme could be done through NACE. The commission would report on the success or failure of Mexico's compliance with the goals and timetable established and agreed by the three countries.[35]

Additional to this programme would be an initiative to enhance Mexico's environmental quality control and analysis capabilities (monitoring equipment, laboratories, technical assistance, computer support, etc.), with the cooperation of the USA and Canada. Existing facilities in Mexico could become regional nodes of a national network for environmental quality control centres. Smaller local facilities could become available as secondary nodes of the network. The local nodes of the network could carry out low cost analysis of samples, a critical element in the testing process, while complete and more expensive analysis would be carried out in the regional nodes, following the results of the pre-analysis of samples.[36] Financial support for both programmes could be secured through NACE using some of the options mentioned above (polluter pays, development bank, contributions from the three governments, donations in kind by the private sector, polluter fees, etc.).

The harmonisation of environmental standards is another area where

Mexico could have also provided alternatives during the supplementary negotiations. Optimally, these standards are set to protect the environment and public health based on the best available scientific data. But these standards reflect also the social value of environmental quality in each society (its willingness and capacity to pay for higher standards). Societies with different levels of development (resources and needs) tend to have different environmental standards. Mexico should present a detailed programme and timetable on how to proceed with the harmonisation programme under NAFTA. It is in its best interest to specify what standards should be harmonised first, based on their importance for the protection of human health and the environment (drinking water standards, exposure to hazardous substances, etc.).[37] Additional consideration should also be given to the social and economic costs to meet them, and the scientific data supporting them. The timetable for harmonisation could go from one to 15 years.

Besides potential differences in the existing standards between Mexico, the USA and Canada, another major problem for Mexico is not having a corresponding standard when a dispute emerges based on environmental issues. In these cases, the dispute resolution panels would be the ones imposing harmonisation without any consideration of its social and economic cost for Mexico. To avoid this situation, Mexico could have proposed a moratorium on bringing cases to the dispute resolution panels if the dispute is based on a standard agreed by the three countries to be harmonised in the near future. The harmonisation of product standards could have been managed through NACE. The commission would also be responsible for establishing long-term proposals to adopt process and best available technology standards in North America. The commission would provide support to diminish distortions in the harmonisation process through technology transfer, credits to those sectors most severely affected and upgrade of their pollution control equipment.

NAFTA and its Potential Environmental Implications for Mexico

The Free Trade Agreement could aggravate existing environmental problems in the border region and in other parts of Mexico if the supplementary agreements fail to deliver concrete measures to expand environmental protection. Expected economic growth from the agreement (relocation of industries, higher investment in trade and services, etc.) could encourage further urbanisation, worsening already critical deficits in those public services that are key to social well-being and the environment (water supply, sewage, solid waste, transport, etc.) or other environmental problems (industrial and agricultural hazardous wastes, pollution of water basins, air pollution, etc.).[38] In the short-term, these effects are likely to be concentrated in the border region,[39] but in the longer term, they could expand to Mexico's major urban areas and other parts of the country as industries and investment move inland.[40]

NAFTA could also introduce a new range of environmental problems, particularly in the management of natural resources. The discussion on this topic under NAFTA has focused exclusively on oil. However, there are other valuable natural resources in Mexico likely to be affected by the agreement. Water, a key resource in Northern Mexico and the Western part of the USA, is one of the best examples. Economic sectors with an elevated water consumption in the west part of the USA (agriculture, electric utilities, aluminium, steel and other manufacturing sectors) could relocate to Mexico to avoid increasing restrictions on water access and higher prices in the USA. National status granted to US and Canadian capital under NAFTA facilitates the relocation of water-intensive sectors to Mexico. Recent modifications to the Mexican Water Law (Dec. 1992) allows private investment (in principle this includes foreign capital) in water distribution systems and water treatment plants. A steep increase in the demand for water due to the relocation of US capital with high water consumption could aggravate social problems associated with the management of water resources (high social deficits in urban and rural areas, uneven distribution, gaps in water consumption).[41] The prospect of further decline in water availability in this part of North America (a global warming scenario), together with a continuous rise in demand (population and economic growth), and the deregulation of water control in Mexico, support the need for the creation of a North American water market on a longer term basis. For a country with strong social imbalances this could have important and critical socioeconomic consequences.[42]

US and Canadian capital in other economic sectors may also try to gain access to natural resources (agricultural soil, forestry, fisheries, biodiversity, mining) in Mexico following a similar pattern. Major concerns for Mexico should be the social consequences of this process (increasing polarisation in the access to these resources, its impact on poverty, income distribution, migration, etc.) and the enforcement of measures to guarantee the conservation of the resources.[43]

Another set of implications will arise from the implementation of

NAFTA. Extra pressure could be imposed on Mexico if the harmonisation of its environmental standards is done too fast.[44] Micro- and small industries could suffer if they must comply with North American environmental standards in the short term.[45] Production costs in these industries could increase up to 30 per cent due to pollution controls.[46] Although small industries in Mexico are an important source of employment, they are often handicapped.[47] Small industries in sectors expected to be winners under NAFTA (leather and footwear, textiles, construction and its suppliers, furniture, glass)[48] are sectors with pollution problems. Part of the benefits expected in these sectors could be lost in the case of small industry, with a significant impact on employment.[49] Expected problems in other sectors under NAFTA (machinery, metal products, chemicals, rubber and plastic products) could be aggravated due to environmental considerations (higher pollution control costs).[50] A progressive harmonisation process, together with financial and technical support to help the small industry comply with the new environmental standards, could prove to be a significant contribution for Mexico's employment problems.[51]

Conclusions

The NAFTA process has placed the debate on the North American environment in a trinational context, encouraging the mobilisation of environmental groups in the trade policy arena.[52] For the first time, environmental groups have made a serious effort at shaping international trade policy with far-reaching ramifications for the future character of bilateral and multilateral trade policy.[53] Environmentalists were also successful in achieving a higher priority for the environment among the discussions of trade and development, thus creating a scenario in which the environment could be expected to influence the final negotiations of the Uruguay round of GATT.

NAFTA has also unsettled the environmental community. It triggered a division among the different groups according to their ideology. The definition of the groups, against or in favour of the agreement, helped furnish each one with a clearer identity. This is likely to have an influence on the membership and resources of each group in the near future.

The final draft of the supplementary negotiations on the environment caused disappointments among many environmentalists in the three countries. As mentioned above, important issues presented by these groups as a condition for their endorsement of NAFTA were not incorporated into the final draft of the supplementary agreements.[54] What the environmentalists sought was a broader democratic participation in a process that is likely to shape economic growth for the next decade in the region. But this objective confronted two major obstacles: the mistrust and reluctance of the business community to allow public participation to interfere with their decision-making process and operation, and the opposition of the bureaucracies in the three countries to allow even minimal interference with their notion of national sovereignty.

A realistic assessment of the supplementary agreements has to recognise an implicit risk that the agreements will not transcend the low level of cooperation and management achieved by the previous La Paz agreement between Mexico and the USA. Unfortunately, the La Paz agreement is only a general framework, often too general, to solve and manage common border environmental problems. The La Paz agreement has never been able to offer a comprehensive approach to manage the border environment in its ten years of operation, nor has it been able to provide the resources to implement it. The supplemental agreements of NAFTA could have the same fate if there is not a clear allocation of adequate financial resources for its operation.

Finally, it is worth noting that the implementation of NAFTA has more extensive environmental risks for Mexico than for the USA and Canada. These risks are not restricted to the border area; in fact, they are likely to affect other parts of the country as well. The supplementary agreements on the environment do not provide Mexico with resources or better opportunities to remove structural constraints on protecting and managing its environment.[55] At the most, they will provide only the border region with resources for environmental clean-up and infrastructure.[56] While the priority given to the border is understandable given the extent of its environmental problems and its political value *vis-à-vis* the attention provided to this region in the USA, it would be a costly mistake not to invest in improving and strengthening Mexico's overall environmental policy and Mexico's environmental management system.[57] Failure to improve environmental management could not only jeopardise economic benefits expected from NAFTA in Mexico. It could also prove to have a very high social cost.

Notes

1. See Mumme (1993).
2. The elimination of non-tariff trade barriers, particularly the downward harmonisation approach associated with international trade liberalisation under the GATT regime, is a good example.
3. The Office of the US Trade Representative (USTR) carried out a Review of US-Mexico Environmental Issues (25 February 1992) challenged by many US environmental groups as incomplete and unreliable. The Sierra Club sued the US Trade Representative for failing to comply with an environmental impact assessment of NAFTA, but lost. A new suit was presented and won by the Sierra Club in July 1993. However, this decision was revoked by a court of appeal in September 1993. Canada also carried out an environmental review on NAFTA (October 1992). It is unclear if Mexico formulated an environmental review. If one was done, it was never made public.
4. Although Mexico's environmental agency (SEDESOL) has been hampered by budgetary constraints in the past, Mexico has made significant efforts in recent years to develop a more efficient enforcement programme. In 1991 the national investment in addressing environmental concerns totalled US$1.8 billion (0.7 per cent of Mexico's GDP). SEDESOL's budget increased from US$6.6 million in 1989 to more than US$77 million in 1992.
5. See Mumme and Sánchez (1992).
6. It is worth noting that the designs of a significant number of these standards are being done by US and Canadian consultants.
7. For a report on the state of Mexico's environment, see World Bank (1992a).
8. It is unclear how long it will take Mexico to reach similar levels of environmental protection to those in Canada and the USA. Its current efforts decentralise environmental protection to the states and municipalities and allow a higher participation of the private sector. Most of Mexico's states now have their own environmental legislation. Nevertheless, environmental protection is still in its early stages in Mexico.
9. NAFTA makes reference to the Montreal Protocol on Substances that Deplete the Ozone Layer, The Convention on International Trade in Endangered Species of Wild Fauna and Flora, the Basle convention on the Control of Trans-boundary Movements of Hazardous Wastes and their Disposal. The NAFTA contracting parties agreed to uphold the principles of these environmental conventions and protocols. However, NAFTA has not been linked to many other international environmental agreements.
10. Article 753(3) of chapter 7 and Article 905(3) of chapter 9 both explicitly state that any member country may impose higher levels of environmental standards than those that could be achieved through international ones.
11. North American Free Trade Agreement, Article 754(5), August 12, 1992.
12. The risk assessment methodologies are designed to ensure that the exporting country meets all the requirements of the importing country.
13. North American Free Trade Agreement, Article 904(4), 12 August 1992.

14. The OECD has produced a consensus on 'guidelines' for incorporating environmental and trade principles into trade and environmental agreements. This could also result in clarification or modifications of the GATT.

15. National Wildlife Federation and Pollution Probe, Binational Statement on Environmental Safeguards that Should Be Included in the North American Free Trade Agreement (NAFTA) (Washington, DC: National Wild Life Federation, 28 May 1992.).

16. Compared to the rest of the environmental groups, the Sierra Club maintains a stronger position on the functions of the NACE. For the Sierra Club, NACE should also have the ability to use government information to compel industries to supply information through domestic courts (*Sierra Club's NAFTA Scoreboard*, 4 May 1993). The Sierra Club seeks also to make governments and individual companies liable for environmental pollution (Press release, Sierra Club, 4 May 1993).

17. Natural Resources Defense Council, *Environmental Safeguards*, 1992.

18. See Hudson and Prudencio (1993).

19. Co-signatories are the Defenders of Wildlife, the National Wildlife Federation, the Environmental Defense Fund, Natural Conservancy, National Audubon Society, World Wildlife Fund, and Natural Resources Defense Council.

20. The information presented in this section is taken from a number of statements published by the environmentalist groups and telephone interviews with the Sierra Club, National Resources Defense Council, Arizona Toxics Information, Texas Center for Policy Studies, Border Ecology Project, and Asociación de Grupos Ambientalistas in 1993.

21. See *North American Agreement on Environmental Cooperation between the Government of Canada, the Government of the United Mexican States and the Government of the United States of America,* Draft, 1993.

22. The accord defines 'effective enforcement' so as 'to allow government agencies and officials not to act to prevent, halt or penalize violations'. Persistent pattern is defined as 'a sustained or recurring course of action or inaction'.

23. The North American Agreement on Environmental Cooperation establishes the Commission for Environmental Cooperation which creates a Council consisting of cabinet-level representatives of the Parties, a Secretariat and a Joint Public Advisory Committee.

24. Chapter 45 excludes from the supplementary agreements any statute or regulation, or provision thereof, directly related to worker safety or health.

25. *Inside US Trade*, 20 August 1993.

26. *Inside US Trade*, 21 May 1993, Special Report.

27. Monetary enforcement assessments shall be no greater than $20 million for the first year of the agreement, or no greater than .007 percent of total trade in goods between the Parties thereafter (Annex 34).

28. See Kelly (1993).

29. Mexico was probably convinced it would have been almost impossible to sell the agreement in the USA without trade sanctions. Given Mexico's priority to have the agreement approved by the US Congress, it is not difficult to understand why they agreed to trade sanctions.

30. The groups supporting the trade agreement have gained prominence in Washington since the 1992 presidential election, in part because some of their staff members are now members of the Clinton administration. They have also shown their willingness to compromise to increase their influence at the highest levels of the Government (Keith Schneider, 'Environmentalists fight each other over trade accord', *The New York Times*, 16 September 1993).

31. Their campaign began with a very aggressive advertisement, '8 fatal flows of NAFTA', in the *New York Times* (21 September 1993).

32. James Gerstenzang, 'White House Unveils Fund to Clean Up Border', *Los Angeles Times*, 14 September 1993, p. A16.

33. Ibid.

34. US assistance to help Mexico improve its enforcement capacity has been limited to training a handful of federal inspectors in SEDUE and now SED-ESOL. Canada expanded its cooperation with Mexico on the environment in 1992 through $1 million dollars to improve environmental enforcement and monitoring. Mexico acquired a mobile laboratory and other equipment. It also obtained assistance in the creation of technical environmental standards for air pollution and management of hazardous substances and waste. Canada has not provided training assistance for SEDESOL staff (Canadian Environmental Report, 1992).

35. See Sánchez (1993).

36. Without the pre-treatment, the chemical balance of samples and the contaminants they contain can change, thereby jeopardising the value of the most sophisticated analysis.

37. A one to five year harmonisation period could be used for these types of standards while a 10 to 15 year period could be used for those standards not critical for human life and the environment.

38. See Sánchez (1991).

39. An additional problem in the border area is the generation of hazardous wastes by the *maquiladoras*. Obtaining national status under NAFTA, *maquiladoras* will no longer be required to return their hazardous waste to the USA. Mexico has no facilities to manage the amount of hazardous wastes that legally could remain in its territory.

40. Recent findings by a team of researchers at Princeton University suggest there may be a positive relationship between economic growth and air quality, but these findings have not been empirically replicated, do not apply to other forms of pollution, and fail to speak to the specific question of trade. For a report on the Princeton study, see Keith Bradeshar, 'Lower Pollution Tide to Prosperity', *New York Times*, 28 October 1991.

41. Geographical proximity to the USA could facilitate the relocation of small and medium-sized companies to Mexico.

42. For more on this scenario, see Sánchez (1992).
43. One of NACE's major tasks would be to coordinate a sound management of natural resources in North America. In the meantime, social and economic gaps in Mexico increase the polarised access to these resources between economic sectors and social groups.
44. The Institute for International Economics in Washington DC has already proposed to carry out the harmonisation of environmental standards in North America in three years.
45. In 1991 there were 41,422 plants and 162,963 workers employed in microindustries, 7,289 plants and 268,433 workers in small industries, and 1080 plants and 165,953 workers in middle-sized industries in Mexico (Source: Dirección General de Industria Mediana y Pequeña y de Desarrollo Regional, CANACINTRA, México, enero de 1992).
46. The US report on NAFTA and the environment quotes a study based on 445 individual manufacturing industries showing pollution abatement costs close to two per cent of value added (USTR, *Review of US-Mexico Environmental Issues*, 25 February 1992). In Canada, average expenditure for pollution control in companies with less than 50 employees was $20,000 in 1989. Companies with more than 50 employees averaged almost $1 million that same year for pollution expenditures (Canadian Environmental Report, 1992). It is difficult to compare this data to small industry in Mexico. Data on the costs for pollution controls mentioned above were provided by companies selling environmental equipment in Mexico.
47. They pay lower wages, but usually have to pay higher prices for capital than do larger units. The small-scale sector tends to be neglected by government policy-makers. Small units often operate beyond the threshold of government assistance, including institutional credit. The small industry characteristic of lower capital cost per job than larger plants carries over into its use of other inputs (UNIDO (1979)).
48. See INFORUM (1990).
49. A comparative study of small industry in Canada and Mexico stresses the vulnerability of Mexican small industry to the agreement. See del Castillo and Vega (1991). That vulnerability would increase if harmonisation of environmental standards is done too fast.
50. See del Castillo and Vega (1991).
51. The National Council of Environmental Industrialists in Mexico (Consejo Nacional de Industriales Ecologistas) states that 10 billion dollars would be invested in the environmental industry in Mexico in the next three years (*El Financiero*, 6 April 1993). NAFIN, a federal agency in Mexico, recently created a North American Environmental Fund (50 million dollars) to provide credits to Mexican industry for environmental protection (*El Financiero*, 6 April 1993).
52. See Mumme (1993).
53. See Mumme (1993).

54. Among other issues, public participation in the operation of NACE, access to information on the state of the environment in the three countries, right-to-know laws, clarification of the dispute panel procedures in NAFTA, clear financial commitments for the operation of NACE and the border clean-up and management, and a strong and independent Secretariat in NACE.

55. The EC experience with workplace and environmental standards offers some lessons for NAFTA. Progress has been made rapidly because the task has been to harmonise national laws and regulations already in place that express member states' shared values for workers' safety and environmental protection. However, financial support has been provided to the weaker member states to increase their standard of living and strengthen their economy (See Morici (1993a)).

56. It is very likely that the financing of the environmental clean-up will be done through credits from international institutions (e.g. the World Bank). This is an effective way to distribute its cost among the rest of the Mexican society, and a form of subsidy to past, present, and future polluters.

57. Among the most urgent needs are the creation of human resources for environmental management and environmental auditing, monitoring equipment, environmental information systems, environmental infrastructure, pollution control infrastructure, waste treatment facilities, public participation, and a new integrated approach for environmental management with strong pollution prevention measures. Although all these structural actions are critical at the federal level, it is among the states and municipalities where they are mostly needed. It is at the local level where significant changes are required to improve the environmental situation in Mexico.

CHAPTER 8

IS THERE AN ALTERNATIVE?
THE POLITICAL CONSTRAINTS ON NAFTA

Adolfo Aguilar Zinser

The central question in Mexico's current economic and political debate is to decide if the country has alternative development options and what the range of those options might be. Nowhere is the issue of alternatives more divisive and critical as in relation to NAFTA. Originally dismissed by its current proponents and defenders as a 'non-option', NAFTA is today portrayed as the 'only option'. In fact, it has become the central component of the neo-liberal economic reform carried out by President Carlos Salinas's administration, and thus has been elevated to the rank of 'inevitable' and 'absolutely necessary'. The arguments to sustain the alleged 'necessity' and 'inevitability' of NAFTA range from the most abstract and philosophical, to the most circumstantial, mundane and trivial. They have mixed straight economic considerations with geopolitical notions. Nonetheless the strongest defence presented by NAFTA's proponents and sympathisers is still that the agreement should not be construed as anything more than a regional trade instrument designed to increase trade flows among the three partners, stimulate economic growth and allow each country to benefit from its comparative advantage. However, as drafted by the negotiators, the pact is already much more than a trade agreement. Indeed, its most significant binding provisions are a whole body of rules related to investments, not trade. Consequently NAFTA could be described, really, as an investment pact.[1]

The extent to which NAFTA has been debated, criticised, supported and condemned in the USA and Canada – discussion has been much less in Mexico because of the rigidity of its political system – has broadened the false notion that NAFTA is simply a trade liberalisation agreement. In fact, out of this debate and considering the disparities and peculiarities of the three economies, numerous proposals have emerged related to what could be a better, more responsible, progressive and fair agreement for regional trade in North America. Economists, environmental activists, labour leaders, politicians, journalists, civic leaders, of the United States, Canada and Mexico have come up with a rich menu of alternatives, some of them ambitious and unrealistic, but others reasonable and practical. In any event a better deal than the one negotiated by George Bush, Brian Mulroney and Carlos Salinas is conceivable.

Of the many questions that a better North American trade agreement would have to address, the most serious are the disparities between Mexico and its two other partners, particularly the United States. There are many issues that have unavoidable consequences for the implementation of any trade agreement in North America. The US economy is several times the size of the Mexican economy, salaries in Mexico are in all areas and in every region just a fraction of what the most poorly paid US or Canadian worker earns;[2] the average levels of technological capacity at which Mexico's economy operate bear no comparison with levels of technological developments in the USA and Canada, and infrastructure in Mexico lags way behind. Given these differences, disparities between Mexico and its partners are simply not to be corrected by the invisible hand of market forces. A paramount effort has to be undertaken jointly by their governments to close this gap, at least to a point where comparative advantages among the three economies can truly reflect the social cost of factors of production. The need to narrow this gap is not simply to benefit Mexico, but – as has been anticipated in Europe's integration experience – to prevent disruptions and social damage in all three economies. From this perspective some of the most attractive options offered by NAFTA critics are:[3]

1. The harmonisation of norms. There are at least two areas where common norms should be observed by the three countries: labour standards and the protection of the environment.[4] The task is not only to establish mechanisms gradually to bring the working conditions, wages and labour and trade union rights of Mexicans to levels comparable to those enjoyed by Canadian and US workers, but also to establish the basic rules of a tri-national social protection framework. The European Social Charter is as relevant to North America as has been the integration of Treaty of Rome countries with diverse levels of *per capita* incomes.

The protection of the environment is also a critical element of any modern instrument for regional economic development. Under NAFTA, Mexico has the potential for attracting investment for industries which would be highly detrimental to the environment. These industries would be avoiding stricter environmental regulations in the USA and Canada.

Firms should be made to comply with tough, but realistic, environmental rules common to the three countries. Harmonisation of labour and environmental norms in a social and environmental charter will not be possible unless special resources are devoted to this purpose and NAFTA makes no provision for these kinds of transfers.[5]

2. Compensatory financing. One of the major falsehoods advocated by NAFTA proponents is that equitable regional trade and direct investments can be promoted without devoting special resources to facilitate these flows.[6]

Again, as the European case illustrates, regional economic integration at any level is an expensive proposition; without applying special funds to key areas, disruptions and inequalities within and between countries will be exacerbated. Finance to compensate for the negative impact is needed in the North American Agreement in at least three major areas:

(a) Resources are necessary to facilitate the transition, to compensate for disruptions and to help workers adapt to the displacements caused by the liberalisation of trade itself. To be competitive in an open commercial environment, industries need to have available special funds for technological and other essential improvements. Regular financial markets do not have the resources or the flexibility to address these demands.

(b) Special financing is needed to pay for the expensive cost of gradually harmonising environmental and labour standards. Industries alone cannot absorb the financial burden of implementing new mechanisms of environmental protection. Governments should also have minimum necessary resources to improve social conditions to guarantee safety and health standards for workers and to improve labour productivity.

(c) The investments expected with NAFTA cannot possibly materialise if expensive regional infrastructure developments are not made.

3. Enforcement rules. Without a fair, equitable and effective mechanism of enforcement, NAFTA is not a viable proposition. The question of enforcement has proved to be one of the most controversial issues at the negotiating table. However, countries in North America should be ready to create a Trade Commission empowered with sufficient authority to

enforce the whole set of rules to be included in a good agreement.[7]

4. Addressing regional disparities also means creating a mechanism to protect areas of the economy where indiscriminate free market criteria could have devastating social and economic effects. This especially is the case for Mexico's agricultural sector, particularly the production of basic grains. Nearly three million Mexican families barely survive in agricultural areas where they have no chance of ever competing with crops produced in US and Canadian fields.[8] Ignoring this reality could only lead to social conflicts and generate waves of migrants seeking jobs in the USA.

5. A realistic North American trade and investment deal cannot simply ignore, as happened in the case of NAFTA, that the main exchange between Mexico and the USA is not goods but people. Thus, labour mobility should be part of the deal.

6. An adequate model of North American trade cannot operate success-fully if it does not have as a framework regional industrial policies that promote equitable and socially profitable comparative advantages. As it is drafted, NAFTA abrogates the authority to design and implement industrial policies. This dimension of NAFTA is designed to be applied in particular to Mexico. The absence of an industrial policy is already causing the destruction of industries where Mexico could be competitive to the benefit of the whole North American market and this is provoking major economic and commercial disruptions in the country.

   If at least a number of these and other proposals presented by critics had been incorporated, NAFTA could have been improved substantially and transformed into a model of gradual integration among partners with very contrasting levels of development. What does not exist presently is the willingness of the current governments of the three countries fully and seriously to consider these options. Not even the change of administration in the USA from a pro-business Republican administra-tion under President Bush to a Democrat government under President Clinton, with a different political and economic philosophy and a more generous social agenda, has succeeded in altering the original version of NAFTA.

   The shortcomings of the NAFTA text, however, eventually became so evident and the pressures of opposing groups in the USA so signifi-cant and intense that, once President Clinton decided to support the ratification of the deal signed by his predecessor, he looked for a compromise. To accommodate labour and environmental demands without reopening the text for a redrafting, two parallel agreements on those issues were negotiated between the three co-signers.

The parallel agreements drafted by the new leaders of Canada and the USA with the five year-old Salinas administration did not amount to a full and serious reassessment of the original agreement. They simply included minimum provisions for a limited protection of the environment and labour rights, designed to preserve the original text while at the same time pleasing NAFTA critics in the US congress so as to persuade them not to block the ratification of NAFTA. Regardless of how some controversial issues in the parallel agreements are resolved – such as the enforcement mechanisms of the adopted rules – NAFTA will remain intact. This illustrates the remarkable resilience and power of the constituencies who have defended the original version. Nevertheless, what the negotiation of the parallel agreements represents is at least an implicit recognition that better and more comprehensive agreements are possible.

Discussions about NAFTA have ultimately revolved around antagonistic views regarding what the national interests are. In each country the issue of national interests raised by NAFTA has taken a particular turn. However, fears and expectations feed into each other, building a very peculiar political and ideological scenario around NAFTA. Mexico appears the most enthusiastic over the possibility of joining an exclusive North American economic club. The Mexican regime champions itself as a true reformer breaking away from the import substituting nationalistic economic strategies of previous governments, and ready to reconcile its national aims with its former foe, the United States. Driven by hope or persuaded by government propaganda many Mexicans, particularly those in the urban middle classes, see NAFTA as a right of passage to unseen prosperity. Criticism to NAFTA has been mute, timid or deliberately silenced by the government. There are nevertheless a number of areas where concerns have been repeatedly expressed. The most important is the issue of sovereignty. Concerns range from the denunciation that Mexico is surrendering its oil resources to US interests, that the country is giving up its regulatory powers necessary to design development, industrial and agricultural policies, to the outright conviction that Mexico is, by virtue of NAFTA, falling under the political and strategic influence of Washington.

NAFTA came onto the Mexican scene almost at the same time as the collapse of the old nationalistic economic system and its replacement by the neoliberal paradigm. This sudden and dramatic shift was carried out under the assumption that Mexico had no option but to adopt an orthodox pro-business policy, to abandon expensive social welfare programmes and to move decisively into the world economy with a particular emphasis on the US market. This reversal of politics came at the same time as a rapid deterioration of the traditional political consensus and the collapse of the ruling party's prestige and credibility. In this context, critics of the NAFTA initiative were easily portrayed by the Salinas government as adversaries of free trade either because of their leftist and out of touch ideological inclinations, or simply due to narrow partisan ambitions and motivations. Although objections to the free trade proposal were made both within the National Action Party (PAN) and the Party of the Democratic Revolution (PRD) (the two main opposition parties of right and left respectively), the pro-government media presented the anti-NAFTA argument as coming mainly from the left, in particular, the main focus of opposition was identified with intellectual and political sectors associated with Cuauhtémoc Cárdenas, the presidential candidate of a broad coalition of centre-left forces in the 1988 election, who has since then been one of the main political adversaries of President Salinas and his ruling Partida Revolucionario Institucional (PRI).[9]

This characterisation promoted by the Mexican government propaganda machinery was one of several factors contributing to the suppression of a genuine internal debate about options related to NAFTA. Anyone expressing reservations about NAFTA could be portrayed, very simplistically, as either an enemy of the president, a protectionist, a Cardenist, a populist or, if his or her views are manifested abroad, as a traitor to the motherland.[10] Given Mexico's presidential authoritarianism, anyone carrying those labels feels at risk of political or economic retaliation. Overwhelming government propaganda portraying NAFTA as a giant step towards modernisation, combined with the paramount political significance President Salinas attached to his initiative, have in effect reinforced traditional authoritarian constraints on the flow of information and free speech in Mexico. People concerned with the consequences of free trade, and genuinely committed to offer valuable alternative views to enrich the negotiations, prefer not to take the risk and remain silent; at most, some air their disapproval and make their suggestions in private. Anyone who dares publicly to manifest his or her views against NAFTA is perceived by others as an isolated radical. Critical opinions have not only been directly or indirectly silenced, but also information about the course of negotiations and the content of NAFTA has been secret and controlled to suit the government's interests. Government propaganda and official statements replace any independent information or dissenting opinions.

It is true that many of Salinas's opponents see NAFTA as the nucleus of a new ideological paradigm that puts Mexico at the mercy of large foreign and national corporations, and which surrenders the country to the strategic interest of the USA. However, this is by no means the only concern Mexicans have. A second criticism comes from mainstream economic sectors, who do oppose the Salinas government, but who are nevertheless directly affected by trade liberalisation. Small and medium-sized manufacturers, as well as many agricultural producers are in this situation, but their views are seldom voiced publicly. There are also those critics of NAFTA, particularly among academic experts, who accept or even favour the option of free trade, but who see the agreement signed by President Salinas as a short-sighted instrument that favours only the interests of large corporations at the expense of Mexico's fundamental development concerns.[11]

The combination of political, ideological and economic factors have contributed to cast NAFTA's image in Mexico in terms of three basic sets of perceptions. First is the widespread notion that NAFTA is part of an inevitable trend of globalisation that Mexico cannot resist or evade, and it is also the only opportunity left to develop the country's troubled economy. Secondly, no matter what Mexico wants from NAFTA, it is the USA who decides its scope, its limits and largely the specific content of the deal. Because of immediate economic necessity and of the size and power of the United States, Mexico's negotiating position is too weak to set the agenda. To be part of NAFTA, Mexico has no choice but to accept whatever deal the USA is ready to offer. At most, while being careful not to undermine the agreement, Mexico was able to resist the inclusion of critical concessions such as those related to its oil resources (as happened in the final stages of the negotiation with the Bush administration) or refuse to endorse harsh provisions (as has been the case with the commercial sanctions and the enforcement mechanisms) demanded by the USA for the parallel agreements.

Thirdly, there has been the notion that regional integration is also part of an inevitable globalisation trend. The argument runs as follows: Mexico has traditionally seen itself as part of Latin America. However, despite all efforts at integration, Mexico's trade with its Latin American partners is insignificant and cannot be substantially improved in the foreseeable future. Thus, without turning its back on Latin America,

Mexico's real option is not in Latin America but in North America where it enjoys the advantage of sharing a large common border with the richest economy of the world. Therefore, if Mexico does not move decisively and without fear and hesitation to join NAFTA, it will be left out and lose a golden opportunity to share North American prosperity.

Inspired by these ideas, Mexico entered the NAFTA negotiations and the parallel agreements with virtually no agenda of its own, and therefore with few, if any, alternatives to test and explore. It was evident from the outset that the Mexican negotiators wanted Mexican goods to gain preferential access to US markets. However, even beyond the desire to open export opportunities for Mexican industries, was the driving need to attract financial capital, thus making NAFTA a powerful instrument of foreign investment promotion, and this was a key consideration. Mexico approached the negotiations with a flexible attitude regarding all trade related matters, offering the most attractive conditions for the transfer of capital across borders. Substantially lower wages, access to natural resources, a favourable regulatory climate and fiscal advantages were emphasised by the Mexican promoters of NAFTA as some of the incentives open to US and Canadian firms should the trade agreement be signed. The uninhibited pro-investment nature of NAFTA gave the agreement a clear neoliberal identity in Mexico as well as in Canada and the USA.

In the USA NAFTA was originally seen by its promoters as an opportunity to reward the Mexican government for its sweeping economic reforms. With NAFTA, it is argued, the USA will not only consolidate Mexico's pro-business economic programme, but will contribute significantly to promote Mexico's growth and development and the creation of jobs, thereby consolidating its neighbours political and social stability. In addition to these political implications, NAFTA was also seen as an opportunity to gain access to Mexico's rich natural resources, particularly oil, and to take advantage of its large and cheap labour market. Through a series of measures and safeguards US firms would be allowed to move into Mexico under privileged conditions. NAFTA's format had the crucial advantage for the USA of making Mexican cheap labour available in Mexico and not through the controversial process of migration. Thus, NAFTA was portrayed as the best of both worlds: as an instrument to cut down migration, but at the same time taking advantage of Mexico's abundant work force and low wages.

Reflecting these interests and expectations, the US negotiators fixed the agenda. What they brought to the table was not a great vision of how a free trade agreement could become in the future the solid foundation of a truly prosperous, dynamic and mutually beneficial relationship. On the contrary, the US agenda was typically an assortment of specific demands conceived by bureaucrats who had long waited for Mexico to come around to the US position. From the outset, the USA conditioned its participation in NAFTA negotiations to exclude any discussion about labour mobility across the US-Mexican border, and to include Mexico's oil in the trade and investment agenda. The Salinas administration has to accept these demands.

The willingness of Mexico to join the North American free trade scenario on US terms did not, however, happen as a result of pressure from Washington or international power games, but was an autonomous decision of President Salinas. The reversal of the PRI's nationalistic attitudes and its eagerness to embrace the USA was indeed prompted by its domestic troubles rather than by US pressures. In fact, the Salinas government overwhelmed the Bush administration with its commitment to 'leave the past behind' and make the USA an offer it could not refuse: to accept a partnership with the USA no Mexican government had wanted since 1910.

In the USA – as well as in Canada – NAFTA emerged at the same time as the Reagan economic revolution had created its own domestic problems. In this context, NAFTA was not seen simply as a trade deal with a deserving partner by which the USA would gain access into its market in exchange for oil and other valuable resources. Rather, NAFTA was also identified from the outset with a whole set of economic policies and financial interests seen as hostile to US workers and unions.

In fact, the United States never saw in Mexico a serious trade competitor whose products could displace domestically produced goods in the US market. Protectionism against Mexican exports has never really been the issue. With the exception of a few products, the Mexican economy, unlike the South Korean, the Chinese or even the Brazilian economy, does not provoke fears in the USA of an aggressive exporter against whom US producers have to be protected. Instead, the contro-versy arose because NAFTA would give US firms the opportunity to move out and reduce substantially their labour, environmental and other socially related costs by investing in Mexico. This would be, according to NAFTA critics in the USA, at the expense of wage levels and environmental standards in the USA, and would undermine trade unions' bargaining power by allowing US corporate management to take advantage of unprotected Mexican workers.

The clear investment orientation of NAFTA was easily construed by its critics in the USA and Canada as evidence of a carefully designed corporate strategy to regain competitiveness by reducing labour costs and taking advantage of other Mexican offers – all at the expense of US workers. Cheap Mexican labour, and lax environmental regulations, were broadly identified as the main reason why corporate North America wanted NAFTA.

To some extent, although not with the same intensity and success, the US government, as well as other supporters of NAFTA in the US business community, reacted to criticism with the same attitudes of anger and intolerance displayed by the Mexican government. Opponents of NAFTA were branded in the USA as protectionist, selfish and enemies of progress.

More than any other recent international economic issue, NAFTA has triggered in the USA a domestic reaction of considerable significance and magnitude. This is clearly the consequence of the social and ideological implications of the initiative. Put simply, it is the rich against the poor, workers against corporations, environmentalists *versus* polluters and abusers of the environment. In anticipation of its ratification process, the debate reached its highest levels of intensity in the summer of 1993. To support their arguments about the exploitation of workers, opponents of NAFTA portrayed Mexico's conditions in such negative terms that proponents began to denounce critics as racist and anti-Mexican. With this added connotation the debate turned again to the issue of supporting NAFTA's ratification and thus Mexico's development, thereby helping President Salinas and his party to preserve power, maintain political stability and to continue with the neoliberal economic reform. Promoters of the deal tended to identify the opponents, in both Mexico and the USA, as having the same protectionist, ideological and even partisan motivations. Consequently, and given the proximity in 1994 of presidential elections in Mexico, failure to ratify NAFTA would allegedly facilitate the decline of the PRI, the collapse of Salinas's economic reforms and encourage the ascendance to power of anti-free trade, anti-US, ultra-nationalistic and populist forces. Likewise, if NAFTA were not approved by the US Congress, it would have been because special interest groups, protectionist and anti-Mexican forces within US society would have prevailed. These arguments show not only how simplistic the debate on NAFTA had become, but also how it had moved away from economic and commercial considerations to become a source of bitter political and ideological confrontation.

This antagonism has effectively neutralised the opportunity to examine carefully and without passion the potential consequences of the agreement, to assess options and to examine possible alternatives. With the defeat of Bush and the election of Clinton the debate has not been dissipated, but, on the contrary, the ambivalent support given to NAFTA by the new president only helped to emphasise the confrontation between pro- and anti-NAFTA forces in the USA and to increase the vulnerability, impatience and intolerance of the Salinas regime in Mexico.

One positive development that has come out of this debate is the enrichment of social interactions between the three countries. The dialogue among different social groups in Mexico, the USA and Canada is truly a revolutionary change in the framework of the relationship. Thanks to NAFTA, government officials, diplomats and business groups are no longer the only interlocutors of the relationships between Mexico, the USA and Canada. A wide number of civic and social organisations, ranging from environmental groups, labour unions, academics, journalists, human rights activists, opinion leaders, community organisers and non-governmental organisations, have come in contact with each other to compare notes, share information, assess the impact of NAFTA in their respective countries, and even to discuss, adopt and promote alternatives to improve or replace the current pact. These interactions are indeed the source of the numerous viable proposals mentioned in this chapter. Alternatives to NAFTA have to be found not only through exploring economic conditions and opportunities, but also through opening up the political process, giving time to the debate, and listening to concerned social groups in all three countries.

Notes

1. FitzGerald also emphasises the investment provisions of NAFTA. See chapter 9.
2. In 1992 the average hourly compensation, including benefits, for production line workers in the United States was $16.17; in Mexico it was $2.35.
3. See also Castañeda and Heredia (1993).
4. NAFTA's side agreements on labour and the environment, announced in August 1993, only require that each partner respect its own national laws. There is no attempt to impose a common norm or standard.
5. For further details, see *El Cotidiano* (1991).
6. See, for example, Belous (1993) and Wilson and Smith (1992).
7. Although the NAFTA text devotes a great deal of attention to dispute settlements, only time will tell how effective they are in practice. Furthermore, the side agreements on labour and the environment provide a route –

PART III

INTERNATIONAL DIMENSIONS

CHAPTER 9

THE IMPACT OF NAFTA
ON THE LATIN AMERICAN ECONOMIES

E.V.K. FitzGerald

The NAFTA negotiations not only marked the virtual completion (rather than the initiation) of a free trade area in North America, but also suggested that NAFTA itself may quite rapidly evolve through a customs union into a wider economic community – if not by design, then by institutional response to problems of regulatory practice. The potentially negative 'economic externalities' arising from this development are, naturally enough, a source of considerable concern for other Latin American and Caribbean countries, which fear the diversion of international trade and foreign investor interest that might slow export growth and delay macroeconomic recovery after a strenuous decade of monetary stabilisation and fiscal retrenchment.

The aim of this chapter is to set out some of the elements required for an economic analysis of this issue, and although no definite conclusions (still less predictions) are presented here, an attempt is made to assess the likely impact of NAFTA on trade and capital flows. What will be argued is that, while the direct consequence of NAFTA itself should be quite modest 'trade creation' and very limited 'trade diversion', the indirect consequences might include a considerable diversion of international capital flows towards Mexico, to the possible detriment of productive investment elsewhere in the region. Further, the chapter suggests that the institutional consequences of NAFTA within North America may be much greater than is currently anticipated, and will probably be such as to delay further links between the USA and other Latin American economies.

The chapter consists of three main elements. First, a 'baseline scenario' for Latin American trade and finance in the next decade is outlined, which draws on recent work by the World Bank and the Inter-American Development Bank, as a framework for the argument. Second, an attempt is made to identify the main consequences for this scenario of the foreseeable outcomes of NAFTA trade and capital flows in the region. Third, some tentative conclusions are drawn as to the implications of NAFTA for regional economic institutions in Latin America itself.

Prospects for Latin American Trade and Finance

Trade and Growth

The World Bank (1993) confidently forecasts a 'substantial turnaround in economic performance in Latin America' by the end of the century. These projections are worth examining as a baseline scenario, even though they are based on somewhat fragile key assumptions about the world economy: (i) economic recovery consolidates in the USA and spreads to the EC and Japan during 1993, so that the Group of Seven (G7)[1] returns to its long-term potential growth rate in 1994, yielding a projected growth rate of 2.7 per cent for the 1992-2002 period; (ii) further fiscal consolidation within the OECD countries will not only support steady growth in the medium term, but also keep real interest rates well below their 1980s levels (real LIBOR[2] of about three per cent for the 1990s); (iii) world trade itself will grow at nearly six per cent over the 1992-2002 period, considerably faster than in the past decade (or even the 1965-90 average of 4.5 per cent), with Latin America increasing its (lost) share of world trade; (iv) non-oil commodity prices will stabilise in real terms – a break from the previous decline; and (v) economic policy improvements in Latin America conducive to macro-economic openness, monetary stability and fiscal restraint will be sustained.

This 'baseline' scenario leads to a forecast GDP growth rate in Latin America of 3.9 per cent for the 1992-2002 period, compared to 1.9 per cent for the previous decade, with rising savings rates and a greater reliance on private investment (and direct foreign investment) as sources of growth. However, as the World Bank itself admits 'there are downside risks to these projections', particularly doubts about: sustainability of adjustment in some major economies (eg. Brazil); world market growth and supply capacity to underpin accelerated export growth; continued capital inflows to sustain import levels (eg. Argentina, Mexico and Venezuela); and future real world interest rates. In the 'low' case, GDP growth in the G7 countries is expected to fall to 2.0 per cent, and world trade to 3.0 per cent, during 1992-2002. This would lead in turn to a reduction from the 'baseline scenario' of 3.3 percentage points in the annual growth of Latin American exports, 3.6 points in imports, and 2.1 points in GDP growth – in other words, a return to the experience of the 1980s. Thus, the regional recovery is still highly contingent on external factors.

The reliance of Latin American exports upon market growth in the USA and Latin American partners is clear from Tables 9.1 and 9.2. On the assumption that this pattern of trade is not likely to shift radically over the coming decade, the central issue in practice is whether NAFTA will significantly reduce the exports of Latin American producers other than Mexico to the USA or to each other. It is possible that (say) Japanese or European investment in new plant in Mexico (or Canada) for the US market might subsequently lead to increased exports to their home markets and thus displace existing Latin American exporters, but this effect is unlikely to be significant for reasons of both comparative production cost and product type, and we shall ignore it here.

Table 9.1
Direction of Latin American Trade in Manufactures

| | (% of world trade) 1991 | | (growth rate) 1981-91 | |
	Origin	*Destination*	*Origin*	*Destination*
High Income Countries:	4.0	1.1	0.9	6.9
of which				
USA	2.1	0.7	4.4	7.8
EC	1.1	0.2	-1.9	4.6
Japan	0.5	0.1	-3.1	6.9
Other Countries:	0.7	0.7	3.6	1.8
of which				
East Asia & Pacific	0.2	0.1	13.4	13.1
Latin America	0.5	0.5	1.9	1.9
All Countries	4.7	1.7	1.2	4.7

SOURCE: World Bank (1993)

Capital Flows

The belief in rapid Latin American recovery is also derived from the remarkable resurgence of private capital flows in recent years. Two thirds of net capital flows to middle-income countries are now private (World Bank, 1993), mostly from financial intermediaries other than commercial banks. The World Bank estimates that these portfolio flows increased from about $6 billion a year in the late 1980s to some $34 billion in 1992. For Latin America as a whole, total portfolio investment inflows rose from $1.4 billion in 1989 to $19.2 billion in 1992, although bonds and American Depositary Receipts (ADRs) remain the predominant form of asset and direct equity investment in 1992 still represented less than 5 per cent of the total. In 1991, moreover, of $4.7 billion foreign investment in Latin American ADRs, $4.3 billion was captured by Mexico and, within this, $2.0 billion by Telmex alone.[3] It should also be remembered that the debt crisis is far from over, and the outflows of interest and reserve replenishment have reduced the net capital inflow of $56 billion to the region recorded in 1992 to a $26 billion net transfer on a financial basis and a zero net transfer on an expenditure basis (Table 3a). Under all these definitions, Mexico has clearly been the only significant 'gainer', the rest of the region experiencing negative net transfers on both financial and expenditure bases.

Table 9.2
Direction of Total Latin American Merchandise Trade

	(% of world trade) 1991		(growth rate) 1981-91	
	Origin	*Destination*	*Origin*	*Destination*
High Income Countries:	3.5	2.6	1.3	3.5
of which				
USA	1.8	1.4	3.6	4.5
EC	1.0	0.7	-0.7	2.0
Japan	0.3	0.2	-3.2	4.7
Other Countries:	1.0	1.0	2.1	0.9
of which				
East Asia & Pacific	0.1	0.2	7.0	8.9
Latin America	0.7	0.7	2.1	2.1
All Countries	4.5	3.7	1.5	2.7

SOURCE: World Bank (1993)

It is widely agreed that the bulk of these private flows represent repatriated flight capital, some high risk funds and only a small proportion of longer-term institutional investment. However, the scope for further growth in flows from the OECD economies towards emerging markets as a whole is held to be considerable (World Bank, 1993). Possibly as much as $40 billion a year could be reached by the end of the century on the assumption that emerging stock markets' present share in world market capitalisation (six per cent) will be maintained and eventually rise towards these countries' share of world GDP (about 13 per cent).[4]

Table 9.3a
Net Transfer of Financial Resources to Latin America and the Caribbean (LAC), 1992, $ billion

	Mexico	Brazil	Argentina	All LAC
Net Capital Inflow	22.7	9.7	9.2	55.5
less net profit and interest paid	7.4	8.3	4.2	25.6
equals net transfer on financial basis	15.3	1.4	5.0	35.9
less net additions to reserves	3.1	16.9	2.6	25.9
equals net transfer on expenditure basis	12.2	(15.6)	2.5	-

SOURCE: United Nations (1993)

Table 9.3b
Portfolio Investment in Latin America (US$ millions)

	1989	1992
Equity Investment from Abroad	434	5,570
of which: Closed-end Funds	416	293
ADRs etc	-	4,377
Direct Equity Investment	18	900
Bonds	833	11,732
Commercial Paper	127	840
Certificates of Deposit	0	1,100
Total	1,394	19,243

SOURCE: World Bank (1993)

Flows of Foreign Direct Investment (FDI) have grown quite rapidly to developing countries as a whole, from $10-15 billion a year in the 1970s and 1980s to almost $40 billion in 1992, the growth having been concentrated on relatively high-technology areas in services and manufactured exports, with 70 per cent of flows going to just ten countries. Within Latin America, of the $24 billion recorded FDI in the three years 1988-91, by far the greatest amount was in Mexico ($10 billion) and Argentina ($5 billion), with Chile, Colombia, Brazil and Venezuela receiving only $1-2 billion each. For Latin America in particular, uncertainty as to country creditworthiness appears to be the main factor affecting equity portfolio capital inflows, although the combination of continued recession and low real interest rates in the USA is also important (Calvo et al, 1992).

Although the problem of capital flight seems to have been contained for the present, a large part of the private portfolio is still held outside Latin America (at least $200 billion on conservative estimates – a sum comparable with total regional money supply in local currency). The risk of resumed outflows is still high (Calvo, 1992), although the decline in US interest rates has slowed the outflows in two ways: first, by making US securities less attractive; and second, by reducing the Latin American debt service burden and thus domestic monetary instability. However, it might be argued that when this capital does return to Latin America, it will be 'country-specific' – comparing the expected return in the economy of origin with that of (say) New York, rather than being substitutable between countries. What is more, the reflux of private capital has led to large current account deficits in a number of countries, resulting in real exchange rate appreciation. Despite official declarations to the effect that these deficits are no concern of the government once the budget has been balanced, private sector investors presumably continue to believe that the authorities will be forced to act as lender of last resort to banks in difficulties if the flows are reversed (IMF, 1993).

In sum, the future growth projections for Latin America rely on considerable private capital inflows, but this would have to be based on competition with other emergent economies and could hardly be expected to exceed $30bn a year, while even on past trends these would be concentrated on a few large economies in the region, particularly Mexico. The scale of the existing long-term liabilities also implies that a decline in these predominantly short-term inflows would immediately result in large outward net transfers or dangerous declines in reserves.

What are the Potential Externalities from NAFTA for Latin America?

Trade

NAFTA does not represent a major change in the trading arrangements between the three partners, particularly since the entry of Mexico to the GATT. In fact, by 1990 Mexico was already one of the largest exporters of manufactures from Latin America – particularly in machinery and transport equipment – as well as being a major energy supplier (Table 9.4). Mexico also sells 78 per cent of these exports to the USA and Canada, as opposed to 31 per cent in the case of Brazil and 19 per cent in the case of Argentina; in contrast, Mexico sells a relatively small proportion (9 per cent) of its exports to Latin America, compared to Brazil (20 per cent) and Argentina (38 per cent). In other words, Mexico is far more integrated to North America already than the rest of the region – and also enjoys a far higher degree of intra-industry (and intra-firm) integration based on technology transfer and market linkages (Table 9.5). Its closest competitor as an exporter of manufactures is Brazil, which only has half the North American market share of Mexico (1 per cent as opposed to 2 per cent), but which has nearly three times the market share in Europe and the rest of Latin America (Table 9.6). In other words, it can be argued that the two countries are no longer competing with one another – although this is probably based more on market access (including transport cost) than on product differentiation as such.

Table 9.4
Major Manufacturing Exports from Latin America and Mexico

	$ bn. 1988-90		% growth, 1970-90	
	Mexico	Latin America	Mexico	Latin America
All Manufactures	10.3	38.4	17.8	16.2
Chemicals	1.6	6.5	14.9	14.1
Basic Manufactures	2.2	14.0	15.1	15.7
Machinery and Transportation Equipment	5.7	13.2	22.0	19.0
Misc. Manufactures	0.9	4.8	13.6	15.1

SOURCE: IDB (1992)

This is why independent studies such as those by the Brookings Institution (Lustig et al, 1992) and the Institute for International Economics (IIE) (Hufbauer and Schott, 1993) indicate that the immediate trade gains from NAFTA will be relatively small. The IIE suggests that NAFTA does little more than complement GATT and that 'the scope for potential trade diversion is quite limited'. Even those sectors potentially most affected – particularly textiles and apparel, automobiles and parts and agriculture – should be liberalised under the Uruguay Round by 1994-5 in any case. Indeed, the effective export market segmentation noted above will be deepened by Mexico diverting its export effort away from Europe and the Pacific, opening new opportunities for the rest of Latin America, particularly Brazil. However, it is probably true that NAFTA quite deliberately blocks the potential for future expansion of exports from leading Latin American exporters (particularly Brazil, but also Colombia and Chile) to North America in sectors where stricter rules of origin apply: automotive goods, computers and other electronic equipment, machine tools, steel mill products, textiles and apparel, major household appliances, industrial machinery and bearings (USITC, 1993).

Table 9.5
Destination of Manufactured Exports from Latin America, 1990 (%)

	USA	Canada	EC	Japan	Latin America	IIT *
Mexico	76.5	1.4	7.0	1.0	9.4	59.0
Brazil	28.6	2.1	21.3	4.1	19.5	31.5
Argentina	17.5	1.5	14.8	3.1	38.0	15.6
All Latin America	45.8	1.8	12.9	2.4	24.5	38.0

* IIT = Index of Intra-Industry Trade

SOURCE: IDB (1992)

Trade generation within NAFTA will clearly benefit Mexico most. Moreover, an official US survey of recent modelling research and sectoral prospects (USITC, 1993) states that the recent swathe of Computable General Equilibrium Models of NAFTA projects a once-and-for-all rise in US GDP of 0.5 per cent at most,[5] which could translate into an equivalent expansion of Latin American exports to the USA worth some $100 million at best. Mexico-US trade will obviously expand considerably, but not spectacularly: estimates range from five to 27 per cent as the once-and-for-all rise in trade, and a corresponding rise in Mexican GDP of up to ten per cent. When spread over a decade this would add about one percentage point per annum to the growth of trade and welfare in Mexico – a considerable, but not overwhelming improvement. Little impact is expected on third-country trade by the USITC. The key finding, however, from the studies surveyed is that most output expansion is expected in sectors where scale economies can be expected (especially heavy industry) rather than sectors (e.g. *maquiladoras*) where there is presumptive comparative advantage based on unit labour costs. This implies not only an increase in investment levels but also Mexico 'moving up the learning curve' towards increased productivity of both labour and capital. This last point is underlined by the Colegio de México model (Sobarzo, 1991) where the gains from inter-industry trade are analysed by making scale economies and imperfect competition explicit, so that trade and welfare expansion arise from fewer firms serving a larger market using factors of production more efficiently. This model reveals that the high growth projections can only be achieved by massive new investment in Mexican industry, expanding manufacturing capacity by 20-30 per cent by the end of the decade.

Table 9.6
Destination of Manufactured Exports from Mexico and Brazil (1990)

	$ billion		Market Share (%)	
	Mexico	Brazil	Mexico	Brazil
North America	9.2	5.0	2.0	1.1
Other Latin America	1.1	3.1	1.9	5.5
EC	0.8	3.4	0.1	0.3
Other OECD	0.1	0.7	0.1	0.3
Japan	0.1	0.7	0.1	0.6
Asian NIEs	0.1	0.7	0.1	0.4
Rest of World	0.3	2.6	0.4	3.1

SOURCE: IDB (1992)

Capital Flows

NAFTA is more an investment than a trade project, in a number of senses. First, as pointed out above, much of the trade liberalisation was inherent in Mexico's membership of GATT since 1985. Second, the anticipated expansion of intra-industry trade will only come about through large investments in efficient plant and infrastructure. Third, the 'locking in' of macroeconomic policies by NAFTA membership should encourage flight capital to return and new portfolio investors to enter the Mexican stock market. Fourth, higher rates of growth should induce increased private investment in all other sectors of the economy. Fifth, and far from least, the considerable trade gap that Mexico plans to run in the medium term will require a sustained net inflow of foreign savings totalling as much as $100bn over the coming decade.

The impact of this project on capital flows towards Latin America is bound to be considerable, if only because Mexico is already by far the most important destination of capital inflows in the region. Working with the somewhat optimistic benchmark figure mentioned above of $30bn a year flowing into Latin America as a whole during the next decade, it is reasonable to surmise that Mexico could absorb up to two-thirds of this total – with Brazil and Argentina absorbing much of the rest. This figure would be consistent with both the gross private inflows to Mexico required to meet the 'foreign savings' target and balance continued public debt service on the one hand, and the relative attraction of Mexico for overseas investors on the other.

It is necessary to distinguish here between three types of flow: portfolio investments; bank credits; and Foreign Direct Investment. There is considerable evidence to indicate (Calvo et al, 1992) that the bulk of the recent inflow of portfolio capital to Latin America is associated with the 'return' of flight capital (or at least the reinvestable earnings thereof) attracted by high interest rates and pegged exchange rates. While its high degree of liquidity remains a major problem for monetary authorities, the origin of these funds would seem to imply that the flows are likely to be quite 'country specific' – in other words, other things being equal, the Mexico City stock market would not attract Argentine capital as much as Buenos Aires, but would attract Mexican funds held abroad. In fact this modality is very attractive to Mexican investors because it combines privileged knowledge of local business conditions with high liquidity and tax protection. Moreover, in the case of US and EC institutional funds, which at present do not make up a large proportion of portfolio flows but which hopefully will do so in the future, the additional security and reporting transparency that will arise from NAFTA will make Mexico City the most attractive of the emerging markets.

It should also be borne in mind that privatisation transactions worth some $39 billion were undertaken in Latin America during 1988-92, about 70 per cent of the developing country total (World Bank, 1993), and some $22 billion by Mexico alone. Although this figure does not translate directly into foreign investment, due to local purchases and debt-swap transactions, the positive effect on fiscal balances and investor confidence do clearly attract both portfolio flows and FDI. However, most of the major privatisations in Mexico and elsewhere in the region have already taken place or are under way, so that this factor cannot be expected to predominate in the medium term.

Bank credit and syndicated bond issues have only recently started to return to Latin America, a full ten years after the Mexican debt crisis. Mexico itself has already emerged as the most attractive client (including both government issues to bolster reserves and state enterprise borrowing), and there are at least four reasons to suggest that this degree of concentration will continue in the future. First, loans to the private sector will tend to follow FDI flows, as US firms will be considered as implicit guarantors of funds in firms in which they have an interest and the modernisation of payments and reporting procedures should reduce investor risk. Second, the Mexican public sector will remain attractive due to the permanent interest rate spread above US prime rates and the implicit protection against exchange risk provided by a parity band defended by both the Bank of Mexico and the Federal Reserve.[6] Third, the increase in US and Canadian direct investment in Mexican banks and insurance – on a conservative estimate, raising their share of the Mexican financial market from 8 to 15 per cent (USITC, 1993) – will reassure lenders, although it is probable that direct loans to Mexican firms from the USA will be replaced by the transactions of new US and Canadian bank operators in Mexico. Fourth, and perhaps most interestingly, in the absence of US regulatory reform, long-term investment in Mexico's universal banking system will be particularly attractive to US and Japanese banks. Once established as financial groups in Mexico, they will be able to operate commercial banks, investment funds, insurance, leasing and factoring business simultaneously.[7]

The US Trade Commission survey (USITC, 1993) indicates projections of $25-53 billion in extra FDI flows towards Mexico during the rest of this decade, and although there is 'little empirical basis for such estimates ... such investment flows will provide Mexico with greater benefits than will the reduction in trade barriers'. If and when the NAFTA FDI boom comes about, in the terminology of trade theory this will both reflect 'FDI creation' (or at least reallocation within NAFTA) and some FDI diversion from elsewhere in Latin America. The investment obligations of NAFTA (and related dispute settlement provisions) accord national treatment to NAFTA investors, remove most performance requirements on investment in the region, and open up new investment opportunities in key Mexican sectors such as petrochemicals and financial services. This gives foreign investors in Mexico far better (and believable) guarantees than elsewhere in Latin America.

If world capital markets worked in a textbook fashion, then any increased attraction of investment in Mexico would tend to raise world interest (and savings) rates slightly and marginally divert funds from all other globally traded assets. Thus the net effect on Latin America might be appreciable, but it would certainly be very small. However, in reality global capital markets are still highly segmented in terms of domestic versus overseas investment within the OECD, between the OECD and emerging markets, and between Latin America and Asia. This segmentation arises from information problems, regulatory regimes, and institutional relationships which are slow to change. Thus, new FDI in Mexico is likely to be diverted from existing plans to invest in the USA, Canada and elsewhere in Latin America (Aghevli, 1990; IMF, 1992b).

In contrast, the effect of the increased competitiveness of Mexico in competing for extra-regional export markets such as the EC or Japan on the basis of diverted FDI is likely to be counterbalanced by the increased aggregate import demand generated by the growth of the NAFTA countries (Hufbauer and Schott, 1993). To this could be added the probable decline in extra-regional export market penetration by Mexico (and possibly also Canada) as their existing investments in export marketing are diverted towards NAFTA partners.

The most significant impact of NAFTA, therefore, is the diversion by companies (based both inside and outside NAFTA) of funds originally intended for investment elsewhere in Latin America. This may be important where pre-existing levels of protection are relatively high (eg. in textiles) so FDI might be diverted to Mexico at the expense of more efficient producers elsewhere in Latin America – this, rather than trade diversion from existing plant, is likely to have a significant impact on countries such as Brazil and Colombia. This effect will be exacerbated by the implicit or explicit discrimination against non-NAFTA producers through restrictive rules of origin, to which component-outsourcing FDI and horizontally-integrated FDI are particularly vulnerable. In the case of outsourcing, NAFTA can be expected to disrupt trade networks and firms engaged in the electronics and garment industries: this would obviously affect Asian suppliers of *maquiladoras* immediately, but also limit the future potential for investment in electronics exports elsewhere in Latin America. Similarly, in the case of horizontally-integrated industries, restrictive rules of origin will disrupt intrafirm trade and may effectively prevent multinationals elsewhere in Latin America expanding plant in order to export parts to sister plant within NAFTA. Indeed, the USA explicitly intends (USITC, 1993) that the limitation of duty drawback will contribute to the establishment of a North American market by discouraging the creation of 'export platforms' in one NAFTA country to serve markets in another member country.[8]

The Implications for Regional Economic Institutions

It had originally been expected that the Uruguay Round would have been completed by end-1990, well before NAFTA was even negotiated, let alone implemented. If this had come to pass, NAFTA would be a complement to rather than a substitute for GATT – which is partly why there is no proper agricultural chapter in NAFTA itself. The resurgence of protectionism in the USA and EC has been a threat to the satisfactory conclusion of the Uruguay Round, which in turn is one of the most serious threats to the World Bank's 'base scenario' discussed above. Indeed 'there is some cause for concern about the popularity of new regional trading arrangements some of which may hurt the cause of multilateral liberalization ... unless world trade grows considerably faster than world GDP, the prospects for sustained economic growth in the basic scenario are likely to recede' (World Bank, 1993). This, in turn, would mean not only slower growth, but also renewed capital flight from Latin America.

Logically, there are two possible responses from the point of view of Latin America: to attempt direct access to NAFTA as a member; or to construct regional customs unions of their own, which could subsequently be linked with NAFTA. Much depends on the Washington position: the Bush Administration appears to have encouraged expectations of bilateral access on the 'satellite model', but support of Congress for new members was never assured (SELA, 1992b); the Clinton Administration appears to be more cautious and Congress even more so. Expanding the membership of NAFTA itself will run up against two major problems: on the one hand, it would in practice require the USA to obtain Mexican consent, which is unlikely to be forthcoming; on the other, the implicit budgetary, fiscal and legislative commitments of the regulatory requirements emerging from the projected trade and financial flows within NAFTA are likely to cause constitutional problems in the USA that will in turn increase Congressional opposition to expansion.

Meanwhile, other regional groupings such as Mercosur[9] have if anything accelerated their attempts at trade integration, although these have been mainly based on mutual tariff reduction rather than institution-building. This has already led to severe financial problems such as exchange-rate fluctuations arising from both market imbalances and national stabilisation programmes. These point to the need for closer macroeconomic policy coordination, particularly if integration is to lead to intra-industry investments as the basis for competitive extra-regional exports (SELA, 1992a). In other words, the real inter-economy regulatory problem in Latin America may relate to capital flows rather than trade as such. However, more research is needed on the economics of capital flows into and out of Latin America – particularly their relationship with trade on the one hand and corporate expansion decisions on the other (FitzGerald and Luttik, 1991) – before reliable conclusions can be reached.

NAFTA itself has no explicit provision for joint regulatory institutions, and even the dispute settlement mechanisms are somewhat imprecise. Historical precedent indicates that the practice of trade relations will lead to the emergence of a felt need for such institutions, and gradual pressure for harmonisation of commercial legislation – which in the case of the USA has considerable constitutional implications. The scale of private capital flows between the three countries will also lead to a need for tax coordination and mutual bank regulation, both of which will require more constitutional change on the part of the USA than on that of Canada or Mexico. Further, there are already signs of the US Treasury acting to support the Mexican peso on a regular basis, and a fixed exchange rate will probably require further monetary coordination in future. Finally, the enormous infrastructural and environmental investments implied by NAFTA itself (Hufbauer and Schott, 1993) will require support from the US Treasury, or perhaps – anticipating the reaction of Congress to such a prospect – pressure on multilateral agencies, particularly the Inter-American Development Bank, to channel funds towards Mexico at the expense of other borrowers.

As we have seen, Mexico is already attracting most of the long-term capital flows into the region, and this is likely to continue for the foreseeable future. This will generate two separate regulatory problems for the rest of Latin America. On the one hand, other countries will have to offer higher rates of return and greater investor guarantees not only to attract new foreign investors, but also to retain their own private capital. To maintain portfolio flows, the primary requirement according to the World Bank (1993) is, of course, 'the maintenance of sound policies in the recipient countries', but the Bank adds that 'what would also help is some rationalization in the fiduciary restrictions on outward portfolio investment from industrial countries, where such regulations vary greatly'. This would require explicit, joint regulatory negotiations with OECD authorities, and thus far greater coordination between Latin American monetary institutions than at present exists.

On the other hand, other Latin American countries will become increasingly exposed to the 'contagion' effect of financial crises in Mexico unless there is considerable progress in the establishment of international prudential regulation of capital markets, and possibly even tax coordination, in order to reduce volatility (IMF, 1992a). Meanwhile, it will probably be necessary to take specific measures in order to reduce the macroeconomic vulnerability of Latin American economies, extending the present practice of sterilising short-term capital flows through central bank reserve management towards high marginal reserve requirements for commercial banks (Calvo, 1992).

In sum, while the direct consequence of NAFTA itself will probably be modest 'trade creation' rather than 'trade diversion', the indirect consequences will include a considerable diversion of international capital flows towards Mexico, to the possible detriment of productive investment elsewhere in the region. Further, this chapter suggests that the institutional consequences of NAFTA within North America will be such as to delay further links between the USA and other Latin American economies, while forcing Latin American monetary and fiscal authorities to take international regulatory coordination more seriously.

Finally, it should be pointed out that the propositions put forward in this chapter are little more than tentative hypotheses which require much more research on the economics of capital flows into and out of Latin America – particularly their relationship with trade on the one hand and corporate expansion decisions on the other (FitzGerald and Luttik, 1991) – before reliable conclusions can be reached.

Notes

1. The G7 consists of USA, United Kingdom, France, Germany, Italy, Canada and Japan.
2. The London Inter-Bank Offer Rata (LIBOR) is one of the key benchmarks for interest rates in world capital markets.
3. The privatisation of Telmex, the Mexican telephone company, represented the biggest transfer of assets from the public to the private sector anywhere in Latin America.
4. Many of these 'emerging markets', of course, are in South-East Asia – not Latin America.
5. See chapter 2.
6. On Mexican exchange rate policy, see Welch (1993).
7. See chapter 4.
8. See chapter 3.
9. Mercosur is an ambitious attempt to build a customs union between Argentina, Brazil, Paraguay and Uruguay by means of intra-regional trade liberalisation and a common external tariff for extra-regional trade.

CHAPTER 10

THE CONSEQUENCES OF NAFTA FOR EUROPEAN AND JAPANESE TRADE AND INVESTMENT IN MEXICO

Gabriel Székely

Early in 1990, international trade specialists and policy makers were faced with the surprising Mexican decision to seek the negotiation of an ambitious trade agreement that would free the flow of commerce with its northern neighbour from all types of tariff and non-tariff barriers. This shift in Mexican policy came on the heels of the expected completion of the 'single market' in the European Community (EC), which was to be fully implemented by 1993. Although we now know that achieving this goal will take much more time than was originally anticipated,[1] leaders of the EC fear that US concerns about the single market might become a self-fulfilling prophecy. At the time, the USA protested at what appeared to be a move towards extending special benefits to European-based businesses alone. NAFTA itself was partly conceived as a means to provide a response should the EC become more restrictive and exclude businesses from non-member countries. With the process of European economic integration no longer so assured, however, the concern that outsiders might be excluded from doing business in the old continent is no longer such a prominent issue of debate. What many fear, however, is that the United States may itself be moving toward a less open and less tolerant trade policy in response to the increasing resentment of groups of citizens who have felt the full effects of the recession in the United States and the rest of the world. In particular, a narrow interpretation of NAFTA could serve the purpose of protecting special interests in the United States to the detriment of foreign firms.

Businesses executives and government officials in the European Community and Japan have expressed concern that several provisions included in NAFTA strengthen protectionist trends in the United States that will have an impact on global trade and investment regimes. Several aspects of NAFTA's chapters on rules of origin and government procurement are discussed in this chapter to highlight the anxieties of European and Japanese leaders. A change in US policy toward protectionism would force these economic powers to reconsider their own international trade strategy.

The threat of relatively closed trading blocs both in Western Europe and North America is a major source of Japanese concern. Domestic groups and several nations in the Asia-Pacific region have been urging the government of Japan to take a tougher stand in trade negotiations with the United States, as well as to lead an effort to establish an Asian Free Trade Area (AFTA). There are several reasons why the Japanese government has not been eager to respond to this challenge: a) the complex nature of the geopolitical landscape surrounding Japan, which means that any power in the region must deal concurrently with China, Taiwan, the two Koreas, and Russia, among other nations; b) Japan more than any other industrial nation, with the exception of Canada, depends heavily on the US economy for its very survival, and it must be cautious not to antagonise the United States by establishing a trade bloc of its own; c) given that prosperity at home depends heavily on foreign trade, Japan is likely to resist as forcefully as it can the demise of the multilateral trading system and the ascendance of regionalism. NAFTA is therefore tolerated as long as the doors of the now enlarged North American economy are kept open to all parties. Yet it is uncertainty about future access to NAFTA, which continues to preoccupy foreign business leaders.

Are these concerns of European and Japanese leaders premature and are we in the midst of a new era characterised by trade policies of exclusion that will bring about rising tensions and conflict among the world's leading economic powers? More specifically, does NAFTA shed some light on the proposition that regionalism is on the rise?

NAFTA itself represents a major accomplishment for US trade policy. In this agreement, the United States has been able to reach a series of compromises with a leading developing economy on a number of issues that had proved intractable in other *fora* involving both industrial and developing countries. These include the fully-fledged liberalisation of US-Mexican agricultural trade,[2] and agreements on the service sector and on intellectual property rights. In fact, it can be argued that a substantial portion of the US agenda in the Uruguay Round of negotiations within the General Agreement on Tariffs and Trade (GATT), has been met in the negotiations with Mexico.[3] Moreover, as regards investment, NAFTA opens for *all* foreign firms opportunities for doing business in Mexico that are truly unprecedented, such as in the financial and energy industries.[4]

In this chapter, a brief review of the central goals that led Mexican and US officials to pursue NAFTA is followed by an analysis of patterns of European and Japanese trade and investment flows in Mexico. Prospects for European and Japanese businesses in the future are discussed with respect to several of NAFTA's leading provisions.

Is Mexico a Champion of Free Trade?

A Mexican official argued in a recent interview that, with respect to his government's views on actively promoting a domestic technology production capacity,[5] 'Mexico's policy is to have no policy at all, instead leaving market forces to determine what should be produced locally and what should be imported from more efficient sources'.

What such a statement suggests is that several decades of indiscriminate trade protection and of holding defensive attitudes toward foreign investment have produced a backlash within Mexican official and business circles. In the 1990s, the 'magic of the market' is expected to produce the good results and the enhanced economic performance that did not materialise during the era of unchecked protectionism.

As Jaime Ros argues in chapter 2, the opening of Mexico's economy began quite slowly in the mid-1980s when special trade and investment agreements with the United States were signed and when Mexico decided to join GATT. After 1988, however, the gradualist approach followed by Mexican authorities gave way to a package of policy reforms that were implemented rapidly and decisively. Though the social effects of the new economic policies are a reason to be concerned, there is little doubt that the overall direction of Mexico's economic policies will not be altered in the future.

Economic growth has been restored, with net GDP increases averaging 3.7 per cent from 1989 to 1992 compared to only 0.5 per cent from 1982 to 1988; public sector deficits have been reduced drastically through spending cuts and more effective tax collection programmes; the terms to service the country's huge foreign debt have been substantially eased following the implementation of the Brady Plan; public enterprises and banks have been sold, often at premium prices, yielding $22 billion to the nation's Treasury by the end of 1992; annual inflation has been curbed from a peak of 159 per cent in 1987 to a single digit by mid-1993 through government price and wage controls and the extensive liberalisation of trade; and finally, international reserves stood at nearly $23 billion dollars in August 1993, which will help the government resist a run on the peso if a speculative attack should be mounted against the currency.[6]

The ongoing efforts to stabilise the Mexican economy will be further strengthened once preferential access to the US market becomes a reality through the implementation of NAFTA. The agreement provides Mexico with a policy tool to oblige the United States to reciprocate now that Mexico has unilaterally curbed import permits from nearly 100 per cent (1983) coverage to a handful of product categories in the early 1990s. The average import tariff has also been cut significantly, to 12 per cent, with a maximum tariff of 20 per cent levied on selected imported goods.

Figure 10.1 shows the disproportionate weight that the United States has with respect to Mexico's foreign trade. The sum of US exports to and imports from Mexico has grown more than three-fold, from $22 billion in 1985 to $72 billion in 1992,[7] in less than three years. The US Department of Commerce estimates that 20,000 new jobs are created for every $1 billion in new exports to Mexico, which means that 540,000 new jobs were created in the United States during this period, since US exports to Mexico rose from $13 billion to $40 billion during these years.[8] Mexico began to run a trade deficit with the USA in 1991 that reached $7 billion in 1992.

Figure 10.1
Mexico's Trade with the World

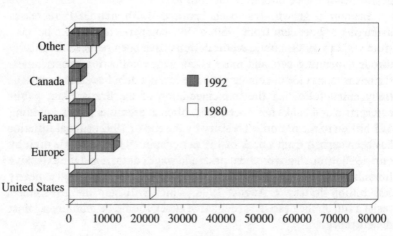

US $ billion

NAFTA, however, will open opportunities in the US market previously unavailable to Mexican exporters and this will help Mexico to compensate in part for the deficit that results from the increased purchase of US products.[9]

More important for the purpose of this chapter is that, by formally joining the North American economy through NAFTA, Mexican authorities will be able to generate the kind of interest among foreign investors that a decades-old policy to diversify the profile of Mexico's economic relations with the world had failed to accomplish.[10] For transnational corporations and financial institutions from industrial countries Mexico will now become an integral part of North American strategy.

European and Japanese Trade and Investment in Mexico

Over the last decade Europe[11] and Japan have become important sources of imported goods and services, accounting respectively for 14.1 per cent and 6.7 per cent of Mexican imports in 1992 (See Table 10.1), although both purchased fewer Mexican goods, representing 8.5 per cent and 2.6 per cent of Mexican exports in 1992. These figures contrast sharply with the role that European countries play in other large economies of Latin America, including Brazil, Argentina, and Chile, where Europe as a whole represents on average 20 to 25 per cent of these countries' total foreign trade transactions.[12] Japan is also a large trading partner of several Latin American countries, often second in importance only to the United States – though much lower import and export flows are involved. The exception is Chile, which in 1992 became the first Latin American economy for which Japan represented its largest trading partner.[13]

Mexico's proximity to the US market, and the extensive role in domestic production traditionally played by US firms, explain why a similar pattern holds with respect to Foreign Direct Investment (FDI) (see Table 10.2). The United States plays a dominant role within the Mexican market, where US FDI in Mexico grew four-fold from $6 billion in 1980, to close to $24 billion in 1992. The US share in total FDI in Mexico, however, was reduced from 70 per cent to 59 per cent during the same period. The reason is that many countries have been investing in the Mexican market both in response to the economic reforms of the last eight years, and in anticipation of the expected benefits that will follow from trade liberalisation within the North American region.

Table 10.1
Mexico's Trade with OECD Countries

	Total Trade[1] (mill $US)	OECD Total (%)	USA	Canada	Japan	OECD Europe	France	UK	Spain
1980:									
Exports	15,570	85.4	64.7	0.8	4.3	15.6	3.6	0.3	7.9
Imports	18,533	81.9	58.7	1.7	4.8	16.3	2.5	2.0	1.7
1985:									
Exports	22,108	88.5	60.3	1.8	7.7	18.6	3.7	3.1	7.7
Imports	13,443	90.0	66.6	1.7	5.4	15.5	2.0	2.1	1.6
1990:									
Exports	30,130	91.5	68.3	2.7	6.3	14.0	2.9	1.8	5.5
Imports	32,924	91.4	68.5	1.3	5.9	15.2	2.1	1.6	1.5
1992P:									
Exports	42,551	93.1	76.6	5.2	2.6	8.5	1.6	0.6	3.0
Imports	57,112	92.3	70.1	1.0	6.7	14.1	2.2	0.9	1.3

[1] This column in US dollars; the rest of the data is presented as the participation of each country in total imports and exports (%)

P Preliminary

SOURCE: International Monetary Fund (various years)

Table 10.2
Foreign Direct Investment in Mexico (in $US billion)

Year	Accumulated Total	USA	Germany	UK	Japan	Other
1980	8.5	6.0	0.65	0.25	0.82	0.78
1983	11.5	7.6	0.97	0.35	1.17	1.41
1986	17.1	11.2	1.40	0.56	1.55	2.39
1989	26.6	17.5	1.70	1.43	1.71	4.26
1990	30.3	19.1	2.00	1.90	1.87	5.43
1991p	35.0	21.6	2.15	2.10	2.00	7.15
1992p	39.5	23.5	2.25	2.70	2.10	8.95

p Preliminary
SOURCE: Mexico's Ministry of Trade and Industry and Banco de México (1992).

The value of these investments in Mexico, however, is low by international standards, especially when compared with the boom of FDI registered in the industrial north during the 1980s; Japan itself invested annually over $20 billion dollars in the late 1980s in the United States alone. Yet the financial flows involved are still of great relevance to a capital-scarce economy such as Mexico's. Thus, the fact that the UK, Germany and Japan had still each accumulated by the end of 1992 over $2 billion in investments (see Table 10.2) is considered a success in Mexico.

Mexican leaders have continued their efforts to attract new capital. They have a strong incentive in that foreign funds are playing a stabilising role in management of the exchange rate. The modernisation of Mexican business firms has resulted in huge imports and a growing trade deficit, even though Mexican exports continue to expand. In 1992, the Mexican trade deficit reached $14.5 billion dollars (see Table 10.1). Government efforts have been successful with FDI inflows averaging $2.8 billion annually from 1985 through 1989 before reaching $4.5 billion from 1990 to 1992.[14] Foreign portfolio investment has similarly increased, with a substantial proportion of these funds coming to Mexico to take advantage of interest rates that are much higher than in industrial countries, of a stable currency sustained by the government's committment to bring down inflation to a single digit, and by high levels of accumulated foreign exchange reserves from the sale of banks and public firms.

With respect to foreign direct investment from all countries, Figure 10.2 shows its distribution by sector from 1985 to 1991. Although Mexican data are quite sparse, the few specialised studies that are available show that most European and Japanese investments are concentrated in manufacturing within the automobile, electronics and petrochemical industries. Volkswagen and Nissan are key participants in the automobile industry; Thompson, Phillips and every single major Japanese electronics producer have manufacturing plants in Mexico as well; and European firms such as ICI,[15] Hoescht and BASF are involved in the petrochemical industry. Within the service sector, telecommunications became quite important in the early 1990s following the privatisation of the government telephone monopoly, Teléfonos de México (TELMEX), with extensive participation of France Telecomm in a joint venture with Mexican and US capital. Also in the service sector are firms involved in the tourist industry, including Spain's Melia hotel chain, France's Club Med, and Japan's Nikko Hotel and the Westin chain.[16]

Figure 10.2
Foreign Direct Investment by Sector

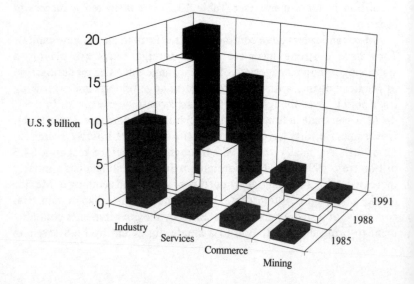

Several sectors will become particularly attractive for foreign businesses in the years to come. According to a study by DRI/McGraw-Hill,[17] the sectors of the Mexican economy that will increase their participation in manufacturing GDP include machinery and equipment, chemicals and basic metals. Other opportunities will result from the parallel agreement on the environment, which could lead to an estimated $8 billion investment to help Mexico reduce pollution and bring the country up to international standards on the environmental front.[18]

Is NAFTA Protectionist? Rules of Origin and Government Procurement

In the area of manufacturing, it is increasingly recognised that Mexico has become over the last quarter-century a world class producer of automobiles, autoparts and electronic products. The Mexican government has maintained for three decades an industrial policy to support the development of the automobile sector and such a policy is still in effect even after an across-the-board trade liberalisation programme was implemented in the mid-1980s.[19] Government policy has been critical to the success of the handful of transnational firms that dominate the domestic market, including Volkswagen and Nissan in addition to the 'big three' from the United States (General Motors, Ford and Chrysler). Only firms currently operating in the Mexican market will benefit from the extended protection of the automobile industry negotiated under NAFTA.

The complaint espoused by European and Japanese firms in this area is that what they consider an already restrictive trade agreement, signed between the USA and Canada in 1988 (CUFTA), has become even worse under NAFTA. In the latter trade agreement, 'regional content' must be from 60 to 62.5 per cent for automobiles in order to qualify for duty-free treatment within the North American market; this level of locally produced parts and components is 20 per cent higher than the 50 per cent required in CUFTA.

The significance of this rule is that those willing to qualify for duty-free treatment will have to invest more money either to help supplier firms from their home market relocate to North America or to develop networks of local suppliers in the particular country where they are currently doing business. For example, in order to meet the NAFTA test, Nissan will establish Japanese suppliers near its $1 billion dollar plant presently under construction in the Mexican state of Aguascalientes. However, not every firm has the resources to follow this path.

In contrast, many Japanese electronic firms will find that the two options presented above will not be helpful in their quest to stay competitive. It would be quite expensive for many Japanese electronic firms to relocate suppliers or to develop local producer networks. Therefore, some firms will choose to forego low-cost labour savings in Mexico and instead will consolidate their production facilities within the most important market (i.e. the United States). In this manner, they will put the whole issue represented by 'rules of origin' to rest since they will no longer have to cross any border in order to sell their products. Other firms, according to executives interviewed, will relocate to China if NAFTA is applied restrictively in this area, taking advantage of the protection resulting from special preferences extended to China by successive US administrations.

Mexico has thus become a potential loser from the application of strict rules of origin. It has had to accept the phasing out of its long-standing policy of requiring companies to meet certain levels of local content, which benefited Mexican firms, and it has had to endorse the concept of rules of origin for the region that may lead several foreign firms to close their plants in Mexico. Mexican negotiators had no choice, however, given the extended fear in the USA and Canada that without such rules many European and Asian firms would use Mexico as a springboard to penetrate further the US market and to displace Canadian producers as well.

However, many assembly or *maquiladora* plants owned by European and Japanese firms in Mexico will not be affected in the way that has been described so far. In fact, NAFTA could be good news for these firms for the following reasons. Before NAFTA, firms that used any inputs that did not originate in the USA – including Mexican labour and other local expenses – had to pay duties when they sent their assembled products back to the United States. This means that, in theory at least, 100 per cent of the inputs used in these assembly plants had to be made in the USA in order to pay no duties at all. Under NAFTA, however, all value added in Mexico now counts toward meeting the regional content test. In electronics, for example, Mexican value added represented in 1990 close to 15 per cent of the final value of the products sold in the USA. On this count, therefore, NAFTA is much more open than the *maquiladora* regulatory regime has been. A typical electronic firm must therefore add to the list of purchases in Mexico additional inputs made in either the USA or Canada to bring the total for all inputs (including value added) up to 60 per cent of the value of output and thereby qualify for duty-free treatment within the North American market. In this example the total level of intermediate inputs that must be sourced in the region is thus only 45 per cent (i.e. excluding value added), and not 100 per cent, which means that on this count too NAFTA is a more open arrangement than the current regime regulating the *maquiladoras*.[20]

It could be argued that manufacturing is not the issue within NAFTA that is potentially the most contentious for European and Japanese firms interested in doing business in the Mexican market. After all, the value of European direct investment in Mexico's manufacturing sector is under $10 billion, and it is about $2 billion for the Japanese. What makes European and Japanese concerns important is that a narrow interpretation of NAFTA's rules of origin will signal a shift in US policy away from its long-standing committment to support and promote free trade throughout the world.

Government procurement has been the subject of difficult negotiations between the USA and Europe for quite some time. The United States insists that non-European firms must be treated more fairly and have an equal opportunity to win government contracts. NAFTA may provide Europeans with some room for negotiation once their firms begin to compete for contracts within Mexico. NAFTA will become a litmus test of how committed the United States is to the principle of equal opportunity to bid for and to win government contracts.

Immediately upon entering into force NAFTA provides that 50 per cent of all federal procurement contracts in North America will become open to bidding by any North American-based business. After ten years, all such contracts will be subject to unrestricted competition in the region. This affects Mexico in particular because it is the one country in the region that has been the most protectionist in this area.

Mexico's annual federal procurement contracts are on average in the $20-22 billion range, with about $10 billion concentrated in the lucrative state-owned energy business. Another important opportunity is the development of Mexico's infrastructure to cope with increased trade and investment flows (i.e., highways, telecommunication services, railroads, ports, and other projects), where increasingly investment by the public sector is being replaced by private enterprise.[21]

There is some ground for European and Japanese businesses to be concerned. In 1992, Sumitomo, the Japanese Trading Company, won a contract to build railway cars which the Los Angeles City Council subsequently rescinded following protests from local unions and industry; the contract was finally awarded to a US company. Similarly, the Mexican transportation ministry had just decided in favour of a Spanish firm to build cars for Mexico City's subway system, when the French-Canadian firm Bombardier publicly protested the decision on the grounds that it did not take into account the interest of a business firm from a fellow NAFTA country.

These episodes raise the question of whether the Mexican government will be in the position to resist political pressure and award contracts based on commercial criteria rather than simply granting preferential treatment to North American firms. Existing fears of NAFTA becoming 'protectionism in disguise' may come true and in the process generate a series of tensions between the USA, Canada and other industrial nations. Moreover, the objective of diversifying Mexico's profile of economic relations with the rest of the world would not materialise under such circumstances.

The issue discussed here is significant not only from the policy point of view, but also for Mexican business firms that are trying to diversify their operations and become more internationally-oriented. In an increasing number of cases, establishing strategic alliances with European and Japanese firms is far wiser than becoming closely linked to US firms which no longer dominate the newest technologies or control the most attractive markets. Thus, it is not in Mexico's interest to alienate potential business partners that may help Mexico reach higher levels of efficiency and productivity in the world economy. This means that in the area of government procurement contracts Mexico will have to act with great caution.

Conclusions

Formally joining the North American economy through NAFTA provides Mexico with a unique opportunity to achieve in the 1990s a substantial diversification of the profile of its international economic relations. Europe and Japan are likely to look at Mexico with greater interest now that it is more closely tied to the US economy. At the same time, however, Mexico has become more vulnerable to sudden shifts in the overall orientation of US trade policy. A turn toward protectionism on the part of the latter country would leave Mexico hopelessly isolated and its fate dependent on that of the US economy.

European and Japanese firms have moderately increased their presence in Mexico's foreign trade and investment sectors over the last decade, though at much lower levels than in other large economies within Latin America. An open NAFTA and the moderate application of the agreement's most restrictive provisions would lead firms in these countries to further expand their business in Mexico. In turn, a stronger connection with the latter is likely to help Europe and Japan to find new areas for expansion into Latin America.

Notes

1. Although the single European market went into effect on 1 January 1993, a number of important issues were still unresolved and many tax rates had still not been equalised.
2. For further details, see chapter 5.
3. By the time NAFTA was signed, in December 1992, the United States had failed to secure agreement within the Uruguay Round for its ambitious agenda.
4. Although oil production remains a state monopoly, there are opportunities for foreign business in many oil-related activities.
5. Interview in Mexico City, May 1991.
6. Details of the current state of the Mexican economy are reported in Banamex (1993).
7. US Department of Commerce (1992) and telephone communication for 1992 data.
8. Quoted in USTR (1992a).
9. See Székely (1991a, pp. 217-28).
10. See Székely (1989, 1777-1797).
11. 'Europe' is used to refer either to the 12 countries of the European Community or to the European members of the OECD according to the data source used.
12. See International Monetary Fund, Direction of Trade Statistics (Washington DC, various years).
13. See Stallings and Székely (1993).
14. See Banco de México (1992); also communication with Mexico's Ministry of Trade and Industrial Development.
15. In 1993 ICI (a British multinational) was split into two separate and competing companies.
16. See Unger (1990); Van Whiting (1993); Székely (1991b).
17. See DRI/McGraw-Hill (1991).
18. See chapter 7.
19. See Shaiken (1987); Benett and Sharpe (1985).
20. See Székely (1992, pp. 44-6). Not all commentators share this interpretation of the impact of NAFTA on the *maquiladoras*. For a different – less optimistic – point of view, see chapter 3.

CHAPTER 11

CANADA'S ROLE IN NAFTA:
TO WHAT DEGREE HAS IT BEEN DEFENSIVE?

Ronald J. Wonnacott

By mid-1990, it had become evident to the Canadian government that the United States and Mexico were on track to negotiate a free trade agreement (FTA). The question was: should Canada participate, transforming the negotiations from a US-Mexican bilateral into a trilateral discussion? This was not an easy decision. The Canadian economy was already having to adjust to free trade with the United States, while at the same time facing a number of recession-related pressures. In this situation, the Canadian government would have preferred to avoid a negotiation that might disturb the carefully balanced provisions of the Canada-US free trade agreement (CUFTA) and that might re-ignite the politically divisive debate on the regional liberalisation of trade that had occurred in the so-called CUFTA election in late 1988. While this was not the time that the Canadian authorities would have selected for facing another round of adjustments, they had no control over this. They were therefore faced with a simple choice: to participate or not to participate in the planned expansion of the Free Trade Area.

They decided – in my view, correctly – to participate. In large part this was for defensive reasons: to avoid the costs of being excluded when trading partners are liberalising their trade and to be at the bargaining table to protect Canada's free trade agreement with the United States. It is therefore important to understand how the CUFTA had been developing since it began in 1989.

The Canada-US FTA: Was it Worth Ensuring?

CUFTA has not been easy to evaluate because of a number of other problems that Canada has concurrently had to face:

1. During the early period of adjustment to CUFTA, there has been an

extended Canadian recession, in large part the result of a slump worldwide – in particular, in the United States. Although economic recovery has been less weak in Canada than elsewhere, Canada only returned to its pre-recession GDP in 1993.

2. In the face of low aggregate demand, the Canadian government introduced a value-added tax (a goods and services tax). Although, as a replacement for the manufacturers' sales tax, it was initially meant to be revenue-neutral, in the event it did increase tax collections and in any case represented another adjustment at a time of serious dislocation.

3. Canada's large shrinkage-resistant fiscal deficit has left monetary policy as the only credible instrument for dealing with macroeconomic problems. Since CUFTA came into effect, the Bank of Canada has pursued a tight money policy that has succeeded in reducing the Canadian inflation rate to below two per cent (given the bias in estimation, this is now indistinguishable from zero). However, this made the recession more severe. In particular, by raising Canadian interest rates and hence the value of the Canadian dollar, it has put a great deal of pressure on Canada's export and import-competing industries. This combination of fiscal impotence and tight money represents the worst possible mix when a country is adjusting to free trade. In short, an attack on inflation by the monetary authorities, no matter how successful it may have been, has focused the pressure of adjustment on Canada's trade-related industries, just at a time when they were under pressure to adjust to increased competition from the United States.

In these circumstances, it has been surprising that the Canadian recession was not worse; unemployment has remained in the 11-12 per cent range, about four per cent above the natural Canadian rate in the late 1980s – this gap is considerably less than the one that opened in the recession of the early 1980s. The most recent recession did, however, extend over a longer period than the one in the early 1980s.

The early evidence is that the recession in the 1990s would have been worse were it not for CUFTA. One of the few robust elements in the Canadian national income accounts during the first three years of CUFTA (1989-91) was the 15.5 per cent growth in liberalised exports to the United States, which substantially exceeded the disappointing rate of growth of US GDP. Moreover, these Canadian exports to the United States also strongly outperformed Canadian exports to the rest of the world, which in fact fell by six per cent. The most persuasive explanation of this pattern was the stimulus to Canadian exports provided by CUFTA's freer access to the US market.[1] This can be viewed as a bonus, since free trade with the United States, like technological change, was required – including adjustment costs – in order to keep Canada competitive.

The situation has now improved. With the inflation fight (at least temporarily) won, Canada has moved to a combination of interest and exchange rates much more favourable for completing the adjustment to free trade with the United States, and the much less important adjustment to free trade with Mexico. However, this more favourable outlook was not yet in view when the Canadian government had to make a decision on NAFTA. That decision was to go ahead, despite the additional adjustment that this decision would impose on the Canadian economy. There had to be strong reasons for this decision.

The Canadian Negotiating Objectives in NAFTA

Canada's stated objectives in this negotiation were:[2]

1. To gain access for Canadian goods, services and capital to Mexico – one of the fastest growing and most promising economies in the world – on an equal footing with the United States.

2. To resolve a number of specific irritants with the United States that occurred within the context of the more intense trade and investment relationship of the early years of CUFTA.

3. To ensure no reduction in the benefits and obligations of CUFTA.

4. To ensure that Canada remained an attractive location for investors wishing to serve the whole North American market.

Broadly speaking, the first two objectives reflected the desire to achieve traditional gains from trade, while the other objectives were defensive, reflecting Canada's desire to avoid the costs of being excluded. By and large, Canada achieved these objectives. Although in some respects the result fell short of these targets, in other respects it exceeded them, with Canada acquiring other benefits as well.

Canada's Traditional Objectives

The Acquisition of Better Access to the Mexican Market

Canada has not secured completely free access, since Mexico will still retain some restrictions on its trade. However, Mexico will be removing its tariffs and many of its non-tariff barriers such as its import licensing requirements and its Automobile Decree, which have severely restricted Canadian exports. Canadian firms will also be able to bid on a significant part of the procurement contracts of the Mexican government and its parastatals such as PEMEX – the national oil company.

With a few exceptions (most notably in some agricultural products where Canada resisted liberalising its trade with Mexico), Canadian exports will enter Mexico on the same terms as US exports – terms that will be far more favourable than in the past. The Canadian producers often cited as beneficiaries of a more open Mexican market are those in automotive equipment, telecommunications equipment,[3] mining and environmental equipment and services, industrial machinery and consumer goods. Increased Mexican demand for Canadian exports will be fuelled not only by the removal of Mexican trade barriers, but also by accelerated growth in Mexico, insofar as it is able to seize the opportunity of freely trading with the United States to reduce its productivity gap and thereby, perhaps dramatically, increase its income. Potential benefits for Canada will go beyond trade in goods, to trade in services and investment. For example, financial services, a previously closed sector in Mexico, will now be open to a substantial degree of Canadian as well as US participation[4] – in particular, in banking where Canadian expertise in branch banking, which the Mexicans wish to develop, may provide an edge over US competitors. Here and elsewhere on the investment side, restrictions will be put in place to prevent any possible future government in North America – for example, in Mexico – from 'implicitly expropriating' foreign assets by huge royalty increases. This sets an important precedent for other countries in Latin America that may be contemplating membership of NAFTA.

The liberalisation of Canadian-Mexican trade has provided Canada with a benefit not explicitly stated in its set of objectives above – the elimination of Canadian barriers against imports from Mexico.[5] Arguably this may not be as important for Canada as the elimination of Mexican barriers against Canadian exports. For example, almost all automotive equipment – Canada's largest import from Mexico by a large margin[6] – has been coming into Canada duty-free due to the Automobile

Pact provisions that safeguard Canadian production (but that also, in this case, have paradoxically provided an incentive for Mexican production for export to Canada). In this case, Canadian tariff elimination under NAFTA may have little impact in increasing Canadian imports. On the other hand, NAFTA's elimination of the Mexican Automobile Decree, which had been seriously deterring Canadian exports, will offer a much greater potential benefit to Canada.

While the effects on Canada of removing its own import barriers may be less than the effects of Mexican removal of barriers to Canadian exports, Canadian benefits from liberalising imports may still be substantial. These will include a benefit to Canadian consumers. Moreover, the greater degree of international competition NAFTA will inject into the Canadian economy will reduce market power and create a more efficient and competitive Canadian economy. Specifically, the ability of Canadian firms to purchase duty-free inputs from Mexico will make them better able to compete on world markets, in particular against US firms selling in Canada, the United States and elsewhere. It has been important to establish this benefit, because competing US firms will secure it and it is competition with US firms in the Canadian – and in particular, the US – marketplace that is likely to represent the greatest challenge to Canadian producers. Thus, paradoxically, trade liberalisation with Mexico may well have its most significant effect on Canadian industry in improving its ability to compete, not in Mexico or even Canada, but in the United States; for Canada, the story of trade liberalisation with Mexico is likely, in large part, to be played out in a third market – the United States – and Canada's ability to compete there will be enhanced by its access to inexpensive Mexican inputs (the reason that the Canadian government has not made an issue of the benefits of duty-free imports from Mexico to Canadian consumers and using industries is that they raise an adjustment problem for *competing* Canadian industries).

Finally, by liberalising imports from Mexico, and perhaps eventually from other low-income countries in the hemisphere, Canada is replacing a policy of aid with one of trade. This implies benefits to both North and South, i.e. benefits to Canadian taxpayers and to Latin Americans who will not only enjoy economic gains from more rapid growth, but will also, more broadly, be able to view themselves as participants in the economic development in the hemisphere – and thereby as contributors to Canada's growth as well as theirs – rather than as the recipients of Canadian charity. Indeed, the hope has been expressed that NAFTA may, in some respects, be a guide to resolving disputes and improving North-South trading relationships.

How NAFTA has reduced irritants in Canada-US trade

While there are some clear accomplishments, such as the improved treatment for Canadian exports as a result of the increased discipline NAFTA provides over US energy regulators, in possibly the most substantial area of change – rules of origin – the record is, at best, mixed. By making these requirements more transparent and less subject to arbitrary ruling by customs officers, and by reforming some unsatisfactory procedures such as 'roll-up' and 'roll-down', border disputes like the one over Honda Civics should become less likely.[7] Indeed, since provision is made for retroactive judgement, it may be possible for Canada to receive a favourable ruling on this case, although this is not guaranteed.

Unfortunately, the risk of arbitrary decisions on rules of origin by customs officers has been reduced at a cost: the 200-odd pages of detail on how these rulings should be made. While this level of detail may provide more transparency for customs officers who devote their careers to this subject, and more importantly, to exporting firms once they have identified which of these 200 pages apply to them, it provides less transparency for analysts who are trying to evaluate the NAFTA forest and have to face all these trees.

There is another cause of concern: the strict rule of origin requirements in autos, clothing and possibly footwear. Unfortunately, more restrictive rules of origin protect the country with the large market – in this case, the United States – not only from outside fourth countries, but also from its NAFTA partners, an issue that will be considered again below.

Canada's Defensive Objectives

Cementing Canada's Gains from the FTA

Canada preserved CUFTA's trade liberalisation with the United States and the original exemptions from it – in particular, culture, automobile safeguards and marketing sectors. There is, of course, the question of whether or not it is in Canada's interest to be able to protect these sectors. The author supports some protection in culture, and views the automobile safeguards as a non-issue. Ensuring that Canadian automobile production is related to sales has long since ceased to be an effective constraint since Canadian production is now running so far above sales; Canadian sales represent less than 10 per cent of Canadian-US sales, while Canadian automobile production is estimated at 17-20 per cent of Canadian-US production. However, setting this question aside for now, NAFTA does allay the fears of its critics who were concerned that FTA exclusions would be brought back onto the table and eliminated or compromised. It also allayed any fears that automobile safeguards would be eliminated ('grandfathering' these while the Mexicans were eliminating their Automobile Decree must have been a minor negotiating triumph for Canada.)

There was one benefit from CUFTA – preference over Mexico in the US market – that could not be saved by NAFTA or any other set of negotiations. This was lost the moment Mexico and the United States decided to liberalise their trade, and the United States thereby decided to give Mexican exports the same favourable access as Canadian exports. (Canada does still, however, retain its preference in the US market over all other countries.)

While Canada's negotiators did not prevent the loss of this Canadian benefit from CUFTA, because it was impossible for them to do so, they were successful in ensuring against an even more damaging possibility: that Mexico would go beyond acquiring the *same* treatment as Canada in the US market, and receive *better* treatment. While that was not possible in tariffs, where Canada already faced zero US tariffs, it was possible in other areas. Had Canada not participated in NAFTA, it might well have encountered this problem in government procurement, where Mexico did acquire better access to these US contracts than Canada was receiving under CUFTA. However, because Canada did participate in NAFTA, it is awarded the same favourable treatment as Mexico.

Improvements in the Canada-US FTA

There are a number of areas in which NAFTA has been cited as improving on CUFTA for Canada. For example, NAFTA has broadened trade liberalisation into new areas; there is now an increased discipline over standards that should reduce the risk of restraints on trade such as the US trade remedy action against Canadian lobsters. Most important, however, has been the harmonisation of tariffs to a lower level in the computer industry. This offers a model in future hemispheric negotiations for avoiding the rule of origin problems that have complicated and deterred trade, first in CUFTA and now in NAFTA.

Ensuring that the United States would not acquire a special location advantage

Canada did not succeed entirely in this objective, since more restrictive rules of origin in certain specific sectors – once again, automobiles, footwear, textiles and apparel – have made it more difficult for firms locating in Canada to service the US market. In the case of automobiles, the problem is most likely to be substantial for transplant companies from outside North America; in the case of apparel, no matter how much the expanding tariff rate quotas (TRQs) may or may not compensate incumbent Canadian firms, if and when NAFTA's more restrictive rules of origin become operational, Canada will become less attractive for new firms considering it as a location.

However, in a much broader and more important sense, Canada has avoided the major across-the-board location disadvantage in all sectors that would have occurred if Canada had opted out of NAFTA. In this case the United States would have become a trading hub having two spoke bilateral agreements – one with Canada and one with Mexico – with perhaps more to come. The resulting problems Canada would have encountered in trying to compete as an industrial location with the United States can most easily be seen by noting that a firm locating in the United States would have duty-free access to all North American markets, but if it were to locate in Canada it would not. By participating in NAFTA and thereby ensuring that it is a trilateral agreement, Canada has avoided this locational disadvantage.

Summary and Conclusions

When the United States and Mexico decided to liberalise their trade, Canada was no longer left with the *status quo* as an option. It had a choice: participate in order to (a) acquire the substantial benefits from free trade with Mexico, in terms of access not only to the Mexican market (with its rapidly growing potential in the future), but also access for Canadian industry and consumers to low-cost Mexican products; (b) protect defensively Canada's interest by seeking appropriate *maquil-*

adora reform and ensuring that Canada would acquire any special benefits in the US market that Mexico might be able to negotiate; and (c) avoid the locational and other disadvantages of being left as an outsider when trading partners are liberalising their trade. These are the same impelling reasons for Canada to participate in the Uruguay Round or any other form of multilateral liberalisation under the GATT: when a country's major trading partners are liberalising their trade, it is very costly to be left out.[8]

Being an insider is the better option, but it is not entirely problem-free. One of the major accomplishments of the negotiators of NAFTA was in dealing with the challenges that arose because we were *in* the negotiations. (See Box 1.)

BOX 1
RISKS IN PARTICIPATING IN NAFTA:
THE MAQUILADORA PROBLEM

Had the *maquiladora* programme not been appropriately dealt with in NAFTA, Canadian industry would have been left with the substantial problem that was erroneously attributed to CUFTA in the 1988 pre-election debate. At that time it was charged that, under CUFTA, *maquiladora* producers, who have always received the special privilege of access to duty-free goods, would secure unrestricted entry into Canada through the United States. It was pointed out that this was not so. True, *maquiladora* products – just like products from other developing countries – receive preferential access to the US market under the GSP (Generalised System of Preferences). Moreover, under old US tariff items 806.30 and 807, products with US content produced in Mexico (or any other country) enter the United States with no duty on that US content. Under CUFTA, however, such products were not automatically able to move from the United States into Canada duty free, since they were subject to CUFTA's rule of (Canadian or US) origin. While this concern was therefore not an issue in CUFTA, it did become an issue as soon as Canada decided to participate in the three-country NAFTA because NAFTA's rule of origin is defined to include Mexican – as well as US and Canadian – content. Consequently *maquiladora* products could come into Canada duty free *via* the United States (or for that matter, *via* direct shipment). Thus, if the 'maquiladora' issue' had not been dealt with in NAFTA, it would have raised a real problem. That fear, however, was not realised since NAFTA will phase out the special *maquiladora* privilege of access to duty-free fourth country components used in the production of exports to NAFTA countries.

Thus, in sum, Canada emerged with an agreement that appears to represent, overall, a substantial improvement on the *status quo*. Whether or not this is the case, however, NAFTA is greatly superior to the real option the country in fact faced. This was not the *status quo*, but instead was the prospect of being left as an outsider as Canada's trading partners began to liberalise their trade. Worse still, a Mexico-USA agreement that would be liberalising bilateral trade would also be managing it – with the most prominent example being in textiles and clothing. No matter how serious one's objection may be to allocating markets in managed trade configurations – and the author would join in such concerns[9] – so long as this allocation is taking place, it is far better, in practice, to be participating and receiving a market share than to be blocked out and receive none.

To return to the original question: to what degree did Canada participate in NAFTA for defensive reasons? A substantial part of the Canadian motive was defensive – a desire to avoid the losses from being excluded. These possible losses included the damage that might result from the development of a hub-and-spoke system, or an even worse variant, and the loss Canada would face were Mexico to acquire better access to the US market than Canada. However, in participating in NAFTA, Canada also acquired the standard gains from extending the domain of free trade to Mexico through the removal of Mexican barriers to Canadian exports and the removal of import barriers to Mexican goods. Precisely how the defensive and non-defensive benefits will compare is an empirical issue.[10] However, two observations can be made. First, the defensive reasons can be expected to have considerable importance. Secondly, politicians and the public place a larger relative weight on defensive reasons than does a trade analyst. Due to their preoccupation with the short-run costs of Canadian firms competing with inexpensive Mexican goods, and disregard for the long-term benefits going to Canadian firms that use these inexpensive goods as inputs, politicians tend to view the 'sacrifice' of Canada's own import barriers as a cost rather than a benefit. By thus downplaying the traditional benefits, they inflate the relative importance of the defensive benefits.

This in turn would have had interesting implications if the United States had not signed NAFTA. In this event, the process of extending liberalised trade to Mexico and beyond would have ended or at least been seriously delayed. There would have been regrets in Canada, but not as substantial as the strong argument for Canadian participation in NAFTA would suggest. The reason is that much of the motivation for Canadian participation has been defensive – a concern with being excluded as the United States and Mexico liberalise their trade. This concern would have disappeared if the United States and Mexico had not liberalised their trade.

There would have been substantial disappointment in an opportunity lost – both to liberalise trade with Mexico and into the hemisphere beyond – although this would have been more keenly felt by trade analysts, who recognise the long-run benefits from the elimination of Canadian barriers to imports from Mexico, than it would be felt by politicians who view this component of trade liberalisation as a short-run cost. However, any disappointment would have been tempered by the fact that Canadians would then have been left free to concentrate on completing the adjustment to CUFTA. An interesting question would have arisen: could Canada extract some of NAFTA's improvements (such as clearer rules of origin) and incorporate them into CUFTA, without incorporating NAFTA's retrograde provisions such as stiffer rules of origin in textiles? So long as the USA views both as improvements (in the case of textiles, a difficult judgement to defend, even in the narrow economic interest of the United States alone), it is not clear that Canada should attempt to open this issue.

There is a major disappointment in NAFTA, even if it is fully implemented. It does not deal with each country's trade remedies (anti-dumping and countervailing duties). These remedies may seriously damage NAFTA, as they have damaged CUFTA. The latter, and in particular its Chapter 19 dispute settlement mechanism, required a negotiated reform of trade remedies within a five to seven year period. This Damocles sword was removed in NAFTA; its dispute settlement now becomes permanent. One can argue that removing this sword has been damaging since it has removed the pressure to negotiate reform; or that it has been beneficial since it has removed the risk that the sword would fall.

Despite some flaws in the NAFTA agreement, it is, in the author's judgement, in Canada's interest to participate fully for both traditional and defensive reasons. This is, in fact, the track that Canada is now on, following the ratification of NAFTA by the Canadian parliament.

Notes

1. Other components in the Canadian trade accounts support this conclusion. During this period, liberalised Canadian imports from the United States also rose by 14%, while the same Canadian imports from the rest of the world rose by only 2.8%. Thus, bilateral reciprocity seems to have been having its expected effect of stimulating trade flows in both directions across the Canada-US border. However, using Canadian trade with the rest of the world as the basis of comparison, CUFTA's boost to Canadian exports seems to have substantially exceeded the stimulus to Canadian imports. The final

      component in this pattern was a 2.5% decline in Canadian exports to the United States in items not liberalised by CUFTA. For more details on changing Canadian trade performance during the early years of CUFTA, see Lipsey et al (1993), pp. 5-6.

2.   As set out in a speech on 12 August 1992 by the Honourable Michael Wilson and Canadian Government (1992) 'North American Free Trade: An Overview and Description', p. iv.

3.   Northern Telecom, which has increased its sales in Mexico over the last five years by over 20 times without free trade, is an example of a Canadian company that is well positioned to take advantage of both better access to the Mexican market and increased demand by Mexicans who will have to improve this particular dimension of their industrial infrastructure.

4.   In financial services, Mexico has recently become a far more interesting market. With its recent real income growth and its reduction in inflation from the three-digit level to about ten per cent, Mexico is no longer the high risk, financially troubled country that it was a decade ago. For further details, see chapter 4.

5.   The stated objectives of politicians in any trade negotiation tend to be 'get down foreign barriers, hang on to our own'. For example, Canadian success in the agricultural negotiations was described as being able to 'expand market opportunities for (Canadian exports of) red meat and grains, while fully retaining our existing system of national supply management for the dairy, poultry and egg sectors' (Canadian Government, 1992, p. ix). One of the most extreme examples of bargaining to retain (indeed, in this case, increase) own trade barriers occurred when the Mexicans insisted on a 25 year period to introduce free trade in used cars from the United States and Canada. Canada then insisted on the same 25 year delay in importing used cars from Mexico. It is easy to see the politics of this, but where is the economics? What is the Canadian demand for used cars from Mexico when used cars can already be brought in duty free from the United States?

6.   In 1991, Canada imported over $1.6 billion of these products from Mexico, while the next largest category was less than $130 million of computers. If all agricultural products had been summed, they would have been the second largest category.

7.   On the rules of origin dispute between the United States and Canada over the import of Honda Civic cars, see Hufbauer and Schlott (1993, p. 41).

8.   If Australia and New Zealand are liberalising their trade, Canada need not participate because few of its markets and supply sources are located there. Because Australia and New Zealand are not our major trading partners we have little to lose by being excluded, and little to gain from participating. In fact there is an increased risk of loss from participating; since our existing trade is concentrated elsewhere, this makes it more likely we will be damaged by trade diversion.

9. One reason is that, by guaranteeing employment in a specific sector in both countries, managed trade restricts specialisation, thereby limiting gains from trade based on comparative advantage and economies of scale.
10. And not an easy one. For example, assessing the (traditional) non-defensive effects on Canada would require an assessment of the benefits of trade creation, the net cost (or benefit) of Canadian trade diversion, the benefit of Mexican diversion of its import purchases to Canada, and the benefit to Canada of reversing its CUFTA diversion of import purchases from Mexico to the United States.

CHAPTER 12

IS NAFTA MORE THAN A FREE TRADE AGREEMENT? A VIEW FROM THE UNITED STATES*

William C. Gruben and John Welch

Some analysts (Pastor, 1992; Weintraub, 1993) consider NAFTA as part of a larger economic integration process that goes beyond narrowly-defined trade policy. Because of US initiatives, issues with only tenuous direct connections to trade have come under negotiation. A harmonisation of national policies, that appears tantamount to a broad movement towards integration, seems under way. But is it? We contend that what looks like integration is simply a continuation of an Hegelian dialectic over trade policy.[1] The dynamics of this dialectic look like efforts toward broad integration, but they may actually veil efforts at protectionism.

Moreover, there is reason to suspect that the current dynamics of 'integration' may ignite confrontations that could end this dialectic in its present form. Indeed, the US attempts at harmonisation through NAFTA's parallel agreements can be compared with an automobile 'chicken race', in which two teenage drivers race towards each other until the first to 'chicken' turns aside. In a chicken race, when neither party flinches, the result may be disaster. In the case of NAFTA and its parallel agreements, the disaster would have been the failure of ratification – and a resultant possible unravelling of Latin America's recent patterns of unilateral trade liberalisation.

To show why an Hegelian dialectic appropriately characterises what is taking place with NAFTA and the parallel agreements, and why economic integration does not, we begin by considering the antecedents

* We would like to thank Sheila Page of the Overseas Development Institute, Jerry O'Driscoll of the FRB-Dallas, and an anonymous referee for many helpful suggestions. All errors and omissions are solely attributable to the authors. The usual disclaimers apply. The contents reflect the authors views and should not be associated with the Federal Reserve Bank of Dallas or the Federal Reserve System.

of the NAFTA negotiations. The events that precipitated NAFTA began, at the very latest, in the 1970s.

Conflict and Innovation in Recent US Trade Postures

From the end of World War II until the late 1970s, US trade policy involved an unconditional interpretation of the Most Favoured Nation (MFN) clause of the General Agreement on Tariffs and Trade (GATT).[2] The United States was the world's principal exponent of a multilateral approach to international trade liberalisation. However, by the late 1970s the United States had become frustrated with GATT. The problems were the caravan effect (GATT negotiations emulate a caravan that moves only as fast as its slowest camel); the free-rider problem (some countries, chiefly less developed countries (LDCs), have benefited from the multilateral system without much lowering their own barriers); and the rise of trade-related issues not covered by GATT, such as Foreign Direct Investment, trade in services and intellectual property rights (Primo Braga, 1989, p. 245). For the United States, these three problems became more frustrating over time. While the caravan effect is self-explanatory, both the free-rider problem and trade-related issues not covered by the GATT deserve more detailed attention. The interlacing of these two issues suggests that they be discussed jointly.

Although many countries had entered GATT because they wanted open foreign markets, they were often less interested in opening their own. For the less developed countries, whose competitive positions against the developed nations were unfavourable in many industries, these predilections were considered understandable. GATT allowed the LDCs to surrender less protectionism than the industrialised nations and offered LDCs special openings to the developed countries under the Generalised System of Preferences (GSP).[3] For some countries, however, these special opportunities were not enough. An historic peculiarity of GATT offered countries a freeway to still more protectionism.

Because pre-World War II protectionists had focused their energies on the tariff, that is what GATT had been designed to lower. Over time, many GATT signatories simply replaced their tariff barriers – which are proscribed by GATT – with other, GATT-legal barriers. Quantity restrictions, expressed through quotas and permits, became commonplace. So did regulations and standards concerning 'product quality'. Export subsidies became popular. Detailed regulations against foreign direct investment surfaced. Some countries chose to become harbours for intellectual piracy – maintaining weak patent and copyright protection in order to become centres for unlicenced production.

During the 1980s, particularly in the LDCs, these innovations in protectionism proliferated in response to terms-of-trade shocks and foreign debt problems. Surmising that the raw materials price booms of the 1970s would continue in the 1980s, many LDCs had devised debt-led growth strategies and found foreign bankers to support them. At the end of the 1970s, however, a shift in US monetary policy incited a sudden rise in interest rates, making debt a tortuous route to any goal. At the beginning of the 1980s, the prices of the LDCs' traditional raw materials exports entered a protracted slump. To address their new balance of payments and debt problems,[4] many LDCs adopted philosophies more reminiscent of 18th century mercantilism than of GATT, and they expressed them through GATT-legal nontariff innovations.

Meanwhile, certain technological developments caused the United States to find foreign protectionist innovations increasingly baneful. Starting in the 1960s, innovations in transportation and communications had inspired a rise in 'production sharing'; for example, firms located one portion of a total manufacturing operation in Taiwan, another stage in Singapore and, perhaps, another in Mexico. By the 1980s, further revolutions in communications and in production technology had allowed a surge in opportunities for US trade in services, to the extent that other countries were open enough to receive it. This surge motivated the United States to push its trading partners to permit more such trade.

Trade in services, however, involves complications that are less common in the goods trade. Much services trade operates most efficiently in locations where producer and consumer physically meet. For trade in services, someone must travel, typically the seller. The service producer will prefer to locate himself and his capital goods inputs at the market so the buyer will not have to travel to use them.

For international trade, however, locating at the market means that the host country's investment rules have an overriding effect on sales opportunities. Rules that restrict foreign investment hinder US services trade. Moreover, because many US service exports involve specialised technological knowledge – embedded in machinery, software or in employees – the profitability and development of such trade often depends on the protection of intellectual property rights. The risk of technology theft has a chilling effect. By the 1980s the accelerating pace of technological development, together with the increasing ease of copying new technology without permission, made such risk steadily greater.[5]

Since these factors made opening trade more attractive to the United States at the same time that LDC innovations in protectionism were raising trade barriers, the United States launched a programme of what came to be called 'aggressive reciprocity'.[6] Section 301 of the Trade Act of 1974 and its revision, 'Super 301', under the Omnibus Trade and Competitive Act of 1988 allowed the United States new manoeuvrability in threatening unilateral trade retaliations. The United States used these threats to extract trade openings from other countries and to motivate trading partners (e.g. Brazil's computer software industry) to tighten their intellectual property protection.

Innovative protectionists soon contrived to apply measures – supposedly designed to open trade – for quite different purposes. For example, the United States used Section 301 and Super 301 to negotiate 'voluntary' export restraints – a US innovation in protectionism in which exporting countries 'volunteer' to restrict their exports to the United States. Foreigners slow in 'volunteering' were not long in receiving threats of 301-related US trade sanctions. The United States also stepped up 'countervailing' actions, such as raising duties, against countries it charged with dumping or other 'unfair' trade practices.[7] In many cases, the merits of these charges have been questionable (Bovard, 1992).

In sum, in the context of US trade policy, two types of dialectics were operative. First, a dialectic operated between forces in the United States that wanted free trade abroad and not so much at home, and foreign countries that also wanted free trade abroad and not so much at home. That is, as one group developed innovations in liberalisation and protectionism, it was countered by those of the other group.

Second, the realignment in trade patterns that inspired the United States' initiatives at the GATT discussions also changed who wanted protectionism and who did not. Some US firms that had favoured protectionism discovered that changes in production technology and in markets had made freer trade agreeable. Other traditional protectionists found that these same changes favoured increased protectionist efforts.

To illuminate this redistribution of protectionist pressures, some details of the dynamics of production sharing deserve attention. Production sharing simply meant that it became more common for US firms to export partially manufactured products for further processing abroad, and then to reimport – perhaps for further processing in the United States before final sale.

As such exchange developed, firms and industries carrying out production sharing inclined increasingly towards trade liberalisation at home (González and Vélez, 1992). After all, producers who import their inputs often benefit from low trade barriers. Manufacturing firms' lobbying efforts on behalf of protectionism began to diminish (Magee, 1990). Moreover, production-sharing US manufacturers became more interested in negotiating liberalised foreign investment laws in foreign countries that made attractive platforms for production-sharing operations. These interests were consistent with those of US service-exporting firms, even though the latter intended to sell the products of their foreign operations abroad.

On the other side of the dialectical process, US labour groups viewed increased US manufacturing operations abroad as signifying fewer union jobs in the United States. The unions accordingly increased their pressures towards restricting trade. They increased these pressures both directly and, in an inspired alliance, indirectly. In an innovative example of indirect pressure, US labour organisations began to chafe over environmental problems in foreign countries. Allying themselves with purely environmental groups, labour organisations accused US firms of moving operations abroad to take advantage of more lax environmental laws or enforcement. They petitioned the US Congress for measures that might impede firms from re-exporting back to the United States. These measures not only could discourage some firms from continuing to operate abroad, even if environmental considerations had not motivated their locations, but could discourage others from establishing foreign operations in the future.

NAFTA as the Next Step

These redistributions of pressures for and against trade liberalisation manifested themselves further in the establishment of the negotiating frameworks that would lead to NAFTA. The opportunities for a free trade agreement had increased with the decline of protectionist pressures from US manufacturers. US labour organisations, however, urged negotiation for parallel agreements without which, they argued, NAFTA itself would incite unfair competition.

The progress of the parallel negotiations offered evidence to suggest that protectionists saw them as a second chance to sink NAFTA. As one after another side agreement appeared to be reached on environmental and other issues, none was adequate. Disparities between US and Mexican labour and environmental laws – or their enforcement – increasingly attracted charges of what the AFL-CIO called (in a phrase that drew on the rhetoric of the old manufacturing protectionists) 'social dumping' (AFL-CIO, 1992).

The major sticking points in the parallel negotiations implied a great deal about the US agenda. Although all three parties concurred that violation of the parallel covenants ought to incur penalties, the USA was unique in arguing that the penalties ought to include selected revivals of protectionism. Canadian and Mexican negotiators, perceiving a contradiction in the use of protectionism to achieve free trade, favoured fines.

For US protectionists, the parallel negotiations not only offered additional opportunities for US intransigence, but presented the Mexicans with a similar invitation. The United States' increasingly-expressed interest in the harmonisation of labour protection, for example, meant that Mexico's concerns about the treatment of its workers in the United States might also find expression.

Finally, while the parallel negotiations looked like a fuller move towards integration than a free trade agreement would offer, they also offered more opportunities to sink the agreement through intransigence and contentiousness. It is important to consider why parallel negotiations may be seen as a more attractive avenue for sinking NAFTA than what the agreement offers on its own. The parallel negotiations offer such an avenue because, instead of addressing issues that are purely and fully linked to international trade, they impinge on domestic policy. Changes in labour standards and environmental policy will have more comprehensive direct effects on Mexican businessmen than will changes in trade policy. Mexican businesses with no connection to trade with Canada or the United States would be affected. Parallel agreements, accordingly, offer new opportunities to ignite Mexican opposition to NAFTA. In sum, what some have argued is a series of moves towards integration can also be seen as the redistribution of pressures for and against protectionism. Labour groups, accelerating their efforts, allied with some environmentalists against the agreement. As manufacturing groups increasingly favour freer trade, they seek allies among the banking community, for whom protectionism lowers the likelihood that loans outstanding to Latin American borrower/exporters (including Mexico) will be repaid.

These same apparent moves towards integration can also be seen as an attempt by US protectionists to broaden their efforts against freer trade by pushing issues that Canadians and Mexicans may perceive to involve their national sovereignty.[8] Moreover, the same parallel negotiations can be viewed as inviting Canadians and Mexicans to push issues that the USA may perceive as involving *its* national sovereignty.

The Negotiated NAFTA: Liberalisation and Protectionism

In arguing that NAFTA does not mean economic integration, we have focused on the parallel negotiations because their design and construction seem to favour protectionism. Those of the official, narrowly-defined NAFTA do not. Nevertheless, even NAFTA is a synthesis of protectionist and free trade pressures.

Nafta does not free trade, but it certainly liberalises it. Over a fifteen-year period, NAFTA initially reduces and ultimately eliminates all tariffs and most non-tariff barriers between Canada, Mexico and the United States. Moreover, NAFTA is a 'GATT-forward' agreement: no signatories can increase their tariffs on imports from countries within or outside the free trade area.

Although full elimination of tariffs will take fifteen years (Table 12.1), about 70 per cent of goods imported from Mexico will enter the United States without tariffs as soon as the agreement goes into effect. At the same time, 50 per cent of US exports to Mexico will be tariff-free. Other less obvious merchandise trade barriers will also fall. In the traditional in-bond or *maquiladora* industries, performance (export) requirements[9] and restrictions on domestic sales[10] evaporate when the agreement goes into effect.

Moreover, NAFTA addresses much more than merchandise trade. In a tri-national context, the agreement realises the United States' long-held goals of liberalising trade in services and foreign investment rules abroad, and tightens the protection of intellectual property. It is important to note that, in this context, NAFTA represents an achievement the United States has failed to realise in a broader multilateral context.[11] Although NAFTA opens Canada and the United States, it accomplishes its most significant liberalisations in Mexico. NAFTA expands Canadian and US companies' ability to establish or purchase a business in Mexico, and facilitates their ability to sell out if they want to leave. NAFTA also loosens previous restrictions for such companies on expanding operations. NAFTA removes restrictions on profit remittances to foreign countries. Local content requirements are eliminated, although NAFTA-wide content rules will exist. Through NAFTA, Mexico extends temporary work permits to service providers from Canada and the United States, and removes licensing and performance criteria.

Despite much liberalisation, however, NAFTA initially retains protectionist elements and some of them persist indefinitely. As Table 12.1 shows, NAFTA protects sensitive sectors – such as agriculture, minerals, banking, and textiles and apparel – by stretching out the phase-in time. This protection is temporary. However, as the synthesis of liberal and protectionist pressures, NAFTA contains other types of protection that are not only permanent, but raise trade barriers above pre-NAFTA levels.[12] In a number of sectors – notably automobiles, textiles and apparel – NAFTA imposes North American content rules and some of them constitute actual increases in protectionism.[13] Under the Canada-United States Free Trade Agreement, for example, automobiles could be imported duty free if they contained at least 50 per cent Canadian/US inputs. For auto imports to receive NAFTA benefits, the North American rule is 62.5 per cent. Likewise, for textiles or apparel to qualify for 'free' trade under NAFTA, they must be made in North America from the yarn or fibre forward.[14] This NAFTA covenant extends and strengthens the protectionism inherent in the broader, multinational Multifibre Agreement.

Table 12.1
NAFTA: Schedule of Tariff Reductions

Category Date	US Imports from Mexico (% of total)	Mexican Imports from USA (% of total)
A. Effective on Date of Agreement	53.8	31.0
B. 5 Years After	8.5	17.4
C. 10 Years After	23.1	31.8
C+ 15 Years After	0.7	1.4
D. Duty Free Before Agreement	13.9	17.9

SOURCES: USITC (1993), pp. 1-2 and 1-3.

Nevertheless, NAFTA unequivocally liberalises trade in North America.

Indeed, that appears to be why the parallel negotiations have become targets for protectionists. It is also noteworthy that the agreement offers only minimal opportunities for trade diversion, in which efficient non-NAFTA producers would be squeezed out of trade with NAFTA countries simply because NAFTA reduces trade barriers among North American countries, but not for others (Primo Braga, 1992).

Trade-related Effects on the United States: Output and Employment

Although the most famous NAFTA-related interjection is, according to Ross Perot, the 'sucking sound' of jobs going to Mexico, a flurry of more serious attempts to gauge the effects of NAFTA has appeared.[15] These studies do not all take the same approach and their results vary considerably.[16] Some involve static models. A few are dynamic. Some accommodate capital flows, but most do not. Others are historically based. The majority involve computable general equilibrium (CGE) models, are highly disaggregated and find positive, but small, welfare and output effects for the United States.[17] After all, Mexico begins NAFTA as a small market relative to Canada, and the United States has already signed a free trade agreement with Canada.

Most CGE models assume either rigid wages and flexible employment, or flexible wages and full employment. The former typically find small percentage gains in employment, while the latter find gains in wages. Both types, of course, show similar income gains. In a model that accommodated a little more fully characteristics of the real world – with somewhat flexible wages and less than full employment – the effect of NAFTA would probably include less employment growth than the rigid wage models, less wage growth than the full employment models and about the same income growth as both. Static CGE models without capital flows typically show the smallest effects, regardless of NAFTA country.[18]

Some static CGE models incorporate increasing returns to scale.[19] As output grows, income grows even more. Even these show only small percentage gains in real income, real wages and employment. The empirical importance of scale effects, as opposed to pure improvements in efficiency from greater competition, remain small (Tybout and Westbrook, 1993; Backus, Kehoe and Kehoe, 1991). Dynamic models portend larger effects on growth, especially for Mexico (Romero and Romero, 1991). Even here, the percentage effects remain small for the United States.

Two other branches of the literature are less consistently sanguine about the effects of NAFTA for the United States. The first branch, whose foremost representative is Leamer (1992), offers arguments based upon factor price equalisation through trade and migration. These arguments are consistent with the Stolper-Samuelson theorem that opening trade will decrease the real wage in the United States because of its scarcity of unskilled labour. However, Hinojosa-Ojeda and Robinson (1992) argue that the relative sizes of the US and Mexican economies and NAFTA's long phase-in period mean the Stolper-Samuelson effect will be small; it would be swamped by the other, growth-enhancing effects of the agreement.

A second branch of the literature regards NAFTA from an historical point of view. Although some of this literature (Hufbauer and Schott, 1992a; Weintraub, 1992) offers conclusions consistent with those of the CGE models, a series of briefing papers from the Economic Policy Institute does not.[20] These papers derive historical parallels, abstracting from individual industry experiences, to hypothesise about the US macroeconomy. Their narratives typically assume, for example, that what has happened in the auto industry is an accurate guide to what will happen in the US macroeconomy. For the Economic Policy Institute, the results of NAFTA for the United States are negative.

An interesting artifact of the Economic Policy Institute papers is their argument that 'free trade' over the last fifteen years has, despite US employment growth during that time, been a principal cause of the movement of jobs to other countries. In fact, however, US policy can be shown to be increasingly protectionist over this period. Apparently the Economic Policy Institute views the recent increases in protectionism in the United States as consistent with an overall free trade stance. The authors do not discuss the empirical evidence presented by Gruben (1990a and 1990b) and Truett and Truett (1993) that jobs that 'went' to Mexico during this period would otherwise have 'gone' to Asia. The Economic Policy Institute authors not only dismiss the United States' increases in employment and declining unemployment rates during this period, but are unprepared to confront the claim that jobs move to other sectors in an economy, not to other countries.[21] Nevertheless, arguments that picture massive movement of jobs to Mexico carry much public weight. Moreover, such arguments are the focal point of the larger protectionist movement in the United States.

Sectoral Effects

If most studies of the impacts of NAFTA suggest overall expansion for the United States, why have protectionists turned so much of their energy against the agreement? After all, from the point of view of protectionists, much effort appears to have been devoted to the design and construction not only of the parallel agreements, but of the domestic content rules within NAFTA itself. This effort has been spent in response to pressures from those who benefit from it.

In a broad sense, the answer is that the opening of trade shifts resources and production from less competitive to more competitive sectors, inspiring renewed political efforts from the less competitive. According to traditional Hecksher-Ohlin-Samuelson analysis (H-O-S), the sectors that will prove most competitive (and that will accordingly gain most) will use the nation's relatively more abundant factors of production relatively intensely. Compared to most other countries, and certainly to Mexico, the United States has a relative abundance of physical capital (plant and equipment) and human capital (an educated work force). Industries that require relatively low-skilled labour or low levels of physical capital to make tradeable products will find much to dislike about NAFTA, unless they can establish operations abroad. Organisations of workers with relatively low skill levels may also find that the effort to lobby against NAFTA pays higher returns than most other efforts they can make.

Nevertheless, displacement of workers across sectors of the US economy will likely be small in both absolute and relative terms, because the sizes of the economies and workforces of Mexico and Canada are small compared with those of the United States. Most studies suggest that US sectors that will lose include sugar refining, fruits and vegetables, apparel and textiles, and household appliances. Winning sectors include chemicals, instruments, machinery and equipment, motor vehicles, instruments, and rubber and plastic. Neither the overall output and employment gains of the winners nor the losses of the losers appear to be large, but the fear of major dislocation remains.

Finally, an important reason why lobbying against freer trade can be strong is that it is easier for someone likely to lose a job to know he is likely to lose it than for someone who may gain a job to know he would be the one to gain it. After all, even if a new job appears, someone else might be hired.

Services

As technological advances have augmented opportunities for US trade in services, the United States has intensified its efforts to negotiate openings. Although the increasing importance of such trade can be seen as underlying these efforts, theoretical attempts at incorporating services trade into international trade models have not proved very successful with the possible exception of Hirsch's (1989). The problem of correctly accounting for trade in services and their complementary relations to trade in goods makes projections based on Hecksher-Ohlin-Samuelson (H-O-S) models problematic.

However, as a practical example of the complementary relations between trade in goods and trade in services, one need only observe that the United States has a comparative advantage in high-technology, knowledge-based products. These products are service-intensive in that they typically require a high degree of service support in one form or another. To the extent that such services are traded (at arm's length), the H-O-S models are not far off the mark.

In considering the United States' motivations towards new types of trade negotiations, recall that a large proportion of services require close interaction between the consumer and the producer. The costliness of this interaction, in terms of travel and new infrastructure, will affect the direction of trade not only in the pure services sector, but also in sectors whose goods are highly service intensive. Recall also that trade in services depends on the degree to which foreign investment is permitted in each sector. However, the location of plant and equipment in a foreign country raises issues about the identity of those who will use it. Labour mobility becomes an important issue.

Because of these interrelationships, NAFTA negotiations on trade in services could have led to difficult problems. The United States and Mexico had a gentlemen's agreement that migration issues would not be included in the formal NAFTA negotiations, but that capital and technology flows would be. NAFTA was structured to avoid discussion of more general migration topics by confining labour negotiations to those related to the flow of 'high tech' services. However, the calls for side agreements on labour standards gave the Mexicans grounds to raise more general questions about international migration. The United States had hoped to ignore these.

The services that received the most attention in the NAFTA negotiations were finance, insurance, transportation and telecommunications. The Mexican banking sector had been nationalised during the country's economic crisis of 1982. Until 1988, Mexican policymakers were more interested in capitalising the banking sector than in broadening or deepening banking services. In 1988, the Mexican government began to liberalise controls on bank interest rates. During 1991-1992, Mexico sold its eighteen nationalised banks to the private sector.

NAFTA does not change entry requirements for foreign banks in the United States and Canada, but the agreement's opening of the Mexican financial system is among the most significant achievement of the negotiations. Because the standards for entry are tied to the size of the Mexican banking system, they will change over time. But in the context of the size of the Mexican banking system at the end of 1992, entry into Mexican banking by Canadian or US firms would require the commitment of reserves and paid-up capital of between \$20 million and \$90 million. Requirements will likely go up, not down. Although this means US banks may be slow to move into Mexico, their presence there will grow over time. Moreover, requirements for entry into brokerage, bonding, insurance, leasing, and warehousing are more liberal. One would expect more initial entry by US specialists in these areas.[22]

Transportation services stand to gain under NAFTA on both sides of the border, especially in trucking. Eighty-two percent of freight in Mexico is moved by road (USITC 1991, pp. 4-48). Mexican exports of trucking services to the United States will probably increase if border and inland infrastructure improvements continue to take place in Mexico.[23] The longer term implications of NAFTA include increases in US trucking services as well, but NAFTA would have only a marginal effect on other transport services (USITC 1991, pp. 4-48). Clearly, trade in goods is transport-service intensive and infrastructure development on both sides of the border will be needed.[24]

Trade in telecommunications and related goods trade was given a large boost by the recent privatisation of Teléfonos Mexicanos (TELMEX) in 1991. Basic telephone services are the main traded service between the USA and Mexico with the United States being a net importer of these services. NAFTA should shift the balance of trade in favour of the USA in basic services and especially in related equipment as the investment in this sector increases over the coming years.

Intellectual Property Rights Protection

Because of the importance of intellectual property protection in facilitating services trade and foreign investment, NAFTA's coverage of this topic has received much notice. Moreover, it has been argued that the provisions on patent and trade secrets offer the highest standards of protection achieved in any trade negotiations (USITC 1993, pp. 3-7).

One of the most significant provisions of this section, and in NAFTA in general, is the codification of national treatment. In the present context, this codification ensures that the intellectual property of firms from any two NAFTA countries will be legally treated in the third just as it would be if it had been developed in that country. A second important general provision is the strict limitation on the use of compulsory patent licenses, which will have a strong effect on Canada's process for patenting pharmaceuticals.[25] A third important provision obliges the signatory countries to enforce intellectual property rights against infringement not only internally, but at the border. That is, controls will be developed not only to stop the production of pirated products, but to stop their importation.

Despite these and other provisions, including those for judicial procedures to ensure enforcement, Canada, Mexico and the United States all offered strong intellectual property protection before NAFTA was signed. Indeed, NAFTA implies few significant changes in US intellectual property laws, and will not much change Mexican patent law. Mexico upgraded its patent law in 1991 to a level consistent with those of major industrial countries.[26]

One of the most important aspects of intellectual property protection in NAFTA is that it helps to assure the durability of Mexico's new intellectual property law, and to do so in an international context. Still, differences between the Mexican, Canadian and US legal systems offer opportunities for problems. Under Mexican law, precedent does not automatically control the implementation of law. Protection in most cases is extended to a firm or individual only if that party successfully litigates the issue. The costs of gaining effective protection are accordingly high. But if true integration is indeed the outcome of NAFTA, the effects of such divergences in legal systems clearly should be reduced.[27]

Migration

From the United States' point of view, a *raison d'être* of the NAFTA is the hope that it will ease pressures on migration from Mexico to the United States. Because trade openings tend to equalise real wages across countries (factor price equalisation), so the argument goes, incentives for cross-border migration would decline. Results reported by the USITC (1991) from partial equilibrium models show such convergence, most of it from an increase in Mexican wages. Hinojosa-Ojeda and McCleery (1990) model migration, trade, and capital flows with dual labour markets (high wage and low wage) in both the USA and Mexico – and add a *maquiladora* sector. According to their results, NAFTA would decrease migration because wages would rise more in Mexico than in the United States.

The picture clouds when one incorporates Mexico's large and inefficient *ejido* (or collective farm) system, as do Levy and Van Wijnbergen (1992) and Hinojosa-Ojeda and Robinson (1991). Under NAFTA, US exports of maize and soybeans could not only offer severe competition to the *ejidos*, but could accordingly induce significant worker dislocation in this system. The result could involve marked increases in migration to the United States. The Mexican government's recent restructuring of the *ejido* system, so as to facilitate infrastructure and capital goods investment through partnership or leasing agreements with business organisations, may allow more competitive operations. However, these same steps may induce some *ejido* farmers to take their money and leave, even if the extra income might also motivate them to remain in Mexico instead of migrating to the United States. The long phase-in period of NAFTA for agricultural products typical of the *ejidos*, however, gives the farmers more time to make their deals and their decisions before this competition intensifies – smoothing and slowing the transition.

Beyond NAFTA: the Environmental, Workplace and Adjustment Agreements

In the parallel agreements, and even in NAFTA itself, the United States has pushed its agenda in directions that obscure the demarcation between trade issues and public policy actions that only indirectly affect trade. In some contexts, it is easy to see why this act could seem like a small one. For example, if a country's zealous health standards on food imports could be seen as impediments to trade, why not differences in environmental protection and workplace standards?

Workplace conditions and environmental protection have been pushed to the forefront of the NAFTA debate. During the vote on fast-track status, President Bush committed the United States to trilateral side or parallel negotiations on the harmonisation of environmental policies, labour law and worker retraining or other adjustment assistance. Upon assuming office, President Clinton voiced his support for NAFTA on the condition that these side agreements be completed before presenting NAFTA for Senate ratification. These side agreements offered the unalloyed protectionist forces unlikely allies in the form of environmentalists and others.[28] A possible outcome, noted in the introduction, would have been for NAFTA to fail to be ratified because of an *impasse* in the parallel negotiations.

Environmental Concerns

In all three NAFTA countries, environmental problems are considered to be important and legitimate policy issues. Moreover, Mexico's pollution problems, especially those in Mexico City and along the border, have become acute. In the context of the NAFTA negotiations, the chief environmental concern has been that relatively loose regulations constitute an unfair trade advantage. The question, then, is what are the likely environmental effects of NAFTA? The two most common fears voiced about NAFTA are that the consequent economic growth in all three countries, but especially Mexico, will generate more pollution and that Mexico will become a pollution haven for US manufacturers. Although plausible as conjectures, these fears have little basis in fact.

Grossman and Krueger (1991) gauge the interaction between trade, growth and pollution as measured by sulphur dioxide and smoke in a cross-section of countries. Using purchasing-power-parity-adjusted data from Heston and Summers (1991) and data from the World Health Organisation, they find a non-linear relationship between *per capita* income and pollution. At low levels of *per capita* income, higher output (and therefore income) generates higher pollution. But beyond a *per capita* income of $5,000 US (1985), pollution control becomes a normal good. Increases in income cause pollution to fall.[29] Since Mexico's *per capita* income in 1988 was almost exactly $5,000 (at purchasing power parity exchange rates), Grossman and Krueger's results suggest that the increased growth in Mexico due to NAFTA will improve Mexico's environment.

The evidence likewise shows that allegedly laxer environmental regulation was not significant in motivating US firms to relocate in Mexico. Environmental abatement costs in the United States are low, averaging between 1-2.5 per cent of total production costs (Grossman and Krueger, 1991 and Cropper and Oates, 1992). Moreover, firms that relocated typically had lower abatement costs in the United States before moving than those that did not relocate (Grossman and Krueger 1991, p. 27). This correlation may be spurious, but if one considers that heavy industry typically both pollutes more and requires higher job skills than light industry and that firms that move to Mexico go there for lower-skilled workers, this result is not implausible.

Some US firms have indeed moved to Mexico because of stepped-up environmental regulation in the United States. A number of Californian furniture companies, for example, moved operations to Mexico after California tightened regulations on paint coatings and solvents (Grossman and Krueger, 1991, p. 22). However, the number was small relative to the total number of furniture producers in the state of California, let alone in the rest of the United States.

Some of the environmental concern stems from two inaccurate assumptions. The first is that Mexico continues to be lax in environmental regulation; the second is that NAFTA does not address environmental issues. The first assumption ignores improvements in Mexican policy over the last decade. In 1982, President de la Madrid set up the Mexican Secretariat of Ecology and Urban Development (SEDUE). Under the Salinas administration, SEDUE's budget for enviromental enforcement grew from $4 million in 1989 to about $68 million in 1992 (Hufbauer and Schott, 1993, p. 92). In 1993, Mexican government expenditure on environmental protection approached one per cent of GDP. The powers of SEDUE have been expanded significantly since its creation and the government is preparing market-based environmental reforms such as auctioning pollution rights. Moreover, the Mexican government has closed a number of polluting factories, most notably PEMEX's Azcapotzalco refinery in Mexico City.

Not all environmental concerns are mistaken. Geographically, an important environmental issue is the USA-Mexico border, and with good reason. Environmental damage there is significant. Raw sewage and water problems date back at least to the 1950s. With the development of the border's *maquiladora* plants, beginning in the 1960s, dumping of toxic chemicals has aggravated the dangers. However, the United States and Mexico have already entered into side agreements for the border. The most comprehensive is the so-called Mexican-US Integrated Border Protection Plan, for which the United States has pledged $379 million and Mexico has pledged $466 million (Globerman, 1993, pp. 296-7). Some find the effort not fully convincing, but the programme is an important step.

Furthermore NAFTA does address the environment directly.

Signatories must commit themselves to a number of additional international environmental agreements: the 1973 agreement on endangered species of wild fauna and flora; the 1987 and 1990 Montreal protocols on ozone depletion; the 1989 Basle controls of transboundary waste movement and disposal; the 1986 Canada-USA agreement on transboundary movement of hazardous waste; and the 1982 La Paz, Baja California Sur cooperative agreement on border improvement (Weintraub, 1993). Each country agrees not to lower existing environmental protection, or health and safety standards, to attract investment. Enforceability of these parts of the agreement will be difficult, but NAFTA's dispute settlement mechanism allows US groups to voice their protests in a formalised judicial environment that can enforce its decisions. This conflict resolution mechanism, together with NAFTA's codified proscriptions, makes competitive lowering of standards unlikely.

Clearly, Canadian, Mexican and US concerns are important, but a collapse of NAFTA is unlikely to improve environmental quality while there is reason to expect that successful implementation of NAFTA would do so. Considering Grossman and Krueger's results, and Mexico's upgraded environmental policy, opposing NAFTA on environmental grounds raises legitimate questions about disguised agendas.

Workplace Conditions

US labour organisations typically express concerns that Mexico's workplace regulations – including those related to safety and health, child labour, benefits and hours of work – will send US firms over the border. Mexico's workplace regulations are strong and, in some cases, tighter than those in the United States. Mexican law establishes the minimum working age as 14. Persons aged 14 to 16 may not work more than six hours per day and are prohibited from working in occupations designated as hazardous. Minors may not work more than a 48 hour week (Weintraub, 1993, pp. 28-9). Mexican regulations on maternity leave, sick leave and profit-sharing are more generous to workers than those of the United States. Yet legitimate concerns about enforcement remain, and probably will. There is little else to say directly about such issues, *per se*.

From the point of view of political economy, however, there is more to say. For those whose goal was to sink NAFTA, negotiations for parallel agreements on the workplace had much to recommend them. On the one hand, such negotiations raised issues of national sovereignty that complicated the Mexicans' (or for that matter the Canadians') ability to come to agreements, however disposed towards agreement these nations' negotiators might have been otherwise. And the Mexican and Canadian negotiators may not have been well-disposed at all. It is one matter to agree upon issues directly pertinent to the purchase and sale of goods and services between your country and another. It is another matter to agree upon how you will regulate the day-to-day events of the workplace, many of which have little to do with foreign trade. And it is yet another to explain to your political constituents – in a period when bipartisan politics is becoming increasingly viable in Mexico – why you made an agreement that affects how they manage their businesses when many of their businesses do not involve tradeable products.

On the other hand, the Mexicans might reasonably have seen such negotiations as an invitation to raise workplace issues of their own – issues that US negotiators might have regarded as intrusions on US sovereignty. In negotiations that addressed how the Mexicans might enforce a labour law, the Mexicans might have found it reasonable to raise issues about US restrictions on migration to jobs north of the Rio Grande. Indeed, the Mexicans might have believed that US negotiators should have no reason to take offence if they demanded that US laws on worker profit-sharing be made equivalent to those in Mexico.

Adjustment Assistance and Retraining

Programmes that assist and smooth relocation of displaced workers are fully consistent with the application of the theory of economic welfare to trade policy. Yet the creation of such programmes does not depend on a trade agreement between the United States and other nations. President Clinton expressed an interest in creating such programmes independently of NAFTA. However, not only will fiscal budgetary problems make such programmes difficult to pass in the future, but similar promises of adjustment assistance were made during the 1980s without being honoured.[30] Part of the problem lies in the fact that labour unions in the United States would like to see such assistance become an entitlement (Weintraub, 1993, pp. 29-30). This makes for a highly contestable political situation and one which will lower the likelihood of such programmes.

Conroy and Glasmeier (1992/93) argue that current policies are inadequately designed and constructed to account for the dislocations that NAFTA will bring. They suggest that the European Community's approaches to funding special adjustment programmes be followed. We concur that worker dislocations deserve care. However, Sala-i-Martin and Sachs (1991) do observe that the United States, at least, insures regions against income shocks. They show that a one dollar reduction in a US region's *per capita* personal income triggers a 34 cent decrease in federal taxes and a six cent increase in federal transfers. In the European Community, they note, the comparable tax reduction is only about half a cent. They argue that 'the current European tax system has a long way to go' before it can compare with the United States (Sala-i-Martin and Sachs, 1991, pp. 20-21).

Others (Fishlow, Robinson and Hinojosa-Ojeda, 1991) argue that a development bank is in order, in part, because of worker dislocations and the disparity in infrastructure between the United States and Mexico. Their proposed North American Development Bank and Adjustment Fund, or NADBAF,[31] is meant to mitigate these disparities and would function in a similar way to the World Bank, the Inter-American Development Bank and the European Bank for Reconstruction and Development (for Eastern Europe). It is not clear, however, that a trinational bank would achieve better results than the regional programmes which already exist, especially at the state levels. In Mexico, the Solidarity programme (PRONASOL) is well established. In the United States, individual states along with the federal government already have a number of unilateral and joint US-Mexico infrastructure projects underway.

A final point about an investment bank should be made. The major role of the European Community's Regional Development Fund was to transfer investment resources to the poorer nations such as Portugal, Spain, Greece and Ireland for infrastructure projects and adjustment. Most expected the major dislocations to occur in the lesser developed countries and not in the developed one. And such dislocations might cause large migration from the poor countries to the rich ones. Although Fishlow, Hinojosa-Ojeda and Robinson's (1991) proposal takes a similar view of the relationship between Mexico and the United States, the context in which the proposal was brought to the US congress was different. The main concern of US legislatures is US infrastructure and adjustment assistance – not NAFTA – generated problems in Mexico. Hence, any comparison with Europe again seems inappropriate.

Whither NAFTA?

NAFTA and the parallel negotiations have been collectively characterised as a move towards greater economic integration. They do present
characteristics consistent with integration. They offer a framework for
harmonising much more than directly trade-related rules and regulation.
In the context of recent US trade history, however, they may also be
seen as just another process in which protectionist and free-trade
interests compete to synthesise a new policy. US manufacturers'
protectionist lobbying diminishes as labour union pressures increase.
Seeking new allies to replace once-protectionist industrialists, labour
organisations associate themselves with enviromentalists. Meanwhile,
some US manufacturers profess to find new forms of unfairness among
their competitors abroad and so do some agriculturalists. In Mexico,
policy innovations, inter-industry and inter-group conflicts, and major
changes in attitudes manifest themselves.

As a result of these conflicting and changing pressures, NAFTA
liberalises trade on some fronts – particularly in services – and
aggravates protectionism on others – as in the rules for increased
domestic content for automobiles and textiles. Here, the worst fears of
those who support multilateralism instead of bi- or tri-lateral free trade
agreements appear to be realised. Yet the cost to the United States if
NAFTA collapsed would not be confined to the small consumer- and
producer-surplus triangles outlined by trade theorists and calculated by
computable general equilibrium models. Indeed, it could be that the
defeat of this trilateral agreement is what would realise the worst fears
of multilateralists. For the collapse of NAFTA could trigger a chain
reaction leading to very unattractive consequences for GATT.

Any failure to implement NAFTA would signal to the rest of Latin
America that a strategy of structural readjustment through trade
liberalisation would not bring improved access to the US market. Since
the reward for this process of readjustment is implicit in IMF and World
Bank programmes, their effectiveness would diminish. The incentives
for free trade in the context of the GATT would likewise become
suspect. After all, in recent years, Mexico has adhered as closely as any
country to the strategies of deregulation, privatisation (unilateral) trade
liberalisation, broadening and deepening of financial markets, and
monetary and fiscal stability. These strategies become less viable when
one's principal trading partner refuses to ensure market access.

Despite the weaknesses in NAFTA, this agreement offers an
important opportunity not only to increase trade in North America, but

to signal US commitment to free trade in general – and to free trade in particular with respect to intellectual property rights protection, trade in services and trade-related aspects of foreign investment. Failure to take advantage of this opportunity may impose costs to the United States that go well beyond the static benefits of increased integration with Mexico.

Notes

1. We use the term Hegelian dialectic, in the context of trade policy, to signify the process by which innovations in trade liberalisation are countered by innovations in protectionism – and are succeeded by some synthesis that is temporarily acceptable to each of the two competing sides – followed by yet another innovation in liberalisation countered by yet another innovation in protectionism, followed by yet another synthesis, *et cetera*. It should be noted that Kane (1988) poses the evolution of financial regulation in the same way, while Gruben (1993) describes NAFTA as a game that leads to a dialectical progression.
2. The MFN clause requires a member nation that lowers tariffs on specific products from a given country to lower them to all nations. However, less developed countries (LDCs) receive 'special and differential treatment' that exempts them from certain aspects of the MFN in the interests of economic development. In supporting the unconditional interpretation of the MFN, the United States persistently contested the policy of special and differential treatment.
3. The GSP allows virtually duty-free entry of designated products from designated developing countries (i.e. LDCs) into the United States and other developed nations.
4. Latin America's debt-led commercial policies, which mixed export incentives with import restrictions, did help Latin America begin to generate balance-of-trade surpluses from 1983 on. Even so, the region's external debt continued to mount. That is, the regional surplus in the balance of goods and nonfactor services remained too small to offset the deficit in the factor services balance (interest, profits, and dividends) (Primo Braga, 1990).
5. For a discussion of the acceleration in technology, the rising ease of appropriating it without permission, and other issues related to the United States' increased interest in the protection of intellectual property, see Mody (1990).
6. It is important to note that the United States continued its programme of aggressive reciprocity even after Latin American countries began to lower their trade barriers in the broad-based liberalisation efforts of the late 1980s and early 1990s. This pattern is one of many that raises questions as to how many of the United States' announced efforts on behalf of free trade are really

acts of disguised protectionism.

7. During the period 1970-75 and 1980-85, US countervailing actions went up by more than 1,000 per cent (Nam, 1987).

8. As an example of pressures brought to bear in this direction before the side agreements were signed, the *San Francisco Chronicle* noted that Missouri Congressman [Richard] 'Gephardt is playing Doubting Thomas, insisting he won't vote for NAFTA unless it is accompanied by side agreements on jobs and the environment so tough they may be impossible for Mexico and Canada to swallow' (*San Francisco Chronicle*, story 17 in stack).

9. For example, automobile manufacturing US subsidiaries in Mexico must export at least two units of value added for every unit imported. NAFTA eliminates such requirements.

10. Currently, the maximum a *maquila* can sell to the domestic market is 50% of production, but this restriction is generally not binding. Since the imported value of the product still faces Mexican tariffs if sold domestically, the reduction in tariffs will affect *maquilas* more than the removal of this restriction.

11. At the 1982 GATT ministerial meetings, the United States attempted to launch a new round of negotiations focused on these issues, but was defeated. These same issues have been addressed in the subsequent Uruguay Round but, from the perspective of US goals, with only limited success.

12. See Morici (1993b), Johnson (1993), Barry and Siwicki (1993), Krueger (1992 and 1993) and USITC (1993).

13. Except for the automobile, textile and apparel sectors, NAFTA content rules are 50% North American.

14. Exceptions include silk and flax (Barry and Siwicki, 1993, p. 138).

15. Space precludes a systematic treatment of these studies, but more comprehensive overviews than what we offer can be found in Lustig et al (1992) and Globerman and Walker (1993).

16. Although most of these studies were performed before the text of the agreement was finalised, we agree with Weintraub's (1993) conclusion that nothing in the agreement so far would substantially change the results of these studies.

17. These include Hinojosa-Ojeda and Robinson (1991), Hinojosa-Ojeda and McCleery (1990), KPMG Peat Marwick (1991), Brown, Deardorff, and Stern (1991a and 1991b) and the USITC (1991). See Brown (1992) for a survey.

18. See Brown (1992, pp. 35-7), Hinojosa-Ojeda and Robinson (1991 and 1992), Hinojosa-Ojeda and McLeery (1990), Roland-Holst, Reinert, and Shiells (1992). See also chapter 2 in this volume.

19. Roland-Holst, Reinert and Shiells (1992) and Brown, Deardorff and Stern (1991a and 1991b).

20. See, for example, Faux and Lee (1992) and Blecker and Spriggs (1992),

21. For more detailed critiques of the Economic Policy Institute papers, see Hinojosa-Ojeda and Robinson (1992), Weintraub (1992), and Gruben (1993).

22. See also chapter 4.

23. In recent years a large share of infrastructure investment in Mexico has been private. Toll roads are a particularly commonplace example.

24. The necessity of border infrastructure improvement is discussed below in the context of Texas (Cobb and Molina, 1991).

25. The Canadian Patent Act currently offers patent protection of twenty years for filing for new pharmaceutical products researched and discovered in Canada. However, for other pharmaceutical products, compulsory licenses could be issued after only seven years from the date of marketing approval. This licensing regime was argued to be discriminatory against companies not conducting research in Canada, and was seen as contradicting the national treatment goal of NAFTA. It should be noted that the national treatment provision of NAFTA would also require the United States to change its laws so as to permit inventors to rely on research performed in Canada and Mexico to establish an invention date (USITC, 1993).

26. Mexico will, however, be required to amend its law to reverse the burden of proving infringement of process patents, placing the burden on the accused infringer.

27. See Alejandro Junco, 'The Case for an Internal Mexican Free-Trade Agreement', *Wall Street Journal*, 22 March 1991. Under Mexican law, precedent is extended when favourable decisions are delivered in five consecutive cases.

28. Some have likened this coalition to that of Baptists and bootleggers, who sometimes join forces to restrict the sale of alcoholic beverages in the southern United States. Although both groups have the same goals, the purer motivations of the Baptists allow them greater effectiveness in rallying public support and in influencing lawmakers. The bootleggers, of course, are happy to fund such efforts.

29. Other studies reviewed by Globerman (1993) find a similar relationship.

30. Smith (1990) and Faux and Lee (1991).

31. A proposal put before the Congress in 1993 eliminates the adjustment fund incorporating only the development bank. It is referred to as NADBANK.

PART IV

CONCLUSIONS

CHAPTER 13

WHO WILL BENEFIT?

Victor Bulmer-Thomas, Nikki Craske and Mónica Serrano

It is a necessary condition for the success of any economic integration scheme, such as NAFTA, that each of the partners obtain net benefits: the welfare gains in terms of employment, production and consumption must outweigh the welfare losses. This is not a sufficient condition for the success of the scheme, since the welfare losses are associated with interest groups that may have the power to block or reverse the move towards integration. In the case of Mexico, however, there is a widely-held view – even if poorly articulated – that the benefits of NAFTA will not only outweigh the losses, but that the losers will also be numerically small and politically ineffective.

This optimism may be premature – at least as far as the number of losers is concerned. Yet it is an extraordinary reversal of the conventional wisdom adopted in the theory of economic integration since 1950,[1] which assumed that free trade areas between developed and developing countries would not be in the interests of the latter. This assumption was based on three main propositions: (1) The higher level of initial protection in developing countries would subject them to massive producer losses following the adoption of free trade within the integration scheme.[2] (2) The developing country would be unable to compete successfully in manufactured trade, where initial trade barriers were greatest and where trade would be likely to expand fastest. (3) Even if trade in primary products became subject to unrestricted free trade after integration, the gains to the developing country were likely to be small because (a) initial tariffs in the developed country were already modest and (b) price and income elasticities for primary products are low.

This argument, although deficient in a number of ways (e.g. the exclusion of trade in services), commanded a high level of support among economists across the ideological and political spectrum and was one of the reasons why developing countries looked for unilateral trade privileges rather than reciprocity in their relations with OECD members. The hypothesis could never be tested, however, since there were no examples of integration schemes among countries at widely different levels of income per head.

NAFTA is the first example of an integration scheme, other than those based on colonial or ex-colonial links,[3] between a developing (Mexico) and developed (Canada and the USA) countries. Yet the initial response has been the exact opposite of what conventional wisdom would predict. While the main interested parties in Mexico have expressed enthusiasm, Canada has been lukewarm or at best neutral, while the greatest reservations have been expressed by pressure groups in the United States.[4] NAFTA, of course, is more than just an economics project and the political complexities (see below) go some way to explain these differential responses. Nevertheless, Mexico's perception of future economic benefits from NAFTA is much more optimistic than conventional customs union theory would predict and this requires some comment.

Economic Change

While Mexican policy-makers might accept, with some qualification, the third of the propositions listed above, they would reject the first two. Since Mexico's application to join GATT in 1985, trade liberalisation has advanced rapidly to the point where average tariff rates are no longer far out of line with Canada and the United States.[5] However, the crucial difference is to be found in the manufacturing sector. Mexico expects to secure its greatest concentration of employment and producer gains in precisely those industrial sectors (e.g. automobiles, cement) where conventional theory assumed the developing country would be unable to compete. There are even those who argue that Mexico will be able to compete effectively within NAFTA in certain services (e.g. private medical care), where the developed countries have often been assumed to find their comparative advantage in trade with less developed countries.

The argument that industry is the vehicle through which Mexico will extract its main benefits from NAFTA is, indeed, ironic. Built behind a high tariff and quota wall, protected from international competition and subject to oligopolistic tendencies, (part of) Mexican manufacturing is now expected to be the standard-bearer in a free trade agreement with two of the most advanced industrial countries in the world. Yet, however ironic, the argument has some force. Over half a century of import-substituting industrialisation (ISI), coupled with aggressive corporate restructuring in the 1980s, has led to the creation of a number of world-class firms where profitability has been retained despite the elimination of much of the previous protection from import competition.

Mexican industrialists still face a number of severe handicaps. The cost of capital is much higher than in the rest of North America (see chapter 4); the physical infrastructure (including transport and telecommunications) leaves a great deal to be desired; some skilled workers and managers are in short supply. With the elimination of capital controls and the liberalisation of trade, however, Mexican manufacturing firms now have access to technology and capital equipment on much the same terms as their competitors in the rest of North America. At the same time, these companies enjoy certain advantages denied to their rivals: an abundance of unskilled and semi-skilled labour on low real wages and a legal framework which imposes lower social and environmental costs.

It is small wonder, therefore, that labour and the environment have proved to be such controversial elements in the NAFTA package. Opponents of NAFTA in Canada and the United States, aware that outright opposition is unlikely to succeed, have concentrated their attention on side agreements that could have undermined Mexico's competitive advantage (see chapter 7). If their efforts have been largely thwarted, it is less a tribute to Mexican negotiating skills (considerable though these have been) and more a recognition by political leaders in the United States that draconian side agreements could lead to an unwelcome diminution of national sovereignty for all three countries.

Mexico's static comparative advantage in (certain) manufacturing sectors appears to have been retained, but that still leaves unresolved the basis of the country's long-run dynamic comparative advantage.[6] Here a number of factors, by chance or by design, have combined to strengthen Mexico's ability to compete on the basis of low real wages. First, the increasing vigilance of US authorities on the US-Mexican border and more stringent penalties for employment of undocumented workers will make it increasingly difficult for Mexico's surplus labour to seek employment in the United States. Secondly, the ejidal reforms (see chapter 5) coupled with agricultural trade liberalisation are expected to lead to a massive outflow of low productivity workers from the countryside to the cities. Thus, Mexican industry is assured of an almost infinitely elastic supply of (unskilled) labour at a fixed real wage for the foreseeable future.[7]

The wage differential is not sufficient to guarantee Mexico success under NAFTA, but - provided Mexico can keep the difference in labour productivity below the difference in wage rates – it is a powerful incentive for Mexican firms to expand exports to the rest of North America as well as a strong source of attraction for foreign capital to locate new plants in Mexico. In some cases, however, no realistic wage differential will ever compensate Mexico for the difference in labour productivities and it is in these activities that Mexico will suffer its greatest production and employment losses.

The most obvious example (see chapter 5) is basic grains production and livestock. The geographical and economic disadvantages faced by many Mexican producers are so severe that it is difficult to believe they can be overcome through agrarian reform, revision of property rights and access to capital. On the contrary, the long transition period (fifteen years) negotiated by Mexico before full liberalisation of agricultural trade suggests that not even the Mexican government has any confidence in the ability of small-scale agriculture (including the ejidal sector) to compete with the rest of North America.

Another example is the *maquila* industry on the northern border. With all firms in Mexico now facing the same tax and tariff regulations, the competitive advantage of border industry will be steadily eroded except in those products where transport costs form a very high proportion of the final price. Furthermore, the strict rules of origin in some sectors (e.g. textiles) will work to the disadvantage of a number of *maquiladoras* that had previously enjoyed duty-free privileges on all imports (see chapter 3). Border firms will also be more exposed, and will suffer accordingly, from the efforts to clean up the environment that will follow the implementation of NAFTA.

A third example is provided by those services that can be traded and where labour costs form only a small part of the final price. Banking (see chapter 4) may fall into this category, although the Salinas government was careful to adopt an ultra-cautious approach to trade liberalisation. Road transport could also be affected with US road haulage firms in a strong position to take advantage of the loss of protection enjoyed by Mexican firms before NAFTA.

There will certainly be a regional dimension to the distribution of these production and employment losses across Mexico. The new jobs are unlikely to emerge in the same states that suffer employment losses. The contrast between a poor South and a rich North is likely to increase as traditional agriculture declines in states such as Chiapas, Guerrero and Yucatán, while the growth of industry and services clusters around urban conglomerations in the states of Mexico, Nuevo León and Sonora.

It is tempting to draw parallels with the reallocation of resources in the United States itself after the civil war in the 1860s or in Great Britain after the abolition of the Corn Laws in 1846 or in Puerto Rico following the adoption of Operation Bootstrap in the 1940s. Economic integration among neighbouring countries or states of countries can be an immensely powerful force if the initial change in relative prices produced by trade liberalisation becomes permanent. Although NAFTA differs from these other schemes in several important respects (the exchange rate, for example, is not permanently fixed), it is also likely to produce a major reallocation of resources (at least in Mexico) with substantial employment and production losses needing to be covered by even greater gains.[8]

The gross benefits of NAFTA, on which the architects of the scheme prefer to dwell, are therefore crucial. While the traditional calculation of benefits suggests only modest gains (see chapter 2), this is not a fair test. The summation of welfare triangles is a very inadequate basis for measuring the impact that NAFTA can be expected to have on Mexican society. Mexico, at least, is playing a longer game and that almost certainly could be said of the United States as well. The impact of NAFTA on the long-run rate of capital formation is crucial and this will be affected not only by the move to a free trade area, but also by the impact of NAFTA on the credibility of government policies, the irreversibility of the current changes and the access to finance by the private sector.

It is consideration of these wider benefits that has stimulated the debate on alternatives to NAFTA – a debate that became more intense as it became clear that the scheme was facing considerable opposition in the US Congress. If the objective is in fact something other than free trade, then it is by no means certain that a Free Trade Area is the optimal route to this (undefined) goal. Here, however, there are two very different approaches to a resolution of the dilemma.

The first, and more traditional, argues that Mexico is losing control over many instruments of economic policy in exchange for only modest gains. If, in fact, the main purpose of NAFTA is to give greater credibility to government policies, this could be achieved through granting independence to the Central Bank, joining the OECD, providing guarantees for foreign investment and completing the Uruguay Round of GATT negotiations with Mexico as a signatory to all measures on intellectual property rights etc. This approach is not limited to critics of the PRI administration. Indeed, the Salinas government, while remaining wedded to NAFTA as its first priority, has clearly accepted the force of this argument and gone some of the way to implement it.[9]

The second, and more radical, approach is to argue that a Free Trade Area does not go far enough. To extract maximum benefits from integration, so the argument runs, Mexico needs at least a customs union with its partners. With all three countries obliged to apply the same Common External Tariff to trade with third countries, there would be more chance of the level playing-field to which Mexico aspires. If this is extended to a Common Market, as some prefer (see chapter 8), then labour mobility would be assured. Mexican labour, and not merely Mexican and foreign capital, could then expect to share widely in the benefits from integration.

At the heart of all discussions of NAFTA, as well as alternatives to NAFTA, is the question of costs and benefits. While critics of NAFTA have tended to exaggerate the costs and ignore the benefits, supporters have done the opposite. It is clear from the chapters in this book that the potential benefits are likely to be substantial and that these, under realistic assumptions, will outweigh the costs. Yet, while this may satisfy some, it leaves unresolved two further questions: first, are there any mechanisms in which the gainers can compensate the losers and secondly, what instruments are at the disposal of the state to compensate the losers? These questions are important because, in the absence of compensation mechanisms, the losers could become a vocal and potentially disruptive influence on the process of economic integration.

If displaced maize producers in Chiapas become semi-skilled workers in automobile factories in Sonora, the compensation mechanism needs no refinement. Similarly, if the shoe manufacturer forced out of business by imports establishes a successful textile business, then market forces have served their purpose well. If, however, the farm worker becomes unemployed in the neighbouring city, then the compensation mechanism can only work through state intervention. Progressive taxation, income transfers and retraining schemes are the instruments used by governments in developed countries to tackle these problems in one country, while inter-country transfers are used (e.g. in the European Community) to absorb the adjustment costs of integration schemes.

No such inter-country mechanism has been created under NAFTA and none is likely to emerge in the next few years. Thus, the Mexican state will be left with responsibility for absorbing the costs of adjustment and compensating the losers from NAFTA. With the role of the state severely curtailed by privatisation and deregulation in the 1980s and in the absence of a compulsory system of social security, this will be a difficult task to accomplish. The state's favoured instrument, the welfare programme known as PRONASOL, will reach some of the losers, but many (if not most) will be excluded. The harsh reality is that even rich countries have difficulty in compensating the losers from resource reallocation so that it is unrealistic to expect Mexico to succeed where Britain, France and the United States have failed.

All these changes will be watched closely by the rest of the Latin American republics, many of whom have indicated their desire to join NAFTA. As chapter 9 shows, there is the danger of investment diversion as a result of NAFTA and it is natural that republics should seek to mimimise the damage through joining the scheme themselves. It seems increasingly improbable, however, that – with the possible exception of Chile – NAFTA will be extended southwards. Although there are many (mixed) motives on the part of the United States for acceding to NAFTA, it is clear that it is much more than a simple free trade agreement between two neighbouring countries. The political agenda behind US support for NAFTA is plainly visible and the same arguments lose force when applied to other Latin American countries. Furthermore, the fragile coalition needed to build congressional support for NAFTA would be difficult to reestablish in the case of other republics. The rules of origin, plausible in the case of three countries already so closely integrated even before NAFTA, could present a severe problem for other countries seeking to join.

Thus, NAFTA is likely to remain – to all intents and purposes – a North American club with a dynamic that goes far beyond the limits of tariff-free trade. In particular, NAFTA is likely to have an impact not only on the political relations between Mexico and its northern neighbour(s), but also on the political process in Mexico itself. It is indeed now generally recognised that trade policy influences domestic politics (Rogowski, 1987, p. 206; Gourevitch, 1986), and consequently it is to be expected that NAFTA will have implications for Mexico's political system. However, it must also be recognised that both the institutional changes within the economy and the political changes taking place have their roots prior to the emergence of NAFTA. The outcome of the 1988 presidential elections, which many claimed to be fraudulent, left the in-coming administration with problems of legitimacy (Berberán et al, 1988; Cornelius and Craig, 1991; Molinar Horcasitas, 1991).[10] Despite the expectations for political change in the aftermath of the 1988 elections, Salinas chose to prioritise the economic over the political and a radical neo-liberal economic reform was implemented. By 1993, although some changes had taken place in the political sphere, these fell short of expectations.[11]

The political implications of these economic reforms, of which NAFTA is part, are neither direct nor automatic and therefore the debate regarding the political impact of NAFTA remains in dispute. Furthermore, many of the results will only become apparent in the long-term. As some of the chapters in this book suggest, expected changes in employment, rural migration as well as uneven regional effects are likely to exert significant strains on Mexico's political system. The limited democratic context in which NAFTA developed led to its legitimacy being questioned. The traditional use of Congress and other political institutions to give a democratic veneer to the undemocratic decision-making process was becoming increasingly problematic in a Congress where the PRI only enjoyed a bare working majority.[12] Problems of legitimacy were also reflected in the development of NAFTA. It has been argued that keeping negotiations restricted to an inner circle within the Mexican government (la Comisión Inter-Secretarial) and certain prominent sectors, such as the Consejo Asesor del TLC, could be justified by the requirements of negotiating strategies (Rubio, 1992, p. 118).[13] However, the insulated policy-making process in which NAFTA negotiations were conducted proved useful to the opposition both in its efforts to criticise the agreement, as well as in its overall strategy to advance its political position. Furthermore, neither the government nor the opposition should be seen as homogeneous entities; both have a range of opinions. Amongst the opposition parties, the left (in particular the PRD) has been more vocal in its criticisms, with the right-wing PAN more positively inclined towards NAFTA and the government's economic policy generally. At the same time, there is a substantial body within the PRI which is unenthusiastic about the Agreement, even if this opinion is not voiced publicly.[14] Finally, during the three years that the negotiations took place the PRD was unable to consolidate itself as a party, and as a result it failed to develop a consistent and coherent position *vis-à-vis* NAFTA, allowing the government to maintain firm control over the agenda of the free trade negotiations.[15]

Domestic Political Change

The arguments surrounding the political impact of NAFTA have been taken to extremes with one position predicting increased democratisation, and the other arguing that it will result in the strengthening of authoritarianism.[16] Those who support the former see a direct link between economic liberalisation and political opening (Delal Baer, 1991; Rubio, 1990, 1992), but with no concrete evidence to support this claim. Those who argue that the agreement will lead to increased authoritarianism base their arguments on analysis of the impact of economic liberalisation on the socio-political arena; however, they fail to recognise the political openings at the margins which have occurred (Cárdenas, 1991b; Gilly cited in Smith, in press). It remains unclear what the political impact will be, since the link between economic reforms generally, and NAFTA in particular, with the political arena is not necessarily direct nor consistent. Although elements of both closure and opening can be detected, what is certain is that no political elite will manoeuvre itself out of power. The Salinas administration is aware that the economic reforms have had negative socio-political consequences, which has forced it to respond with a variety of measures, and in the light of NAFTA it is likely that some of these consequences will become more complex and that new political pressures will arise. It is already clear that the US factor has gained weight in domestic politics – not solely in terms of closer surveillance of Mexican political practices, but also in the use that opposition parties have made of the US card.[17]

The two extreme outcomes predicted by these analyses are not only simplistic, but they fail to take into account that an agreement such as NAFTA has never existed before. Whilst it is true that economic integration between the USA and Mexico is not a new phenomenon, the institutionalisation which will accompany the implementation of the agreement is likely to become an important factor within Mexico's political process. The democratisation argument relies on the assumption that economic change will be a catalyst for changes in the political system through the gradual erosion of the long-standing control by the centre, the greater decentralisation and delegation of economic policy-making, and the articulation of new coalitions, as well as the setting of limits to arbitrariness and presidentialism. Yet not only is the relationship between economic liberalisation and democratisation unclear, but past experience has indicated that economic liberalisation can proceed in authoritarian states.[18] In the absence of the institutionalisation of processes of negotiation between the regime and civil society, it will be difficult to guarantee both the permanence of the changes so far achieved and also further progress towards democratisation.

The more negative argument highlighting authoritarianism has been a recurrent theme among strong opponents to NAFTA. Not only have these views been based on the idea that the US government has played an important role in supporting Mexico's authoritarian system due to its stability, but by implicitly supporting the government's prioritisation of the economic over the political, it has reduced the pressures for political change. The partial recomposition of the traditional Mexican political system, evident in the second half of the Salinas administration, is partly due to these constraints. This outcome is used by NAFTA opponents to support their view that we are witnessing a renovation of Mexico's authoritarian system. Yet not only was the electoral recovery shown by the PRI in 1991 a more complex process rather than just the result of authoritarian measures, but the USA also provided the opposition with a valuable forum for advancing its own cause. The results of the 1991 mid-term elections provided indications of a PRI recovery, with the PRI obtaining 61.48 per cent of the votes. Nevertheless, whilst one should not underestimate the weight of fraud, it is clear that other factors have come into play. The 1991 PRI electoral recovery was a complex process involving fraudulent practices, the implementation of a highly sophisticated and electorally driven anti-poverty programme and the mobilisation of abstainers, a practice that placed greater emphasis on floating voters (Cornelius and Craig, 1991; Molinar Horcasitas and Weldon, 1993). It would be difficult to deny that Mexico's electoral practices remain below acceptable democratic standards, but nevertheless the changes which have occurred should not be ignored. Moreover, shifts in the political regime are not only due to government policies, but also to the interaction of the various political actors. First, although opposition parties have played a leading role in the drive towards change, their inability to maintain the pressure for change, and their gradual weakening, particularly in the case of the PRD, restored the initiative to the state and more specifically to the presidency and the official party (Loaeza, 1991a; Valdes, forthcoming). Secondly, not only has the state recovered its prominent role, but until recently showed a noteworthy capacity to focus public discourse and debate on economic issues (including NAFTA) at the expense of political change, and so encouraged the polarisation of the major opposition parties and averted their potential alliance (Crespo, 1991). Furthermore, Salinas's performance has led some authors to argue that he 'won the presidency from the presidency', and that the policies so far implemented have again demonstrated the capacity of the state to generate legitimacy through economic revival rather than adhering fully to electoral processes (Crespo, 1992). Equally important has been the implementation of specific policies, ranging from PRONASOL to the reformulation of state-church relations, which have also contributed to the reversal of the regime's declining fortunes (Gentleman, 1993).

NAFTA's political impact will be most likely in those areas where the implementation of the adjustment programme has already made inroads. These include social policy, the restructuring of the dominant party and its relation with the state, labour-state relations, business-state relations, centre and the periphery relations, and more generally the electoral arena. In addition to the already evident impact that economic liberalisation has had in increasing the gap between the rich and poor,[19] NAFTA is likely to have social consequences, ranging from increased rural-urban migration and changes to the labour market. Following a sharp decline in the percentage of public expenditure allocated to education and health from 17.5 per cent and 1.4 per cent in 1980 respectively to 7.2 per cent and one per cent in 1988, PRONASOL became the central social policy of the administration. This policy has been focused on service provision and the support of small business in the poorest areas. While formally committed to alleviating poverty this has not always been evident in the decision-making surrounding priority issues for PRONASOL. Electoral motivations became apparent from the first stages of its implementation and its effectiveness in the electoral arena has been demonstrated (Molinar Horcasitas and Weldon, 1993). Indeed as some observers have argued, PRONASOL has entailed the exchange of public goods for electoral support, but its characterisation as clientelist and authoritarian may not be accurate given its capacity to change the electorate's perception of the potential value of the vote. Indeed, to the extent to which PRONASOL has forced the government to respond to politically expressed demands, it could further strengthen changing attitudes towards the vote from a mere instrument of protest to one expressing political preferences.[20]

If the electoral effectiveness of PRONASOL proves to be ephemeral and economic policy, including NAFTA, fails to maintain the confidence of the electorate, the social consequences resulting from economic restructuring will possibly lead to increased social discontent bringing back pressure upon the political arena. It is not yet clear whether the changes enacted by the Salinas administration will be sufficient to withstand the social unrest resulting from the expected dislocations. If this unrest cannot be channelled through the system, for example *via* PRONASOL, it could play an important role in forcing democratic change. However, it is possible that the regime will use increased political control, and one cannot discount the use of repression. From this perspective, the survival of the regime is not only dependent upon the strength of the state and the success of economic policy, but equally important is the continued willingness of the US government to accept

Mexico's undemocratic practices. The economic crisis and the austerity programme implemented throughout the 1980s have shaken the basis of the corporate party-state structure, and have led to the reformulation of relations between the state and various sectors. In the aftermath of 1988, there were attempts to renovate the PRI through the development of horizontal structures. This renovation was designed to 'modernise' the party and create spaces for more interaction between the leaders and the membership: in effect, a move towards internal democratisation. The restructuring began with a reorganisation of the popular sector, with the labour and peasant sectors to follow. However, not only have the expected changes within the PRI stalled, but they have even been reversed, with the XVI National Assembly renewing the emphasis on the old corporate structures. Although the low incidence of protest suggested that the PRI-government apparatus remains as the key factor in terms of political control, so far the PRI has failed to renew its relationship either with low-income neighbourhoods through the popular sector, or with peasant organisations.[21]

A crucial element of this restructuring has been in labour relations, where NAFTA will have particular impact. Certain sectors have suffered more in this restructuring. Minimum wages fell between 40-50 per cent and employment grew at a rate of only 0.4 per cent (Heredia, forthcoming). Some observers have argued that this restructuring has laid the conditions for the emergence of a modern corporatism in which unions will cease to function as instruments of political power and will serve instead as coordinators between labour and management (Breña Garduno, 1993). Yet in the absence of a change of regime the possibility of a transition from state corporatism to other social variations, in which both interests' representation is organised from below and class identities transcended, has been questioned. Whilst economic modernisation has introduced significant differences among enterprises, as well as new forms of labour organisation, the pace and direction of these changes has been also affected by state intervention. Wage ceilings and electoral concerns underlie such forms of neocorporatist intervention (Bizberg, 1990). Moreover, the results of strikes such as those at the Ford and Volkswagen plants suggest that a modern labour movement has yet to be fully constituted.[22] Although the relative lack of unrest could be partly explained by the unequal distribution of power between workers and employers, it is important not to underestimate the regime's control.[23] Not only has the Confederation of Mexican Workers (CTM) remained crucial in the process of privatising state-owned companies and throughout the NAFTA negotiations, but the government's control over labour has ranged from the Ministry of Labour declaring a number of strike actions illegal to outright repression of union leaders (Levinson, 1993).[24] Although recent Constitutional amendments have not yet included labour legislation, the revision of article 123 and the formulation of a more flexible federal labour law, placing greater emphasis on productivity and allowing greater flexibility in dismissals due to industrial or market changes, is expected in some circles (Breña Garduno, 1993).

Trade liberalisation has also affected state-business relations. The nationalisation of the banks in 1982 opened a period of increasing confrontation between the state and the business community, leading important business groups actively to support the PAN in the competition for Mexican political leadership. A temporary but vigorous promotion of democracy emerged as an important interval in a long-standing relationship between the state and the private sector (Loaeza, 1991b). Although initial steps signalling the recomposition of business-state relations were evident from 1987, the threat posed by the left in 1988 consolidated the support of big business for Salinas (Maxfield, 1989). To the extent that the impact of trade liberalisation has been uneven and has accentuated differences among domestic business, it has generated changes in business coalitions that could have political implications in the medium- and long-term.[25] Although so far the most visible change has been the support offered by big business to the economic policies of the Salinas administration, together with the apparent erosion of their interest in the democratisation process, the increasing isolation of small and medium-size entrepreneurs resulting from the alliance forged between the state and big business became a significant factor in the PAN's advance in the north of the country (Mizrahi, 1992 and 1994).

Unless accompanied by compensation mechanisms, NAFTA will contribute further to regional inequalities due to the mixed impact it is likely to have on the regions. In consequence, NAFTA will generate additional pressure upon increasingly troublesome relations between the central authorities and regional states. Although traditionally relations between the centre and the periphery were complicated, the post-revolutionary political system displayed significant flexibility in its management of centre-periphery relations.[26] Relations among local, regional and federal authorities evolved towards a tacit understanding that for decades helped to reconcile coordination with acceptable margins of state autonomy. The impact of nearly a decade of negative growth on relations between the central government and regional states has been reflected in greater instability. Evidence of such instability is visible first in the increasing number of state governors who have been removed since 1982; secondly, by the advance of the opposition at the regional level illustrated by the electoral map of the country – with PAN strongholds in the richest northern states and a significant presence of the PRD in the southern states – and thirdly, by the arrival of the opposition to state governorships since 1989, paving the way for increased tensions regarding the distribution of federal and local resources (Heredia, forthcoming; Cornelius and Craig, 1991; Torres Ramirez, 1990 and Van Young, 1992).

Although NAFTA's implementation will no doubt increase the social costs of economic policies, it is difficult to establish a direct link between the agreement and political representation. Notwithstanding this, it could be argued that changes accompanying the reform of the Mexican economy – including the legal framework of land tenure, privatisation of state enterprises and fiscal reform – are likely to modify existing patterns of social organisation and consequently could eventually be reflected in political representation. To date it seems that NAFTA has introduced an additional factor to the pressures that almost a decade of negative economic growth placed on the electoral arena. Elections have gained greater international attention in the light of NAFTA, which may have played a role in the willingness of the government to 'allow' opposition victories and to consider electoral reform in order to smooth free trade negotiations.[27] Transition to democracy entails a complex process of bargaining and negotiations aimed at the institutionalisation of the rules of competition. Some political liberalisation is apparent, yet political liberalisation does not necessarily lead to democratic transition. Such an eventuality might be dependent upon the capacity of the opposition both to continue mobilising the population and to generate a climate where negotiations become unavoidable.[28] Furthermore, we must avoid the assumption that alternatives to the PRI are necessarily democratic. The continued inflexibility of the PRI towards any electoral reform that could threaten its dominant position, together with the opposition's obstinacy with the presidency as its main target, have not only obstructed the process of negotiations but have also revealed the weaknesses of the democratic credentials of these actors (Martínez and Merino, 1991). Nevertheless, during the Salinas administration there has been a series of proposals regarding electoral reform which have reflected complex negotiations taking place between different political actors. Whilst there have been positive features, there has also been the continued negative element of discretionality and uncompromising postures. The difficulties involved in electoral negotiations have highlighted the extent of division and lack of discipline within the PRI, the increasing tension that has underpinned relations between the official party and the ruling elite and, equally important, the distinctive negotiating postures of the main political parties, with the PAN more inclined to compromise and the PRD more often showing intransigence. Indeed, the combination of these factors, together with the unwillingness of the PRD to accept the reform, has ruled out the possibility of enabling the country to approach the 1994 presidential elections with a consensual electoral code. The inability of the political parties to reach a consensual electoral law has again left the prime responsibility for a stable and orderly conduct of elections in 1994 in the hands of the presidential candidates rather than in the rule of law.[29]

The impact that NAFTA and recent deregulation is likely to have on some areas traditionally associated with authoritarianism, such as administrative discretionality, erratic and inconsistent public policies, margins for arbitrariness, discretionary powers of the bureaucracy and corruption, has been wrongly associated with democratisation.[30] Whilst it may be true that NAFTA's implementation could encourage greater accountability, the depoliticisation of economic decision-making, and perhaps greater pluralism through the emergence of new interest groups and coalitions, the democratisation of the political system will ultimately depend upon the emergence of new political institutions.[31] In a country marked by deep social inequalities and where governability and democratic practices are not always considered to be compatible goals (Camou, 1992), it seems difficult to imagine how 'accountability from the top' will unleash a dynamic that will ultimately lead to a democratic transition.[32] Moreover, and despite the apparent gains, the political benefits mentioned above are not linked directly to the agreement nor to economic liberalisation, and as such cannot be taken for granted. Furthermore, the lack of institutionalisation means that these changes can be reversed. Mexico still lacks an independent judiciary, a forum for open, democratic debate (including a discussion of NAFTA itself), and a 'transparent' and accountable electoral system, which are the underpinnings of formal democracy.

Although in November 1992 Salinas raised many of the main issues consistently demanded by the opposition, which could eventually lead to fair and democratic competition, again the PRI's proposals left the issue of the party's over-representation untouched. The PRI remained determined to preserve its absolute majority in Congress and in this way once again made clear its lack of willingness to surrender its position as the dominant party. Nevertheless, over the past years there have been sufficient signs indicating the capacity of opposition parties to force negotiations. With all its limitations the most recent reform seems to offer some room for cautious optimism in areas such as financial limits to election campaigns and, in particular, with regard to verification mechanisms. Yet their enforcement will largely depend on the willingness of political parties to abide by these rules. While it could be argued that in the context of the post- 1988 elections a compromise was simply not feasible for the PRD, and although 1993 has opened a window of opportunity for the opposition to gain control over spaces where the rule of law could prevail, the proximity of presidential elections has again brought to the fore the potential strength of the PRD as an electoral force. It appears that electoral credibility could again emerge as the main casualty. In a regime where the arbitrary use of formal legality allows the government an important weapon, financial ceilings and impartial verification of elections could become an important asset in the hands of the opposition. This could in turn contribute to the formulation and implementation of clear and transparent rules to set limits to the use of public resources and the manipulation of elections, and more broadly to regulate elections. This could be an important step in the process of building a modern democracy under the rule of law. A sound electoral legislation could become an important instrument to ensure increasing levels of fairness in electoral competition, to provide the necessary means properly to handle elections and, more generally, to guarantee greater certainty with regard to electoral outcomes. Yet, as is the case with any legal instrument, the viability of an electoral change will ultimately depend on the willingness and the capacity of relevant actors, including the opposition parties, to enforce the law. While it is is difficult to come to decisive conclusions regarding the links between NAFTA and political opening, it could be argued that the prospect of the agreement has indirectly contributed to the emergence of an environment conducive to negotiations.

Political Relations Between the USA and Mexico

The motivations for, and the consequences of, NAFTA are not limited to the domestic arena. There are also foreign policy implications for all the actors involved. Many of the concerns about NAFTA voiced within Mexico refer to the loss of autonomy regarding foreign affairs and the decline of sovereignty. Although US interests in closer economic links with Mexico were originally tied to energy security considerations, a combination of events led the USA to reassess its relationship with Mexico in the late 1970s.[33] Despite the high levels of tension that accompanied US-Mexican relations throughout the first half of the decade, the gradual recognition of the interdependent nature of most of the issues involved in the bilateral relation, together with the political instability arising from the 1988 Mexican presidential elections, emerged as the turning point in closing this particularly difficult period of US-Mexican relations. The view expressed by Kissinger in 1988 that Mexico represented one of the most important and complex challenges for US foreign policy was increasingly shared within US circles (Cornelius, 1988; Kissinger and Vance, 1988, pp. 917-8; Thorup, 1990). This was reinforced by the general reassessment of US foreign policy resulting first from the increased competition faced by the USA in the international economy and, subsequently, by the impact of the end of the Cold War. While it is clear that a solid consensus has not yet emerged, the conditions generated by this debate provided fertile ground for the initial consideration of the 1990 Mexican initiative for free trade. Yet, as indicated by the subsequent negotiation of the parallel agreements, continued failure to articulate a solid foreign policy consensus has also affected NAFTA (Schlesinger, 1991 and 1992/93; Kissinger and Vance, 1988; Moran, 1990).

Although, as chapter 11 indicates, the reasons for Canada's decision to support the widening of CUFTA into a trilateral agreement was a defensive action, its decision to join the Organisation of American States (OAS) in 1990 had already pointed to a shift towards regionalism in foreign policy (Randall, 1977 and 1992; Ogelsby, 1979).[34] This shift can be traced back to the late 1970s when Canada decided to strengthen its links with Latin America, while more recent expressions include Canada's increasing involvement in the Central America peace process and in the Haitian crisis.[35] Furthermore it is possible that both Canada and Mexico share common interests beyond trade in bringing the USA within a multilateral framework which could check US power and induce US restraint through common interests.

In Mexico, the main foreign policy questions associated with NAFTA have revolved around two main issues: the possible loss of autonomy and the erosion of sovereignty. Although proximity with the USA set the limits of Mexican foreign policy, its long-standing objective was the preservation and search of autonomy *vis-à-vis* the USA. This strategy materialised in a 'legalistic' and relatively independent foreign policy whose underlying rationale was to serve as a break to potential foreign intervention and destabilisation. These considerations, rein-forced by prevailing views about free trade between developed and developing countries, help to explain Mexico's rejection in the early 1980s of US proposals for a North American Common Market[36] (Urencio, 1981; Puyana, 1982). Clearly the idea of integration with the USA was seen as anathema both to Mexican nationalism and Mexican foreign policy. Yet the debate over a common market paved the way for gradual recognition of the ongoing integration between the two economies, and, most importantly, of the need to provide such integra-tion with some measure of control. This perception was subsequently reinforced by the impact of the 1982 crisis on most fronts of the bilateral relation revealing the interdependent nature of contentious issues such as migration, narcotics and the environment. Nevertheless, bilateral relations entered a difficult period characterised by high levels of tension that obstructed the consideration of a managed integration.

Following the 1982 crisis the renegotiation of the debt became the first priority of the Mexican government, consuming most of its energy in the external front and laying the basis for the 'economisation' of foreign policy.[37] Indeed, evidence of increasing economic dependence on the USA set the limits to independent foreign policy goals and marked the return to a *rapprochement* with the USA.[38] Yet, despite the efforts deployed by the Mexican government, and the reversal to pragmatism and restraint in the conduct of foreign policy, high levels of conflict continued to hamper harmonious relations with its northern neighbour.[39] During this period, diverging views about the main issues underlying the bilateral relation, together with continued US obstinacy towards the Central American crisis, provided significant ground for conflict and temporarily eclipsed hopes for managed integration. Yet the impact of the 1988 Mexican elections on US perceptions about stability on its southern flank put an end to the nationalist backlash against Mexico, placing this country back on the agenda of US external priorities. These events paved the way for what many considered a return to the post-war special relation between Mexico and the USA.

Whilst it is true that this shift was favoured by the change of administrations taking place on both sides of the border with the incoming Salinas and Bush administrations, such gradual convergence was also made possible by hopes of progress in the Central American peace process opened by the Esquipulas plan and, equally important, by the recognition by both parties of the need for cooperation effectively to tackle mutual problems such as drug-trafficking and migration. Indeed, while it is generally recognised that the multiple and complex variables and interests underlying the bilateral relation generate a structural tension, the potential for coordination and conflict limitation has also been acknowledged (Rico, 1989; Whitehead, 1991) Evidence of this was apparent not only during the post-war period, when a tacit understanding enabled both countries to maintain harmonious relations, but also in the increasing coherence that characterised US-Mexican relations during the Bush administration.

Although the NAFTA initiative clearly benefited from this improved climate, formal economic integration continued to be considered as a remote possibility. As late as 1989 scepticism with regard to the viability of a free trade agreement was widespread. The report of the US Mexican Bilateral Commission of that year considered sectoral liberalisation as the more feasible alternative (Weintraub, 1984; Castro Martínez, 1990 and Avila, 1991). Nevertheless, the combination of the requirements attached to economic opening – in terms of both access to markets and capital inflows between Canada and the USA, together with the expected economic impact of changes taking place at the time within the EC and Eastern Europe, served as a catalyst to NAFTA.[40] Indeed, the decision of the Mexican government to pursue free trade negotiations with the USA should be seen in the context of market dependence resulting from the shift towards export-led growth.[41]

Mexico entered NAFTA negotiations confident that it would preserve its autonomy in international affairs, and most importantly its sovereignty. Yet the lukewarm opposition offered by Mexican foreign policy to the invasion of Panama, and to the violation of its sovereignty by the extraterritorial enforcement of US anti-narcotics laws in Mexican territory, indicated the subordination of foreign policy to NAFTA.[42] Although following the kidnapping of Alvarez Machaín (a Mexican national) there were hints suggesting a more assertive international response, plans to take the case to the General Assembly in order to request an opinion of the International Court of Justice were subsequently abandoned. Similarly, although Panama's invasion was particularly sensitive since it signalled potential links between anti-narcotic policies and intervention, moderation prevailed over the longstanding pattern of detachment and disagreement with US interventions within the region. More surprisingly, and although subsequently abandoned, Salinas's declarations at the outbreak of the 1991 Gulf War regarding the participation of Mexican troops underlined the Executive's disregard of traditional foreign policy postures. Such disregard was subsequently reaffirmed first by the pressure exerted on the Mexican government in July 1993 to receive and deport 659 Chinese refugees intercepted by the US coastguard without granting them the right to prove their status as political refugees, and by the subsequent forced repatriation of 20 Cubans, which was later on followed by the request to the Cuban government to return eight of them.[43] Not only did these policies suggest the renunciation by Mexico of a foreign policy instrument (common observance of international norms) that in the past encouraged restraint on the USA, but also a conviction that bilateral reassurances by the US government would guarantee the level of harmony reached over the past couple of years and the assumption that the special relationship would ultimately prevail.[44]

Whilst it is true that the levels of coherence that accompanied US-Mexican relations over the second half of the 1980s suggested the recomposition of the US-Mexican tacit understanding, the weight of personalities remained an important factor. Moreover, the rules underpinning the new formula are not obvious. If in the past an 'agreement to disagree' (Ojeda, 1976) provided the basis for the US-Mexican understanding, the path now followed by Mexican foreign policy suggests that Mexico has more often conformed to US views, at the expense of the consistency which traditionally characterised its observance of international norms (including non-intervention). The potential costs of this shift for the defensive strength of foreign policy are yet to be seen. Beyond the criticism that could be made on the binding force of international law and the impact of changes taking place in humanitarian intervention, the relevance of international norms and rules (including non-intervention and limitations on the use of force) in offering some measure of protection to small states has been generally recognised (Hurrell, 1992; Roberts, 1993; Jackson, 1990).

The need for pragmatism was made evident by past experiences where narrow interpretations of what an independent posture represents led to unnecesary confrontation and to a stalemate in foreign policy. Although the current administration has systematically insisted and justified its foreign policy on the basis of pragmatism, what we have so far observed is the realignment and subordination of foreign policy to NAFTA. The decision to proceed with NAFTA was justified on the basis of a more realistic and less defensive foreign policy whose main goal was the effective insertion of Mexico in the international economy. Yet this offensive shift soon made clear the overconcentration of foreign policy on one issue not only at the expense of other goals and regions, but also of its previous defensive roal. Failure to understand that pragmatism and the observance of regulating principles are not necessarily incompatible goals has led the current administration to dismiss the relevance of its legalistic tradition, while remnants of confrontational periods have been evident in areas wrongly considered as unimportant by foreign policy-makers in Mexico.[45] It would be difficult to deny the need for greater pragmatism, but it would be equally erroneous to underestimate the potential value of regulating principles for long-term defensive goals *vis-à-vis* the northern neighbour. As mentioned earlier, the multilateral framework of NAFTA could offer some room for both Mexico and Canada to induce some measure of restraint on US behaviour.

Although some observers have argued that free trade will greatly contribute to economic growth and consequently to Mexico's autonomy, the subordination of Mexican foreign policy to NAFTA negotiations raised concern about the potential costs of greater integration and opened the debate about alternative formulas to institutionalise the bilateral relation. Although the Salinas administration has underlined its preference for free trade, as opposed to economic integration on the European lines, the advantages of the latter option have been emphasised by opponents to NAFTA.[46] Indeed the speed with which NAFTA negotiations were conducted raised suspicions about the ruling elite's medium- and long-term vision of economic integration. Whilst it is true that domestic political and economic considerations underpinned the rapid process of negotiations, the Salinas government placed greater emphasis on having the agreement completed and approved rather than in negotiating the conditions for Mexico's entry into a free trade area.[47] As chapter 12 points out, the negotiation of the parallel agreements was the result of US demands linked to the change of administrations. In consequence, at least in the short-term, the claim that through economic growth NAFTA will further Mexico's autonomy and independence and will contribute to open new foreign policy alternatives is not totally convincing. For the time being, with the exception of the Chile-Mexico free trade agreement which came into force in 1992, attempts at trade diversification have not yet succeeded. Although Mexico became part of the Pacific Economic Cooperation Council in 1990, efforts to become a member of the Asian Pacific Economic Council or the OECD have not flourished. Not only does NAFTA seem to have narrowed the freedom of manoeuvre and the freedom of action for diplomacy, but agreements of this kind could not easily be reduced to trade rules. NAFTA will gradually make in-roads on the parties' sovereignty either through the harmonisation of domestic legal frameworks or through the gradual development of intrusive multilateral rules.

Whilst it is true that trade and investment linkages have steadily integrated the economies of the USA, Canada and Mexico, NAFTA represents a qualitative change that will undoubtedly unleash significant political challenges. The three countries have agreed to deepen and institutionalise their economic links and in such a way to relinquish or share their sovereignties. Although NAFTA has not yet led to the creation of supranational institutions, it has already unleashed a dynamic in which the activities of interest groups, involving farmers, consumers, environmentalists, labour and business have crossed national boundaries. The decisions of these actors will increasingly take into account the subcontinental dimension, and could in turn affect other areas. What seems clear is that this process, together with the impact of the implementation of the dispute settlement mechanism, will bring closer not only the economies of the three actors, but also their political systems.

This expected impact on sovereignty was partly acknowledged by Mexico's increasing reliance on a more dynamic definition of sovereignty.[48] While it could be argued that Mexico exercised its sovereign rights in entering into free trade agreements with its northern neighbours, the impact of this decision on Mexico's autonomy will to a large extent depend on NAFTA's contribution to the consolidation of the international competitiveness of the Mexican economy.[49] The likely impact on Mexico's sovereignty has not been restricted to foreign policy. Given the underlying asymmetry between the USA and Mexico, changes in the capacity of the Mexican government to regulate the economy have already affected, and will continue to affect, its autonomy. What seems clear is that NAFTA has increased Mexico's dependence on the US market and that, given the limited available alternatives, the opportunity cost of breaking the relation with its northern neighbours has already increased. Although the dependence on the USA, and more specifically on the west and south-west of the USA, has clearly increased over the past years, the pattern of US-Mexican relations is still far from complete interdependence in the sense of relations which would be mutually costly to sever (Baldwin, 1980).[50] Although the strategy pursued by the Salinas administration to insert Mexico into the international economy was partly based on the conviction that the advantages embodied in NAFTA would outweigh the costs, the haste with which negotiations were conducted has suggested two possible and interrelated scenarios. Either bargaining 'under duress' took place, by which the alternative of free trade was imposed on Mexico by temporary needs, or 'fair trade' alternatives, which could help to distinguish between strong and weak partners and accordingly grant preferential treatment to the latter, were simply dismissed. What seems clear is that gradual progress towards symmetrical interdependence will depend on the capacity and willingness of the USA to maintain the relationship created by NAFTA as well as on the ability of the Mexican economy to compete under the rules created by this agreement.

Notes

1. The classic statement of the theory of economic integration, couched in terms of trade creation, trade diversion and net welfare gains, can be found in Viner (1950). In the subsequent three decades there were numerous refinements to the theory (e.g. Krause, 1972), but there was virtually no challenge to the notion that developing countries would be better off forming integration schemes with each other rather than with developed countries. Conventional wisdom only seriously began to be revised when first Greece (1981) and later Spain and Portugal (1986) joined the European Community. See Grilli (1992).

2. Developing countries were slow to join GATT after its creation in 1947. As a result, tariff reductions in the various 'rounds' of GATT negotiations mainly affected developed countries, widening the gap with developing countries in terms of the level of protection. Mexico, for example, only applied to join GATT in 1985 when it became clear that its response to the debt crisis needed to include trade liberalisation.

3. The association of Puerto Rico with the United States, or Martinique and Guadeloupe with France (and the European Community), offer clues with regard to the reallocation of resources when poor and rich countries integrate. Nevertheless, political ties in all such cases allow for unilateral transfers from the richer partner at a level which would be unthinkable in the case of independent countries.

4. This has been well illustrated by the populist response to NAFTA orchestrated by Ross Perot, whose campaign has focused on the 'giant sucking sound' of jobs allegedly moving to Mexico as US firms take advantage of lower real wages and lax environmental enforcement. See Perot and Choate (1993).

5. By mid-1993, the weighted tariff average for imports of goods had been reduced to 11.1% with quantitative restrictions lifted on virtually all imports.

6. The degree of integration of the three economies even before NAFTA was considerable. For a pioneering attempt to quantify the extent of integration in product and factor markets, see Roland-Holst, Reinert and Shiells (1993).

7. It is hardly surprising, therefore, that the opponents of NAFTA in Canada and the USA fought so hard for the side agreements signed in August 1993 to include a link between minimum wages and productivity growth. However, Mexico successfully resisted the formalisation of this link, which in any case is increasingly irrelevant as the real minimum wage fell far below the market-

clearing wage in the 1980s.

8. Consumption losses, however, through trade diversion appear to be quite small. See Primo Braga (1992).

9. The most obvious example is the law granting autonomy to the Central Bank, which was submitted to Congress in 1993.

10. This suspicion was raised by the failure of electoral authorities to deliver preliminary figures on the day of the election. The results announced by the Federal Electoral Commission gave the PRI candidate Carlos Salinas 50.74% of the vote, Cuauhtémoc Cardenas (PRD) 31.06% and Manuel Clouthier (PAN) 16.81%. The results of a post-election survey commissioned by the PAN were: Salinas 34-35%, Cárdenas 31-32% and Clouthier 29-31%.

11. Since 1988 these changes have generally favoured the PAN: in 1990 it won its first governorship election in Baja California Norte and the first local government in a state capital, Mérida. In 1991 it was awarded the interim governorship of Guanajuato in negotiations after contested elections and in 1992 it won the governorship of Chihuahua. In contrast, by 1991 the PRD had been reduced to the third electoral force.

12. In the 1988-91 Legislature the PRI's traditional monopoly over Congress was challenged by the opposition achieving control over 240 of the 500 seats of the lower chamber. For the first time the PRI did not have the two-thirds majority needed to make constitutional changes. This changed after the mid-term elections in August 1991.

13. Following the instructions of the executive during the spring of 1990 the Mexican Congress carried out a national consultation. Yet, this was mostly intended as a campaign to win public opinion. The Inter-Secretariat Commision was integrated by representatives from Relaciones Exteriores, Hacienda, Programación y Presupuesto, Trabajo y Previsión Social, the Banco de México, and the Presidencia de la República (Zabludovsky, 1991, pp. 178-183).

14. Information gathered during interviews with PRI and government officials, June 1993.

15. The nature of the PRD as a confederation of political groups established in 1989 helps to explain its inability to consolidate a unifying programme above its various factions. Throughout the sessions of the legislature in which fundamental constitutional amendments have been carried out, the party has remained on the defensive and has proved unable to negotiate or influence this process. Although in 1988 it was considered as the party of the Mexican majority, by 1991 its electoral strength had declined substantially. Beyond the PRD's weaknesses, it is important to emphasise both the context of the hegemonic party system in which the PRD has operated as well as unfavourable conditions ranging from the alliance forged between the PRI and PAN, the results of the government's ambitious anti-poverty programme and low-intensity persecution. For an analysis of the process leading to the PRD consolidation, see Valdés (forthcoming).

16. The debate surrounding the classification of Mexico as authoritarian is not clear-cut. See, for example, Cosio Villegas (1972); Reyna and Weinert (1977); and more recently Cornelius and Craig (1991).

17. Whilst it is true that international pressure favouring democratic change in Mexico has been limited, closer international observance of Mexican political practices was reflected in the increase in the total number of foreign correspondents based in Mexico City (Weingarten, 1993). Throughout the 1980s opposition parties have voiced their claims of electoral fraud in US fora including the media and the US Congress. These moves, which were traditionally considered an anathema to the Mexican political culture, have opened a debate about changes in this arena.

18. There are examples of economic liberalisation without the concomitant breakdown of political authoritarianism; one example would be the Central American regional integration scheme of the 1960s and 1970s.

19. Although the previous claim that economic growth was of little or no benefit for significant portions of the population has been challenged by recent studies indicating a strong correlation between rapid economic growth and poverty diminution, as the experience of the 1980s in Sub-Saharan Africa and Latin America suggests, transitions to market orientated economy can involve significant disruptions and income losses particularly for vulnerable sectors (Haggard, 1991). By 1990, official figures acknowledged this showing that 41.3% of the population were living in poverty (Consejo Consultivo del Programa Nacional de Solidaridad, 1990).

20. Beyond the electoral arena there are several political implications of PRONASOL. First, it has introduced novel forms of social organisation for the PRI reflecting the independent groups which emerged in the 1980s. Secondly, its impact on centralism is not obvious; on the one hand, the control of the Executive over the programme has contributed to the strengthening of presidentialism at the expense of local government, but on the other it has also entailed a measure of decentralisation reflected in its response to local demands and in its unblocking effect on policy implementation at the local level. Moreover, it has given rise to tensions both within the PRI as well in state-party relations. Although earlier characterised as clientelist and authoritarian, Molinar Horcasitas and Weldon have recently defined it as 'pork-barrel' politics similar to those present in democratic regimes (Harvey, 1990, p. 34; Molinar Horcasitas and Weldon, 1993).

21. Although in the late 1980s a significant proliferation of new peasant organisations took place, the creation of the CAP (Congreso Agrario Permanente) in 1989 awakened scepticism as to the reform of the state's relations with the peasantry. Behind the policy of 'concertación', neocorporatist tendencies were apparent (Harvey, 1990).

22. An analysis conducted by GEA (Grupo de Economistas Asociados) suggests that the wage ceiling has forced unions to renounce offensive tactics and instead to negotiate labour conditions with productivity at the centre. Although the negotiation of NAFTA's parallel agreements raised some expectations with

regard to better labour conditions, the official labour sector has maintained its total support for the agreement (*La Jornada*, 10 June 1993).

23. The impact of economic restructuring has not been uniform. It has varied among regions and sectors. Throughout the 1980s rates of growth were mostly negative, but in no way homogeneous; the rate of growth among states including Puebla, D.F., Chihuahua, Jalisco, Michoacán and Quintana Roo ranged from 0.75% to 11.9%. Unionised workers were generally better off than non-unionised. Yet along the border, where only 10% of the labour force is unionised, the minimum wage tends to be higher than in the centre where the unionised rate is 30%. Similarly, between 1982 and 1990, minimum wages fell by 47.7%, but the decrease in manufacturing wages was 19.8%. Finally not only were levels of employment in the manufacturing and construction sectors relatively maintained (between 1980 and 1986 overall reduction in both sectors was of -2.8% and -2.7%), but wage ceilings were in some cases compensated by social benefits. In the case of central government wages, a fall of 52.5% was probably counterbalanced by job security and an expansion of 18.06% in public employment between 1982 and 1988 (Breña Garduno, 1993; Heredia, forthcoming; Cornelius and Craig, 1991 and Bizberg, 1990).

24. Although still important, in electoral terms control over labour has not proved as efficient as in the past, but it has been a crucial factor underlying economic restructuring. This was possibly an important consideration for the return to sectoral organisation within the PRI and to patronage practices reflected in the moderate increase of the labour quota within Congress.

25. The negative impact of liberalisation on medium and small enterprises led the government to consider special programmes both to help their restructuring and to establish links between them and the productive plant (Beristain and Trigueros, 1990; Urquidi, 1990; Hernández Laos and Velasco Arregui, 1990; Urquidi, 1992).

26. For a thorough analysis of Mexican federalism, see Reyes Heroles (1988) and Trigueros Gaisman (1990).

27. In the aftermath of the electoral crisis of 1988, there have been significant opposition victories. For the first time the PAN won a governorship. While it is true that the PAN's victory in Baja California preceded NAFTA, more recently the PAN won its second governorship in Chihuahua (1993). Similarly, widespread mobilisations following other elections (San Luis Potosí, Guanajuato, Tabasco, Michoacán and Guerrero) have resulted in a number of interim governors, some of whom belong to the opposition. Although the PRD has been largely excluded from these arrangements, it is important to note that opposition state governments could play an important role in advancing democracy through constitutional change at the regional level, and we have witnessed some moves in that direction in Guanajuato, Chihuahua and Baja California.

28. This process, identified by Garretón as the 'invisible transition', was an important factor underlying the removal and designation of interim governors in Guanajuato, San Luis Potosí and Michoacán (Garretón, 1989).

29. See, for example, the pessimistic view of José Woldenberg, 'Reforma electoral: la masa se hizo engrudo', *La Jornada*, 3 July 1993 and Rodrigo Morales, 'La reforma: el peor de los mundos', *La Jornada*, 20 September 1993.

30. Although the deregulation that has taken place over the past years has provided the basis for these arguments, one of the first steps in this direction introduced by NAFTA is embodied in the provisions concerning the establishment of a special committee to determine whether the application of domestic law has prevented or frustrated the functioning of the binational panel. The lack of independence of Mexico's judiciary was one of the motivating forces underlying this provision (Smith, 1993).

31. Whilst it is true that the political changes which have taken place in the north of the country have been partly motivated by the impact of US political culture on the attitudes of local entrepreneurs, the advance of the PAN and the success of business candidates, including Ruffo and Barrio (governors of Baja California and Chihuahua, respectively), was strongly motivated by the overall isolation of small and medium-size entrepreneurs from both big business and the central state. In order to break this isolation local business organisations served as the basis of electoral platforms emphasising the need for democracy, local autonomy and accountability (Mizrahi, 1992; Elizondo, 1992).

32. Similarly, it is important to keep in mind how in the past deep economic and social problems have exerted considerable pressure on both the legal and administrative systems, leading to significant distortions. While frustration has often accompanied the functioning of these institutions, deviations from the rule of law – normally supported by reliance on colonial or customary law and 'paralegal' negotiations – have also performed important distributive functions (see, for example, Azuela de la Cueva, 1989).

33. During the late 1970s, in the context of an unstable energy market, the USA put forward a proposal for a North American Common Market. The recently discovered Mexican oil reserves became an important factor underlying US security considerations (Fagen, 1979). For an historical perspective on US interest in free trade, see Martz (1993).

34. Despite the priority that Canadian foreign policy traditionally granted to international institutions and multilateralism, until recently the Canadian government remained reluctant to join an organisation which would have forced it to adopt uncomfortable decisions. In 1972 Canada became a member of the Inter-American Development Bank and achieved the status of permanent observer at the OAS.

35. In the 1970s Canadian aid to Latin America doubled and the promotion of trade and investment was reflected in the absorption by the region of 50% of total manufacturing goods traded with developing countries and 25% of

Canadian foreign direct investment (Mace, 1989).

36. Apart from the asymmetrical nature of US-Mexican relations, other considerations included ideological and cultural differences, the change in the economic model of development and the emphasis placed on 'negative' integration at the expense of schemes involving policy coordination and compensation mechanisms.

37. Foreign policy 'economisation' was not exclusive to Mexico. As in Mexico, Brazil and Argentina experienced similar trends and their margins of autonomy *vis-à-vis* the USA narrowed (Russell, 1990; Hirst, 1990). Although Mexico, together with Colombia and Jamaica, has been responsible for a significant proportion of lobbying, this practice has become common place in the region. Between 1987 and 1989 Latin American countries spent US$ 451 million in promoting their exports and ensuring their access to the US market *(Crónicas de la CEPAL)*, 90-CC-47.

38. The 'economisation' of foreign policy paved the way for a vigorous public relations campaign deployed at the international level, involving the expansion of consulates in the USA, the appointment of press attachés in key embassies, as well as the increasing use of lobbying particularly after 1989. This was partly justified by the need to reverse Mexico's previous neglect towards the US Congress and to counter the negative image associated with narcotic flows. Yet what appears to be an excessive use of lobbying has been criticised not only on the basis of huge costs, but also in terms of the perceived gains in credibility. Estimated costs of lobbying for 1993 to try to ensure the passage of NAFTA were of the order of $30 million. A third feature of this economisation was the setting up of 40 offices of BANCOMEXT around the world in charge of capturing trade opportunities for Mexican enterprises. Whether these offices will play a similar role to the one provided by various instruments during the transition to export-led growth in both Korea and Taiwan is not clear (Eisenstadt, 1992; *El Financiero*, 15 October 1992; *Financial Times*, 28 May 1993 and Haggard, 1990 and 1991).

39. Although evidence of increasing pragmatism could be traced back to the late 1970s, when the in-coming López Portillo administration made clear its intention to avoid the rhetoric and confrontation that had characterised the foreign policy of his predecessor, the combination of the discovery of oil reserves, the personalisation of foreign policy under López Portillo and the ideological drift of Reagan's foreign policy eclipsed these pragmatic efforts.

40. International factors ranging from increasing protectionism, the rapid integration of financial markets and the threat of regional blocs underpinned the shift in Mexico's foreign policy. In North America, as in the transition to the Single European Market, the interests and needs of multinational companies (MNCs) proved crucial. Indeed, the road to NAFTA was encouraged by trade and investment flows and led by MNCs (Gereffi, 1993; Strange, 1991). Similarly, as suggested in chapter 10 and other studies, the interest of Japanese and European investors has been largely influenced by expectations of access to the US market. See the contributions on Europe and

Japan in Roett (1991).

41. The development by Mexico of an export capacity created a new source of tensions. Although partly tackled by a series of trade agreements negotiated since 1986, the 1990 US embargo of Mexican tuna and shrimp offered evidence of this trend. Trade agreements included the 1985 bilateral accord which extended 'injury test' protection to Mexico and reduced the incidence of countervailing duties. This was followed by the 1986 joint statement concerning the prospects for a common framework to regulate trade and investment. The 1989 framework agreement on trade and investment signalled the intention of the two governments to encourage managed economic integration.

42. Although occasionally disagreement and divergent views have emerged, throughout the bargaining process the monopolisation of NAFTA negotiations by the Trade Ministry reduced the Foreign Ministry to a subsidiary role.

43. See *La Jornada*, 16 and 20 July 1993 and *El Financiero*, 31 August 1993.

44. Ironically, trade was the one area where the Mexican government sought a multilateral solution on the basis of agreed international trade norms. Indeed, Mexico took the tuna dispute to GATT claiming that the embargo was inconsistent with obligations owed to Mexico under GATT. The multilateral organisation determined that the embargo, although designed to conserve dolphin, was inconsistent with international trade law (McDorman, 1992).

45. The excessive attention to NAFTA led the Foreign Ministry to dismiss the relevance of arms control and more specifically of non-proliferation. This indifference could help to explain the divergence of Mexico's confrontational posture during the 1990 Nuclear Non-Proliferation Treaty review conference from the pattern of realignment in foreign policy. Mexico's opposition obstructed the achievement of a resolution at a critical juncture.

46. One of the strongest arguments has been linked to the expansion of economic compensations that accompanied the entry into the EC of Greece, Portugal and Spain. In the last decade the EC has doubled its regional funds.

47. While the maintenance by the Mexican government of its state oil monopoly has been seen as a significant achievement, some observers claim that energy was not a driving force in NAFTA as it had been in US-Canada free trade negotiations, and that Mexico's oil exports are likely to halt by the end of the century. Chapter six of NAFTA covers four basic areas: crude and refined oil, natural gas, electricity and coal. Although article 601 confers full respect for the parties' constitutions, it has been argued that this clause does not legitimise the PEMEX monopoly and that there is still room for interpretation. Moreover, current underinvestment in the Mexican energy sector may tilt the balance in favour of greater privatisation. Trade in energy and basic petrochemicals will be subject to gradual liberalisation, possibly of both trade rules and domestic energy markets; equally important is the parties' recognition of the need for 'viable and international competitive energy and petrochemical sectors' (Roett, 1991, p. 16; Lock, 1993, pp. 243-4).

48. In fact, it was the debt crisis that opened a debate about sovereign statehood. Conditionality attached to debt restructuring was regarded as an encroachment on the sovereignty of debtors who often had little or no alternative.

49. Sovereignty has been defined as the situation by which a 'state decides for itself how it will cope with its internal and external problems, including whether to seek assistance from others, and in so doing, to limit its freedom by making a commitment to them' (Waltz, 1979).

50. California and Texas are the states likely to reap the largest benefits from NAFTA. Californian trade in goods to Mexico increased by 13% in 1991 and the combined trade of the two states has been around US$25 billion. Moreover, since NAFTA's rules of origin will set limits to Japanese investment in the *maquiladora* sector, California's main exports – electric and electronic equipment – will undoubtedly benefit (Goldsborough, 1993).

BIBLIOGRAPHY

Aghevli, B. B. et al (1990) 'The Role of National Saving in the World Economy', IMF Occasional Paper No. 67 (Washington, DC: International Monetary Fund).

American Federation of Labour-Congress of Industrial Organisations (AFL-CIO) (1992) *Policy Recommendations for 1992* (Washington, DC).

Appendini, K. (1992a) *De la milpa a los tortibonos: La restructuración de la política alimentaria en México* (Mexico City: El Colegio de México/UNRISD).

Appendini, K. (1992b) 'Los campesinos maiceros en el contexto de la política de liberalización y contrareforma agraria', Paper for the XVII International Congress, Latin American Studies Association, Los Angeles.

Avery, W. P. (1993) 'Agriculture and two-level bargaining in the North American Free Trade Agreement', Annual Meeting of the International Studies Association, Acapulco, Mexico.

Avila, C. (1991) 'El mercado de América del Norte: espacio económico para México', *Comercio Exterior*, Vol. 41, No. 7.

Azuela de la Cueva, A. (1989) *La ciudad, la propiedad privada y el derecho* (Mexico City: El Colegio de México).

Backus, D. K., P. J. Kehoe, and T. J. Kehoe (1991) 'In Search of Scale Effects in Trade and Growth', Federal Reserve Bank of Minneapolis Research Department Working Paper No. 451.

Baldwin, A. D. (1980) 'Interdependence and power: A conceptual analysis', *International Organization*, Vol. 34, No. 4.

Ballew, P. and R. Schnorbus (1992) 'NAFTA and the Auto Industry: Boon or Bane?' *Chicago Fed Letter*, No. 64, December 1992, Federal Reserve Bank of Chicago.

Banamex (1991) *Examen de la situación económica de México*, vol. LXVII (790) (Mexico City: Banco Nacional de México).

Banamex (1993) 'Central Bank Autonomy', *Review of the Economic Situation in Mexico*, vol. LXIX (812) (Mexico City: Banco Nacional de México).

Banco de México (1992) *The Mexican Economy 1991* (Mexico City).

Bank of Mexico (1993) *Annual Report 1992* (Mexico City).

Barraclough, S. (1991) 'Some questions about the implications for rural Mexicans of the proposed North American Free Trade Agreement (NAFTA)', Paper for IX Seminario de Economía Agrícola del Tercer Mundo, Mexico City: Instituto de Investigaciones Económicas, Universidad Nacional Autónoma de México.

Barry, E. and E. Siwicki (1993) 'NAFTA: The Textile and Apparel Sector',

233

in S. Globerman and M. Walker, *Assessing NAFTA: A Trinational Analysis* (Vancouver: The Fraser Institute).

Bayoumi, T. and B. Eichengreen (1992) 'Monetary and Exchange Rate Arrangements for NAFTA', mimeo, University of California, Berkeley.

Bazdresch, C. et al (1992) *Mexico: Auge, Crisis y Ajuste* (Mexico City: Fondo de Cultura Económica).

Belous, R. S. and J. Lemco (1993) *NAFTA as a Model of Development* (Washington, DC: National Planning Association).

Benett, D. and K. Sharpe (1985) *Transnational Corporations vs the State: The Political Economy of the Mexican Auto Industry* (Princeton: Princeton University Press).

Berberán, J., C. Cárdenas and A. L. Morjardín (1988) *'Análisis de los resultados oficiales del 6 de julio* (Mexico City: Editorial Nuestro Tiempo).

Beristaín, J. and I. Trigueros (1990) 'Mexico', in J. Williamson (ed.), *Latin American Adjustment. How Much has Happened?* (Washington, DC: Institute for International Economics).

Berry, S., V. Grilli and F. López-de-Silanes (1992) 'The Automobile Industry and the Mexico-US Free Trade Agreement', Working Paper No. 4152, National Bureau of Economic Research.

Best, E. (1987) *US Policy and Regional Security in Latin America* (London: Institute for International Strategic Studies).

Bhagwati, J. (1989) 'Is Free Trade Passé After All?' *Weltwirtschaftliches Archiv*, Vol. 125, No. 1.

Bhagwati, J. (1991) *The World Trading System at Risk* (Princeton: Princeton University Press).

Bizberg, I. (1990) 'La crisis del corporativismo mexicano', *Foro Internacional*, Vol. XXX, No. 4.

Blanco, H. (1991) 'Naturaleza y alcance del tratado de libre comercio', in SECOFI, *Hacia un tratado de libre comercio en América del Norte* (Mexico City: Miguel Angel Porrúa).

Blecker, R. A. and W. E. Spriggs (1992) 'Manufacturing Employment in North America: Where the Jobs Have Gone', Briefing Paper, Economic Policy Institute.

Bouzas, R. and J. Ros (1993) 'The North-South variety of economic integration: Issues and prospects for Latin America', Paper presented at the Conference on 'Economic Integration in the Western Hemisphere: Prospects for Latin America', University of Notre Dame, 17-18 April, 1993.

Bovard, J. (1992) 'The United States' Protectionist Antidumping and Countervailing Subsidy Laws', Paper presented at Liberty in the Americas: Free Trade and Beyond, a conference sponsored by the Cato Institute and the Centro de Investigaciones Sobre la Libre Empresa, Mexico City, 1992.

Breña Garduno, F. (1993) 'The impact of NAFTA on labour legislation in Mexico', *United States-Mexico Law Journal*, Vol. 1, No. 1.

Brothers, S. D. and A. E. Wick (eds.) (1990) *Mexico's Search for a New*

Development Strategy (Boulder: Westview Press).

Brown, D. (1992) 'The Impact of a North American Free Trade Area: Applied General Equilibrium Models', in N. Lustig, B. P. Bosworth, and R. Z. Lawrence (eds), *North American Free Trade* (Washington, DC: The Brookings Institution).

Brown, D. K., A. V. Deardorff and R. M. Stern (1991a) 'A North American Free Trade Agreement: Analytical Issues and a Computational Assessment', mimeo, University of Michigan, October.

Brown, D. K., A. V. Deardorff and R. M. Stern (1991b) 'Some Estimates of a North American Free Trade Agreement', mimeo, University of Michigan, October.

Brown Jr, G. E., J. W. Gould and J. Cavanagh (1992) 'Making Trade Fair', *World Policy Journal*, Spring.

Bustamante, J. et al (1993) 'Continous survey of flow of undocumented Mexican immigrants as they cross the USA-Mexico border at the cities of Tijuana, Mexicali, Ciudad Juárez, Nuevo Laredo and Matamoros, based on individual questionnaires administered to a randomly selected sample on Fridays, Saturdays and Sundays of every week ever since September of 1987 to the present', mimeo, El Colegio de la Frontera Norte.

Bustamante, J. and G. Martínez (1979) 'Undocumented immigration from Mexico: beyond borders but within systems', *Journal of International Affairs*, Vol. 33.

Calva, J. L. (1991) *Probables efectos de un tratado de libre comercio en el campo mexicano* (Mexico: Ed. Fontamara).

Calvo, G. A. et al (1992) 'Capital Inflows and Real Exchange Rate Appreciation in Latin America: the role of external factors', IMF Working Papers No. 62 (Washington, DC: International Monetary Fund)

Cameron, M. (1991) 'North American Trade Negotiations: liberalization games between asymmetric players', Paper presented at the XV World Congress of the International Political Science Association, 21-25 July, 1991, Buenos Aires.

Camou, A. (1992) 'Gobernabilidad y democracia', *Nexos*, No. 170.

Canadian Centre for Policy Alternatives (1992) 'Which Way for the Americas? Analysis of NAFTA proposals and the Impact on Canada', mimeo, November.

Canadian Environmental Report (1992)*The North American Free Trade Agreement* (Ottawa).

Canadian Government (1992) 'North American Free Trade: An Overview and Description' (Ottawa).

Cárdenas, C. (1991a) 'Pacto Continental de Comercio y Desarrollo',*Nexos*, June.

Cárdenas, C. (1991b) 'Free Trade is not enough'*New Perspectives Quarterly*, Winter.

Castañeda, J. G. and C. Heredia (1993) 'Hacia Otro TLC', *Nexos*, January.

Castro Martínez, P. (1990) 'México y la política comercial estadounidense

1982-88', *Foro Internacional*, Vol. XXX.

Chant, J. F. (1993) 'The Financial Sector in NAFTA: Two Plus One Equals Restructuring', in S. Globerman and M. Walker (eds.), *Assessing NAFTA: A Trinational Analysis* (Vancouver: The Fraser Institute).

Chauvet, M. (1993) 'Crisis de la ganadería: ajuste y restructuración', Mexico: ILET, unpublished preliminary paper

Cobb, S. L. and D. J. Molina (1991) 'Implications of North American Free Trade for Infrastructure and Migration on the Texas-Mexico Border', in Federal Reserve Bank of Dallas (1991): *North American Free Trade: Proceedings from a Conference*, Dallas, June 14.

Comisión Sobre el Futuro de las Relaciones México-Estados Unidos (1988)*El desafío de la interdependencia: México y Estados Unidos* (Mexico City: Fondo de Cultura Económica).

Conroy, M. E. and A. K. Glasmeier (1992/93) 'Unprecedented Disparities, Unparalleled Adjustment Needs: Winners and Losers on the NAFTA "Fast Track"', *Journal of Interamerican Studies and World Affairs*, Vol. 34, No. 4.

Consejo Consultativo del Programa Nacional de Solidaridad (1990)*El combate a la pobreza: lineamientos programáticos* (Mexico City: PRONASOL).

Cornelius, A. W. (1988) 'Las relaciones de Estados Unidos con México: fuentes de su deterioro, 1986-1987', *Foro Internacional*, Vol. XXIX, No. 2.

Cornelius, A. W., J. Gentleman and P. Smith eds. (1989) *Mexico's Alternative Political Futures* (San Diego: University of California).

Cornelius, A. W. and A. L. Craig. (1991) *The Mexican Political System in Transition* (San Diego: University of California).

Cornelius, A. W. and Martin, P. L. (1993) *The Uncertain Connection: Free Trade and Mexico Migration* (San Diego: Center for Mexican Studies, University of California.

Cosio Villegas, D. (1972) *El sistema político mexicano* (Mexico City: Joaquín Mortiz).

Cotidiano, El, 'TLC: Trabajo y Ecología', No. 43, September-October 1991 (Mexico City)

Crespo, J. A. (1991) 'La evolución del sistema de partidos en México', *Foro Internacional*, Vol. XXI, No. 4.

Crespo, J. A. (1992) 'Crisis económica, crisis legitimidad', in C. Bazdresch et al (eds.) *México: Auge, Crisis y Ajuste* (Mexico City: Fondo de Cultura Económica).

Cropper, M. L. and W. Oates (1992) 'Environmental Economics: A Survey', *Journal of Economic Literature*, Vol. 30, June.

del Castillo, G. and G. Vega (1991) 'Perspectivas sobre el libre comercio: un estudio comparado de empresas Mexicanas y Canadienses', *Frontera Norte*, Vol. 3, No. 6.

Delal Baer, M. (1991) 'North American Free-Trade', *Foreign Affairs*, Vol. 70, No. 4.

Dixit, A. (1987) 'Issues of Strategic Trade Policy for Small Countries', *Scandinavian Journal of Economics*, pp. 349-367.

DRI/McGraw-Hill (1991) *The Outlook for Mexico Under NAFTA* (New York).

Economic Strategy Institute (1991) *The Good News or the Bad News. Free Trade with Mexico: The Potential Economic Impact* (Washington, DC).

Eisenstadt, T. (1992) 'Cabildeo y relaciones públicas en Estados Unidos',*Este País*, No. 15.

Elizondo, C. (1992) 'Property rights in Mexico. Government and business after the 1982 Bank nationalization', DPhil Thesis, University of Oxford.

Encinas, A., J. de la Fuente and H. Mackinlay (1992) *La disputa por los mercados: TLC y sector agropecuario* (Mexico City: Ed. Diana).

Fagen, R. (1979) 'Mexican Petroleum and US National Security',*International Security*, Vol. 4, No. 1.

Faux, J. and T. Lee (1992) 'The Effect of George Bush's NAFTA On American Workers: Ladder Up or Ladder Down?' Briefing Paper, Economic Policy Institute.

Federal Reserve Bank of Dallas (1991) *North American Free Trade: Proceedings from a Conference*, Dallas, June 14.

Finger, M. and T. Murray (1990) 'Policing Unfair Imports: The US Example', Working Paper Series, WPS 401 (Washington, DC: World Bank).

Fishlow, A., S. Robinson, and R. Hinojosa-Ojeda (1991) 'Proposal for a North American Regional Development Bank and Adjustment Fund', in Federal Reserve Bank of Dallas (1991): *North American Free Trade: Proceedings from a Conference*, Dallas, June 14.

FitzGerald, E. V. K. and J. Luttik (1991) 'A Note on the Measurement of Trade and Finance Linkages in the World Accounting Matrix', Working Papers on Money, Finance and Development No. 40 (The Hague: Institute of Social Studies).

Freedman, L. (1991/92) 'Order and Disorder in the New World', *Foreign Affairs*, Vol. 71, No. 1, Special issue, America and the World.

GAO (General Accounting Office) (1991) Briefing Report to the Chairman, Committee on Agriculture, House of Representatives, 'Mexico Trade: Trends and Impediments in Agricultural Trade', January, GAO/NSIAD-90-85BR.

García Rocha, A. and T. Kehoe (1991) 'Efectos del Tratado de Libre Comercio sobre la economía mexicana', in SECOFI, *Hacia un tratado de libre comercio en América del Norte* (Mexico City: Miguel Angel Porrúa).

Garretón, M. A. (1989) 'Popular mobilization and the military regime in Chile: The complexities of the invisible transition', in S. Eckstein (ed.), *Power and Popular Protest: Latin American Social Movements* (Los Angeles: University of California Press).

Garza, H. (1984) 'Desquilibrios y contradicciones de la política exterior de México', *Foro Internacional*, Vol. XXIV, No. 4.

Gavito, J., S. Sánchez and I. Trigueros (1992) 'Los Servicios Financieros y el Acuerdo de Libre Comercio: Bancos y Casas de Bolsa', in E. Andere and

G. Kessel, *México y el Tratado Trilateral de Libre Comercio: Impacto Sectorial* (Mexico City: McGraw-Hill)

Gentleman, J. (1993) 'The impact of the NAFTA initiative on the struggle for democracy in Mexico', Paper presented at the 34th Annual Convention of ISA, Acapulco, March.

Gereffi, G. (1993) 'Cómo contribuye la industria maquiladora al desarrollo nacional de México y a la integración de América del Norte', in G. Vega (ed.) *Liberación económica y libre comercio en América del Norte: consideraciones políticas y culturales* (Mexico City: El Colegio de México).

Globerman, S. (1993) 'Trade Liberalisation and the Environment', in S. Globerman and M. Walker (1993) *Assessing NAFTA: A Trinational Analysis* (Vancouver: The Fraser Institute).

Globerman, S. and M. Walker (1993) *Assessing NAFTA: A Trinational Analysis* (Vancouver: The Fraser Institute).

Goldsborough, O. J. (1993) 'California's Foreign Policy', *Foreign Affairs*, Vol. 72, Spring.

González, J. G. and A. Vélez (1992) 'Intra-Industry Trade Between the US and the Major Latin American Countries: Measurement and Implications for the Initiative for the Americas', Paper presented at the meeting of the Latin American Studies Association, Los Angeles.

Gourevitch, P. J. (1986) *Politics in Hard Times: Comparative Responses to International Economic Crisis* (Ithaca: Cornell University Press).

Grilli, E. R. (1992) *The European Community and the Developing Countries* (Cambridge: Cambridge University Press).

Grinspun, R. and M. A. Cameron (1993), *The Political Economy of North American Free Trade* (New York: St Martin's Press).

Grossman, G. M. and A. B. Krueger (1991) 'Environmental Impacts of a North American Free Trade Agreement', Working Paper No. 3914, National Bureau of Economic Research, November.

Gruben, W. C. (1990a) 'Mexican Maquiladora Growth: Does It Cost US Jobs?' Federal Reserve Bank of Dallas *Economic Review*, January 1990.

Gruben, W. C. (1990b) 'Do Maquiladoras Take American Jobs? Some Tentative Econometric Results', *Journal of Borderland Studies*, Vol. 1, Spring.

Gruben, W. C. (1991) 'Free Trade, Globalization, and US Labor: What Are the Long Run Dynamics?' Paper presented at the conference North American Free Trade: Labor, Business, and Government Policy Perspectives, Industrial Relations Center and the Twin City Labor Management Council, Minneapolis, November 19.

Gruben, W. C. (1993) 'North American Free Trade: Opportunities and Pitfalls', *Contemporary Policy Issues*, Vol. 10, October, pp. 1-10.

Grunwald, J. (1991) 'Opportunity Missed: Mexico and Maquiladoras', *The Brookings Review*, Winter 1990/91.

Haggard, S. (1991) 'Markets, poverty alleviation and income distribution: an assessment of neo-liberal claims', *Ethics and International Affairs*, Vol.5.

Haggard, S. (1990) *Pathways from the periphery: The politics of growth in the newly industrializing countries* (Ithaca: Cornell University Press).

Hamilton, N. and E. Meekim (1993) 'Economic and political liberalization in Mexico and South Korea', *Third World Quarterly*, Vol. 14, No. 1.

Hanson, G. (1992a) 'External Economies, Vertical Integration and Trade: Theory and Evidence from Mexico', mimeo, University of Texas at Austin.

Hanson, G. (1992b) 'Agglomeration, Dispersion, and the Pioneer Firm: Theory and Evidence from Mexico', mimeo, University of Texas at Austin.

Harberger, A. (1991) 'A study of Mexico's real exchange rate', mimeo, University of California, Los Angeles.

Harvey, N. (1990) *The New Agrarian Movement in Mexico 1979-1990* (London: Institute of Latin American Studies).

Heer, D. (1990) *Undocumented Mexicans in the United States* (New York: Cambridge University Press).

Helleiner, G. (1991) 'Consideraciones sobre un área de libre comercio entre Estados Unidos y México', in G. Vega (coord.), *México ante el Libre Comercio con América del Norte* (Mexico City: El Colegio de México and Universidad Tecnológica de México).

Heller, C. (1990) 'Tendencias generales de la política exterior del gobierno de de la Madrid', *Foro Internacional*, Vol. XXX, Jan-March.

Heredia, B. (forthcoming) 'Making economic reform politically viable: The Mexican experience', in W. C. Smith, C. H. Acuña and E. Gamarra (eds.), *Democracy Market and Structural Reform in Latin America* (New Brunswick: Transaction).

Heritage Foundation (1991) 'Refuting Six Myths About the US-Mexico Free Trade Accord', mimeo (Washington, DC), March.

Hernández Laos, E. and E. Velasco Arregui (1990) 'Productividad y competitividad de las manufacturas mexicanas 1960-1985', *Comercio Exterior*, Vol. 40, No. 7.

Heston, A. and R. Summers (1991) 'The Penn World Table (Mark 5): An Expanded Set of International Comparisons', *Quarterly Journal of Economics*, Vol. 106, pp. 327-368.

Hindley, B. (1987) 'Different and More Favorable Treatment – and Graduation', in Michael Finger and Andrzej Olechowski (eds.), *The Uruguay Round: A Handbook on the Multilateral Trade Negotiations* (Washington, DC: World Bank).

Hinojosa-Ojeda, R. and R. K. McCleery, (1990) 'US-Mexico Interdependence, Social Pacts, and Policy Alternatives: A Computable General Equilibrium Approach', mimeo, University of California, Berkeley, October.

Hinojosa-Ojeda, R. and S. Robinson (1991) 'Alternative Scenarios of US-Mexico Integration: A Computable General Equilibrium Approach', Department of Agricultural and Resource Economics, Division of Agriculture and Natural Resources, University of California, Working Paper No. 609.

Hinojosa-Ojeda, R. and S. Robinson (1992) 'Labor issues in a North American

Free Trade Area', in N. Lustig, B.P. Bosworth, and R. Z. Lawrence (eds.), *North American Free Trade* (Washington, DC: The Brookings Institution).

Hirsch, S. (1989) 'Services and Service Intensity in International Trade', *Weltwirtschaftliches Archiv*, Vol. 125, No. 1.

Hirst, M. (1990) 'Brazil: Primeras impresiones sobre la política exterior del nuevo gobierno', *América Latina Internacional*, Vol. 7, No. 24.

Hudson, S. and Prudencio, R. (1993) 'The North American Commission on Environment and Other Supplemental Environment Agreements: part two of the NAFTA package', mimeo, Washington, DC.

Hufbauer, G. C. and J. J. Schott (1992a) *North American Free Trade: Issues and Recommendations* (Washington, DC: Institute for International Economics).

Hufbauer, G. C. and J. J. Schott (1992b) *Prospects for North American Free Trade* (Washington, DC: Institute for International Economics).

Hufbauer, G. C. and J. J. Schott (1993) *NAFTA: An Assessment* (Washington, DC: Institute for International Economics).

Hunter, L. J. R., Markusen and T. F. Rutherford (1991a) 'Trade Liberalization in a Multinational-Dominated Industry: A Theoretical and Applied General Equilibrium Analysis', mimeo, University of Colorado.

Hunter, L. J. R. (1991b) 'Trade Liberalization in a Multinational-Dominated Industry: A Theoretical and Applied General Equilibrium Analysis', in Federal Reserve Bank of Dallas (1991) *North American Free Trade: Proceedings from a Conference*, Dallas, June 14.

Hurrell, A. (1992) 'Teoría de regímenes internacionales: una perspectiva europea', *Foro Internacional*, Vol. XXXII, No. 5.

IDB (1992a) *Economic and Social Progress in Latin America* (Washington, DC)

IMF (1992b) *International Capital Markets: Developments, Prospects and Policy Issues* (Washington, DC)

IMF (1992), *Direction of Trade Statistics* (Washington, DC)

IMF (1993), *Direction of Trade Statistics* (Washington, DC)

INFORUM (1990) *Industrial Effects of a Free Trade Agreement between Mexico and the US*, Report for the US Department of Labor (University of Maryland).

INFORUM (1991) *Industrial Effects of a Free Trade Agreement between Mexico and the USA* (College Park, Maryland: Interindustry Economic Research Fund, Inc).

Jackson, H. R. (1990) *Quasi-States: Sovereignty, International Relations and the Third World* (Cambridge: Cambridge University Press).

Johnson, J. R. (1993) 'NAFTA and the Trade in Automotive Goods', in S. Globerman and M. Walker, *Assessing NAFTA: A Trinational Analysis* (Vancouver: The Fraser Institute).

Josling, T. (1992) 'NAFTA and Agriculture: A Review of the Economic Impacts', in N. Lustig et al (eds.), *North American Free Trade: Assessing the Impact* (Washington, DC: The Brookings Institution).

Kane, E. (1988) 'Interaction of Financial and Regulatory Innovation', *American Economic Review*, May.

Kehoe, T. (1991) 'Modeling the dynamic impact of a North American Free Trade Agreement' (Minneapolis: Department of Economics, University of Minnesota).

Kehoe, T. (1992) 'Assessing the Economic Impact of North American Free Trade', Discussion Paper No. 265, October (Department of Economics, University of Minnesota).

Kelly, M. (1993) 'Who Got What in the Side Agreements?', *Frontera Norte*, Vol. 5, No. 10 .

Kissinger, H. and C. Vance (1988) 'Bipartisan Objectives for American Foreign Policy', *Foreign Affairs*, Vol. 66, No. 5.

KPMG Peat Marwick/Policy Economics Group (1991) *The Effects of a Free Trade Agreement between the US and Mexico* (Washington, DC: US Council of the Mexico-US Business Committee/Council of the Americas).

Krause, M. B. (1972) 'Recent developments in customs union theory: an interpretative survey', *Journal of Economic Literature*, Vol. 10.

Krueger, A. O. (1992) 'Government, Trade, and Economic Integration', *American Economic Review*, Vol. 82, No. 2, pp. 109-114.

Krueger, A. O. (1993) 'Free Trade Agreements As Protectionist Devices: Rules of Origin', Working Paper No. 4352, National Bureau of Economic Research, April 1993.

Krugman, P. (1989) 'Is Bilateralism Bad?' National Bureau of Economic Research, Working Paper No. 2972.

Lajous, R. (1987) 'La agenda bilateral entre México y Estados Unidos', *Foro Internacional*, Vol. XXVII, No. 3.

Latin American Monitor (1993) *Mexico*, Vol. 10, No. 7., August 1993.

Leamer, E. E. (1992) 'Wage Effects of a US-Mexican Free Trade Agreement', National Bureau of Economic Research, Working Paper No. 3991, February.

Levinson, J. I. (1993) 'Comments on labour law in Mexico: The discrepency between theory and reality', *United States-Mexico Law Journal*, Vol. 1, No. 1.

Levy, S. and S. van Wijnbergen (1991a) 'Labor markets, migration and welfare: agriculture in the Mexico-US Free Trade Agreement', mimeo, June.

Levy, S. and S. van Wijnbergen (1991b) 'Maize and the Mexico-United States Free Trade Agreement', mimeo.

Levy, S. and S. van Wijnbergen (1992) 'Maize and the Free Trade Agreement between the Mexico and the United States', *The World Bank Economic Review*, Vol. 6, No. 3, pp. 481-502.

Lipsey et al (1993), 'Inside or Outside the NAFTA?' (Toronto: C. D. Howe Institute Commentary No. 48).

Liverman, D. M. (1991) 'Global change and Mexico', *Global Environmental Change*.

Loaeza, S. (1991a) 'Los partidos y el cambio político', separata, Madrid, Centro de Estudios Constitucionales.

Loaeza, S. (1991b) 'Partido Acción Nacional and the paradoxes of the opposition in Mexico', Paper given at the conference Political Parties and Elections in Mexico, held at the Institute of Latin American Studies, London, May.

Lock, R. (1993) 'Mexico-United States Energy Relations and NAFTA', *United States-Mexican Law Journal*, Vol. 1, No. 1.

López-de-Silanes, F., J. R. Markusen, and T. F. Rutherford (1992) 'The Auto Industry and the North American Free Trade Agreement: Employment, Production, and Welfare Effects', mimeo, Harvard University.

Lustig, N. (1991) 'Bordering on Agreement', Discussion Paper (Washington, DC: The Brookings Institution).

Lustig, N. (1993) 'NAFTA: Potential impact on Mexico's economy and beyond', paper presented at the Conference on 'Economic Integration in the Western Hemisphere: Prospects for Latin America', University of Notre Dame, 17-18 April 1993.

Lustig, N., B. P. Bosworth, and R. Z. Lawrence (1992) *North American Free Trade: Assessing the Impact* (Washington, DC: The Brookings Institution).

Mace, G. (1989) 'Les relations du Canada avec L'Amérique latine et les Caraïbes', in P. Painchaud (ed.), *De Mackenzie King a Pierre Trudeau: Quarante Ans de Diplomatie Canadienne* (Québec: Presses de l'Université Laval).

Magee, S. P. (1990) 'The Decline of Lobbying in the US over Trade Policy, 1950-1986', mimeo, University of Texas at Austin.

Martínez, A. and M. Merino (1991) 'México en busca de la democracia', separata, Madrid, Centro de Estudios Constitucionales.

Martz, J. D. (1993) 'Economic Relationships and the early debate over free trade, *ANNALS, AAPSS*, No. 526.

Maxfield, S. (1989) 'International Economic Opening and Government-Business Relations', in W. Cornelius, J. Gentleman and P. Smith (eds.), *Mexico's Alternative Political Futures* (San Diego: University of California).

McDorman, I. T. (1992) 'The 1991 US-Mexico GATT Panel Report on Tuna and Dolphin: the implications for trade and environment conflicts', *North Carolina Journal of International Law and Commercial Regulation*, Vol. 17, No. 3.

McLeod, D. and J. H. Welch (1991) 'Free Trade and the Peso', mimeo, Federal Reserve Bank of Dallas.

McLeod, D. and J. Welch (1992) 'El libre comercio y el peso', *Economía Mexicana*, Vol. I, No. 1 (Mexico City: CIDE).

Meyer, L. (1990) 'The US and Mexico: The Historical Structure of their Conflict', *Journal of Interamerican Studies and World Affairs*, Vol. 43, No. 2.

Mizrahi, Y. (1992) 'La nueva oposición conservadora en México: la radicalización política de los empresarios norteños', *Foro Internacional*, Vol. XXXII, No. 5.

Mizrahi, Y. (1994) 'Rebels without a cause? The politics of entrepreneurs in Chihuahua', *Journal of Latin American Studies*, Vol. 26, Part 1.

Mody, A. (1990) 'New International Environment for Intellectual Property Rights', in Francis W. Rushing and Carole Ganz Brown (eds.), *Intellectual Property Rights in Science, Technology, and Economic Performance: International Comparisons* (Boulder: Westview Press).

Molinar Horcasitas, J. (1991) *El Tiempo de la Legitimidad Electoral: Elecciones, Autoritarismo y Democracia en México* (Mexico City: Cal y Arena).

Molinar Horcasitas, J. and J. A. Weldon (1993) 'Electoral determinants and consequences of National Solidarity', unpublished paper.

Moran, H. T. (1990) 'International Economics and National Security', *Foreign Affairs*, Vol. 65, No. 5.

Morici, P. (1991) 'Regionalismo en el sistema internacional de comercio y las relaciones México-Estados Unidos', in G. Vega (coord.), *México Ante el Libre Comercio en América del Norte* (Mexico City: El Colegio de México).

Morici, P. (1993a) 'Implications of a Social Charter for the NAFTA', in J. Lemco and W. Robinson, *Ties Beyond Trade: Labor and Environmental Issues under the NAFTA* (Canadian-American Committee).

Morici, P. (1993b) 'NAFTA Rules of Origin and Automotive Content Requirements', in S. Globerman and M. Walker, *Assessing NAFTA: A Trinational Analysis* (Vancouver: The Fraser Institute).

Mumme, S. (1993) 'Environmentalism, NAFTA, and North American Environmental Management', *Journal of Environment and Development*, Vol. 1, No. 2.

Mumme, S. and R. Sánchez (1992) 'New Directions in Mexican Environmental Policy', *Environmental Management*, Vol. 16, No. 2

Murphy, N. C. and R. Tooze (1991) *The New International Political Economy* (Boulder: Lynne Rienner).

Myhre, D. (1993) 'The Unseen Instrument of Agricultural Restructuring in Mexico: The Growth, Crisis and Erosion of the Official Credit System', preliminary unpublished paper (Mexico: ILET).

Nam, C. H. (1987) 'Export Promoting Subsidies, Countervailing Threats, and the General Agreement on Tariffs and Trade', *The World Bank Economic Review*, September.

OECD (1990) *OECD Economic Outlook*, No. 48, December.

OECD (1992) *International Direct Investment: Policies and Trends in the 1980s* (Paris: Organization for Economic Cooperation and Development).

Ogelsby, J. C. M. (1979) 'A Trudeau Decade: Canadian Latin American Relations 1968-1978', *Journal of Inter-American Studies and World Affairs*, Vol. 21. No. 2.

Ojeda, M. (1976) *Alcances y límites de la política exterior de México* (Mexico City: El Colegio de México).

Ojeda, M. (1986) *México: El Surgimiento de una Política Exterior Activa* (Mexico City: SEP Cultura).

Oye, K. (1992) *Economic Discrimination and Political Change* (Princeton: Princeton University Press).

Pastor, R. (1992) 'NAFTA as the Center of an Integration Process: The Non-Trade Issues', in N. Lustig et al (eds.), *North American Free Trade: Assessing the Impact* (Washington, DC: The Brookings Institution).

Perot, R. and P. Choate (1993) *Save Your Job, Save Our Country. Why NAFTA must be stopped now!* (New York: Hyperion).

Primo Braga, C. A. (1989) 'US-Latin American Trade: Challenges for the 1990s', *Economic Impact*, No. 2.

Primo Braga, C. A. (1990) 'US Policies and the Prospects for Latin American Economic Integration', in Werner Baer and Donald V. Coes (eds.), *United States Policies and the Latin American Economies* (New York: Praeger).

Primo Braga, C. A. (1991) 'The North-South Debate on Intellectual Property Rights', in *Global Rivalry and Intellectual Property: Developing Canadian Strategies* (Ottawa: The Institute for Research on Public Policy).

Primo Braga, C. A. (1992) 'NAFTA and the Rest of the World', in N. Lustig et al (eds.), *Assessing the Impact: North American Free Trade* (Washington, DC: The Brookings Institution).

Primo Braga, C. A., R. Safadi and A. Yeats (1993) 'Regional Integration in the Western Hemisphere: 'Déjà Vu All Over Again', mimeo, World Bank.

Puyana, A. (1982) 'La idea del mercado común para América del Norte y las implicaciones para México', in L. Meyer (ed.), *México-EU 1982* (Mexico City: El Colegio de México).

Randall, S. (1992) 'The Politics of North American Free-Trade', Paper presented at El Colegio de México, March.

Randall, S. (1977) 'Canadian policy and the development of Latin America', in Norman Hillmar and Garth Stevenson (eds.), *A Foremost Nation: Canadian Foreign Policy and a Changing World* (Toronto: MacLelland and Stewart).

Reiner, L. (1993) 'Mexico-US Energy Relations and NAFTA' *United States-Mexico Law Journal*, Vol. 1, No. 1.

Reyes Heroles. J. (1988) *El Federalismo Mexicano* (Mexico City: Fondo de Cultura Económica).

Reyna, J. L. and R. Weinert (1977) *Authoritarianism in Mexico* (Philadelphia: Institute for the Study of Human Issues).

Rico, C. (1989) 'Una vuelta en la montaña rusa: Las relaciones mexicanos-estadounidenses después de la posguerra y desafíos del futuro', *Foro Internacional*, Vol. XXIX, No. 3, January-March.

Roberts, A. (1993) 'Humanitarian war: military intervention and human rights', *International Affairs*, Vol. 69, No. 3.

Roett, R. (1991) *Mexico's External Relations in the 1990s* (Boulder/London: Lynne Rienner).

Rogowski, R. (1987) 'Trade and the Variety of Democratic Institutions',

International Organization, Vol. 41, No. 2.

Roland-Holst, D. W, K. A. Reinert and C. R. Shiells (1992) 'North American Free Trade Liberalization and the Role of Non-tariff Barriers', mimeo, Mills College, April.

Roland-Heist, D. W, K. A. Reinert and C. R. Shiells (1993) 'Social Accounts and the Structure of the North American Economy', *Journal of the International Input-Output Association*, Vol. 5, No. 3

Romero, J. and L. Young (1991) 'A Dynamic Dual Model of the Free Trade Agreement', in Federal Reserve Bank of Dallas, *North American Free Trade: Proceedings of a Conference*, Dallas, June 14.

Ros, J. (1992a) 'Ajuste macroeconómico, reformas estructurales y crecimiento en México', mimeo, Kellogg Institute, University of Notre Dame.

Ros, J. (1992b) 'Mexico's trade and industrialization experience since 1960: a reconsideration of past policies and assessment of current reforms', mimeo, Kellogg Institute, University of Notre Dame.

Ros, J. (1993) 'Trade liberalization with real appreciation and slow growth: sustainability issues in Mexico's trade policy reform', mimeo, Kellogg Institute, University of Notre Dame.

Rubio, L. (1990) 'Mexico in perspective: An essay on Mexico's economic reform and the political consequences', *Houston Journal of International Law*, Vol. 12, No. 2.

Rubio, L. (1992) ¿*Como va a afectar a México el tratado de libre comercio?* (Mexico City: Fondo de Cultura Económica).

Runsten, D. (1992) 'Transaction Costs in Mexican Fruit and Vegetable Contracting: Implications for Asociaciones en participación', Paper prepared for the Conference 'Transformation of Mexican Agriculture: Opportunities, Dilemmas and Implications for California', Berkeley.

Runsten, D. and Wilcox, L. (1992) 'Demand for Labor, Wages and Productivity in Mexican Fruits and Vegetables: Preliminary Estimates and Implications for NAFTA', Paper prepared for XVII International Congress of the Latin American Studies Association, Los Angeles.

Russell, R. (1990) 'Relaciones internacionales de Argentina. Cambio de gobierno y política exterior. Las primeras tendencias de la gestión peronista', *América Latina Internacional*, Vol. 7, No. 24.

Sala-i-Martin, X. and J. Sachs (1991) *Fiscal Federalism and Optimum Currency Areas: Evidence for Europe from the United States*, Working Paper No. 3855, National Bureau of Economic Research, October 1991.

Sánchez, R. (1991) 'El Tratado de Libre Comercio en América del Norte y el Medio Ambiente de la Frontera Norte', *Frontera Norte*, Vol. 3, No. 6.

Sánchez, R. (1992) 'Cambios Climáticos Globales en el Norte de México: El Caso del Agua', *Ciencia*, Vol. 43, special issue.

Sánchez, R. (1993) 'Una Alternativa para Mejorar el Manejo Ambiental en México en el Marco del Tratado de Libre Comercio', *Frontera Norte*, Vol. 5 No. 10.

SARH (Secretaría de Agricultura y Recursos Hidraúlicos) (1990) 'Programa

Nacional de Modernización para el Campo 1990-1994' *Comercio Exterior*, Vol. 40, No. 10.

SARH (1992a) *Propuesta de Programa Integral de Apoyos a Productos Básicos*, November, unpublished document, Mexico City.

SARH (1992b) *El sector agropecuario en las negociaciones del Tratado de Libre Comercio Estados Unidos-México-Canada*, unpublished document, Mexico City.

SARH (1993) *Mexican agricultural sector. An overview*, May 1992, unpublished document, Mexico City.

Schlesinger, J. (1991) 'New instabilities, new priorities', *Foreign Policy*, No. 85.

Schlesinger, J. (1992/93) 'Quest for a post-Cold War foreign policy', *Foreign Affairs*, Vol. 72, No. 1, Special Issue, America and the World.

Secretaría de Relaciones Exteriores (1991) 'Informe presentado por el Secretario de Relaciones Exteriores al Senado de la República 1990-1991', Textos de Política Exterior, No. 107, Mexico City, December.

SELA (1992a) *La nueva etapa de la integración regional* (Mexico City: Fondo de Cultura Económica for the Sistema Económico Latinoamericano).

SELA (1992b) *Objectivos de la negociación de los Estados Unidos en la Iniciativa para las Américas* (Caracas: Secretariado Permanente del Sistema Económico Latinoamericano).

Shaiken, H. (1987) *Automation and Global Production: Automobile Engine Production in Mexico, the United States and Canada* (La Jolla: Center for US-Mexican Studies, University of California, San Diego).

Smith, F. J. (1993) 'Confronting differences in the US and Mexican legal systems in the era of NAFTA', *United States-Mexico Law Journal*, Vol. 1, No. 1.

Smith, H. P. (in press) 'El impacto político del libre comercio en México', in G. Vega (coord.), *Liberación económica y libre comercio en el Norte de América: Consideraciones políticas, sociales y culturales* (Mexico City: El Colegio de México).

Smith, R. E. (1990) 'United States Policies and the Labor Sector in Latin America', in Werner Baer and Donald V. Coes (eds.), *United States Policies and the Latin American Economies* (New York: Praeger).

Smith, W. R. (1992) 'Protecting the Environment in North America with Free Trade', *The Backgrounder*, No. 889, The Heritage Foundation.

Sobarzo, H. (1991) *Análisis de los efectos de un Tratado de Libre Comercio entre México y América del Norte: Un enfoque de Equilibrio General* (Mexico City: Centro de Estudios Económicos, El Colegio de México).

Stallings, B. and G. Székely (1993) *Japan, the United States, and Latin America: A New Trilateralism in the Western Hemisphere?* (London: Macmillan).

Stern, R. (1987) 'Intellectual Property', in Michael Finger and Andrzej Olechowski (eds.), *The Uruguay Round: A Handbook on Multilateral Trade Negotiations* (Washington, DC: World Bank).

Strange, S. (1991), 'An eclectic approach', in C. N. Murphy and R. Tooze, *The New International Political Economy* (Boulder: Lynne Reiner).

Suárez, B. (1993) 'Modernización de la agricultura y nutrición', preliminary unpublished paper (Mexico: ILET).

Székely, G. (1989) 'Dilemmas of export diversification in a developing economy: Mexican oil in the 1980s', *World Development*, Vol. 17, No. 11.

Székely, G. (1991a) 'Forging a North American Economy: Issues for Mexico in the 1990s', in R. Roett (ed.), *Mexico's External Relations in the 1990s* (Boulder: Lynne Reiner).

Székely G. (1991b) *Manufacturing Across Borders and Oceans: Japan, the United States and Mexico* (La Jolla: Center for US-Mexican Studies, University of California, San Diego).

Székely, G. (1992) 'Japanese Need Not Apply: why NAFTA is bad news for Japan', *International Economy*, November-December.

Ten Kate, A. (1992) 'Trade Liberalisation and Economic Stabilisation in Mexico: Lessons of Experience', *World Development*, Vol. 20, No. 5.

Thorup, C. (1990) 'In the Eyes of the Storm: The State of US-Mexican Relations', in S. D. Brothers and A. E. Wicks (eds.), *Mexico's Search for a New Development Stategy* (Boulder: Westview Press).

Tornell, A. (1990) 'Real vs. Financial Investment: Can Tobin Taxes Eliminate Irreversibility Distortion?', *Journal of Development Economics*, Vol. 32.

Torres Ramírez, B. (1990) 'Consensus and crisis in Guadalajara, 1965-1975', Paper presented at the Institute of Latin American Studies, London, November.

Trela, I. and J. Whalley (1991) 'Bilateral trade liberalization in quota restricted items: US and Mexico in textiles and steel', University of Western Ontario, Department of Economics, May.

Trigueros Gaisman, L. (1990) 'El federalismo en México: Autonomía y coordinacíon en las entidades federadas', in *Derecho Constitucional Comparado*, Vol. 16.

Truett, L. J. and D. B. Truett (1993) 'Maquiladora Response to US and Asian Relative Wage Rate Changes', *Contemporary Policy Issues*, Vol. 11, January.

Tussie, D. (1991) 'Trading in fear? US hegemony and the open world economy in perspective', in Murphy N. Craig and R. Tooze, *The New International Political Economy* (Boulder: Lynne Rienner).

Tybout, J. and M. D. Westbrook (1993) 'Trade Liberalization and the Dimensions of Efficiency Change in Mexican Manufacturing Industries', Working Paper No. 92-03, Georgetown University.

Unger, K. (1990) *Las exportaciones mexicanas ante la restructuración industrial internacional* (Mexico City: Fondo de Cultura Económica).

UNIDO (1979) *Small Scale Industry in Latin America* (New York: United Nations Industrial Development Organisation).

United Nations (1993) *World Economic Survey 1993* (New York: UN Department of Economic and Social Development).

Urencio, C. F. (1981) 'Ante la perspectiva de un mercado común de América del Norte', *Comercio Exterior*, Vol 31, No. 10.

Urquidi, V. (1990) 'Broader perspectives on development problems', in S. D. Brothers and A. E. Wick (eds.), *Mexico's Search for a New Development Strategy* (Boulder: Westview Press).

Urquidi, V. (1992) 'El convenio trilateral de libre comercio entre México, Estados Unidos y Canadá', *El Trimestre Económico*, Vol. LIX, No. 2.

USDA (US Department of Agriculture) (1991) *Agriculture and the North American Free Trade Agreement: An Interim Review* (Washington, DC), April.

USITC (United States International Trade Commission) (1990a) *Review of Trade and Investment Liberalization by Mexico and Prospects for Future United States Mexican Relations: Phase I* (Washington, DC), April.

USITC (1990b) *Review of Trade and Investment Liberalization by Mexico and Prospects for Future United States Mexican Relations: Phase II* (Washington, DC), October.

USITC (1991) *Review of Trade and Investment Liberalization by Mexico and Prospects for Future United States Mexican Relations: Phase III* (Washington, DC), February.

USITC (1993) *Potential Impact on the US Economy and Selected Industries of the North American Free-Trade Agreement* (Washington, DC).

US Department of Commerce (1992) *US Exports to Mexico: A State-by-State Overview, 1987-1991* (Washington, DC).

USTR (United States Trade Representative) (1992a) *The North American Free Trade Agreement: An Overview* (Washington, DC).

USTR (1992b) *Review of US-Mexican Environmental Issues* (Washington, DC) 25 February.

USTR (1992c) *1992 National Trade Estimate Report on Foreign Trade Barriers* (Washington, DC).

Valdes, L. (forthcoming) 'The PRD: The third option in Mexico', to appear in N. Harvey and M. Serrano (eds.), *Political Parties and Elections in Mexico* (London: Institute of Latin American Studies).

Van Whiting (1993) *Foreign Investment in Mexico* (Baltimore: Johns Hopkins University Press).

Van Young, E. (1992) (ed.) *Mexico's Regions: Comparative History and Development* (San Diego: University of California).

Viner, J. (1950) *The Customs Union Issue* (New York: Carnegie Endowment for International Peace).

Waltz, Kenneth N. (1979) *Theory of International Politics* (Reading, Massachusetts: Addison Wesley).

Weingarten, S. P. (1993) 'Observations of a US labour unionist and former US reporter in Mexico', *United States-Mexico Law Journal*, Vol. 1, No. 1.

Weintraub, S. (1984) *Free-Trade Between Mexico and the US* (Washington, DC: The Brookings Institution).

Weintraub, S. (1990) 'The North American Free Trade Debate', *The Wash-*

ington Quarterly, Autumn, 1990.

Weintraub, S. (1992), 'Modeling the industrial effects of NAFTA', in N. Lustig et al (eds.), *North American Free Trade: Assessing the Impact* (Washington, DC: The Brookings Institution).

Weintraub, S. (1993) 'The North American Free Trade Agreement as Negotiated: A US Perspective', in S. Globerman and M. Walker, *Assessing NAFTA: A Trinational Analysis* (Vancouver: The Fraser Institute).

Welch, J. H. (1991) 'A Preliminary Survey of Issues Surrounding a US-Mexico Free Trade Agreement', mimeo, Federal Reserve Bank of Dallas, March.

Welch, J. H. (1993) 'The New Face of Latin America: Financial Flows, Markets, and Institutions in the 1990s', *Journal of Latin American Studies*, Vol. 25, Part 1.

Whitehead, L. (1991) 'Mexico and the hegemony of the US: Past, Present and Future', in R. Roett (ed.), *Mexico's External Relations in the 1990s* (Boulder/London: Lynne Reinner).

Wilson, M. G. and W. R. Smith (1992) *The North American Free Trade Agreement: Spurring Prosperity and Stability in the Americas*, The Heritage Foundation Lectures Series (Washington, DC).

World Bank (1992a) *Mexico Environmental Report* (Washington, DC), March 9.

World Bank (1992b) *World Development Report 1992* (Oxford: Oxford University Press).

World Bank (1993) *Global Economic Prospects and the Developing Countries* (Washington, DC: World Bank).

Young, L. and J. Romero (1992) 'Steady Growth and Transition in a Dynamic Dual Model of the North American Free Trade Agreement', mimeo.

Zabludovsky, J. (1991) 'El proceso de negociación del tratado de libre comercio de América del Norte', in SECOFI, *Hacia un tratado de libre comercio en América del Norte* (Mexico City: Miguel Angel Porrúa).

INDEX

adjustment costs,
    and Canada, 165, 167
    and Mexico, 14, 18-19, 40,
      208
    and US, 20, 22, 24
    assistance and retraining, 195-
      196, see also PRONASOL,
      compensatory mechanisms
agriculture, 5
    and non-trade barriers, 62
    competititiveness and re-
      structuring, 60
    costs of free trade to, 20
    perspectives for, 69
    sectoral vulnerability of,
      59
    trade, 60-69
    and transition periods, 70,
      72
American Depository Receipts,
    136
anti-trust law (Mexico), 40
Asian Free Trade Area (AFTA),
    150
Asian Pacific Economic
    Council, 223
automobiles, 5
    and export and investment
      boom, 15
Automobile Pact, 166-7
autonomy, maintenance of, 37
    Mexico, 31

balance of payments, 17
Border Environmental
    Commission (BEC), 99, 105
Border Environmental Finance

Bank (BEFB), 105, 106
Brady Plan, The, 151

Brookings Institution, 140
Bush, George,
    President of the United States
      120, 129

Canada
    and the environment, 96
    and Mexican procurement
      contracts, 16
    and 'new issues', 21
    and rules of origin, 168
    and tariff classification, 33
    competitiveness, 167
    NAFTA negotiations and
      defensive position, 81,
      165, 168-9, 170-2
Canada-US Free Trade
    Agreement (CUFTA), 2,
      157, 163-5, 219
    improvement of, 169-70
capital flows, see also FDI,
    and flight capital, 136-7,
      142, 145
    and Latin America, 135-9
    and mobility, 20, 23
    diversion of, 133, 209
    endogenous, 12-13
    into Mexico, 16-17
    portfolio investments, 142,
      155
    private, 135-8
Central America, 8, 219
    and Esquipulas Plan, 220
Chile, 8, 209, 223

China, 158
Clinton, Bill, President of the
    United States, 81, 98, 129,
    192
Colombia, 8
Common Markets, 3
    minimum definition of, 8
    potential development of, 208
    proposed North American,
    early 1980s, 220
computable general
    equilibrium (CGE), 12
    model, projections of, 140,
    185
compensatory mechanisms, lack
    of, 208, 215
    and social tensions, 216-7
Confederation of Mexican
    Workers (CTM), see labour
    relations
constant returns to scale
    (CRS), 12
cross border transactions,
    see financial services
customs unions, 32, 38

de la Madrid, M, 96, 193
debt,
    and Mexico, 3, 39
debt crisis, 136, 151, 220
development options,
    and political system
    rigidity, 119
direct foreign investment,
    see foreign direct investment
dispute settlement
    mechanisms, 31, 36-7, 173
    and environment, 102
domestic coalitions, 2

Echeverría, 92
economic assymetry, 3, 21,
    23, 81, 84

economic integration,
    in North America, 11-28
    'silent' form of, 11, 23
economic sectors, see sectors
economies of scale,
    gains from, 14
ejidos and ejidal reform, 60,
    63, 64, 66, 72-3, 191,
    205
employment, see jobs
environment, see also BEC,
    BEFB, NACE, NRDC, NWF,
    SEDESOL, SEDUE, Water
    activist groups, 98-109
    and implications of NAFTA,
    109-11, 192-4
    and legislation
    enforcement, 96, 97, 102,
    220
    and minimal safeguards of,
    96-8
    and 'norm harmonisation',
    120-1
    and 'normas técnicas', 96
    and 'parallel' (supplementary)
    agreements', 81, 112
    and social costs, 112
    and 'sovereignty', 112
    and standards of, 22-3
    and trade related sanctions,
    101
    and US-Mexican disparities,
    182
    Canada's position on, 101,
    103
equitable regional trade,
    and compensatory financing,
    121
    and enforcement, 121-122
European Community (EC), 2,
    94, 149, 221
    attitudes towards NAFTA,
    157
    future Mexican relations
    with, 7

investment in Mexico, 153-7
US perspective on, 29
European Monetary System
(EMS), 16
European Social Charter, 120
export-led growth, 2
export processing plants, see
maquiladoras

financial services, 5, 21,
43-4, 48-50
and cross-border
transactions, 50-1
global trends in, 43
trade in, 45-8, see also
trade in services
Fideicomisos Instituidos en
Relación con la
Agricultura (FIRA), 65
flight capital, see capital
flows
foreign debt, see debt
Foreign Direct Investment
(FDI), 138, 142-5, 153-6, 178
foreign investment, 17, 38
and Mexican domestic
market, 39
and services, 35-6
and US position on, 30
general law on (Mexico), 37
regulation of, 21-3, 31
foreign-trade zones, 34
'fourth' countries,
and trade barriers, 37-8
free trade zones, 31, 34

General Agreement on Tariffs
and Trade (GATT), 30, 36,
37, 64, 161, 171, 178
and 'GATT-legal' barriers,
178-9
and Mexico, 151
and NAFTA collapse, 197

and Uruguay Round, 145,
150, 207
and 'new issues', 21
Generalised System of
Preferences, 35, 178, 198
government procurement, 149,
157-60
Gross Domestic Product (GDP),
and Mexico, 2-3, 39, 141,
151
per capita (US), 3

ideological implications of
NAFTA, 128
Immigration and Reform
Control Act 1986 (IRCA), 83
import substitution, 2, 205
and Salinas administration,
123
Inter-American Development
Bank (IDB), 105, 133, 146
income gains,
and impact of NAFTA, 13
increasing returns to scale
(IRS), 12, 15,
incremental capital flows,
projected causes of, 15
industrial rationalisation,
gains from, 14
inflation, 3,
annual (Mexico), 43
INFORUM (report of, 1991), 13-
14
and negative macro-economic
effects, 14
on preferential market
access, 16
Institute for International
Economics (IIE), 140
Integrated Border Protection Plan
(proposed), 193
intellectual property rights,
and NICs, 29
US position on, 21-3, 30,

179, 189-90
Israel, and FTA, 21

Japan, see also trade blocs,
    AFTA
    and geopolitical concerns,
    150, 157
    and investment, 7, 153,
    155-6
jobs,
    loss and gain, 7
    creation, 152
    as trade related effect
    (US), 185-6

Kaldor, Nicholas, 13
Kantor, Michael, 100

labour, see also migration,
    20
    mobility, 122, 127
    relations, 214-5
labour standards, 22-3, 194-5
    and 'norm harmonisation',
    120-1
    and 'parallel agreements'
    81
    and US-Mexican disparity,
    182, 188, 191-2
labour productivity (US), 30
    and OECD statistics, 40
land transportation, 5
Latin America, 8
    and contingency of economic
    recovery, 134-5
    and responses to NAFTA, 145
    and economic externalities,
    133, 139-45
    and economic forecasts
    ('baseline scenario'), 133
    and GDP growth, 134
    and trade with Mexico, 125

Less Developed Countries
    (LDCs), 178
    and orthodoxy on
    integration, 203-4
local capital, 20
long term capital formation,
    207
    and credibility of
    government policies in
    Mexico, 207

Machaín, A, kidnapping of,
    221
maquiladoras, 11, 26, 141,
    161, 170, 171, 183
    see also rules of origin
    and transport costs, 206
migrants,
    definition of, 85
    destination preferences,
    89-90
    socio-economic
    characteristics, 88-9
migration, 79-84, 190-1,
    220
    and absence from NAFTA
    negotiations, 80, 188
    and US-Mexican border, 11-
    12, 205
    'careers', 84
    circuits, 85-6
    undocumented (illegal), see
    also IRCA, 81-4, 91-2
minimum concessions, 24-5
Most-Favoured-Nation status
    (MFN), 33, 36, 37-8,
    178, 198
Mulroney, Brian, 120
Multi-Fibre Agreement, 37, 184

narcotics, 220-1
National Wildlife Federation,
    (NWF), 100, 104

Natural Resources Defence
      Council (NRDC), 100, 104
National Action Party see PAN
neo-liberalism, 124
      and reform, 119, 128, 209-
      210
      and identity of NAFTA, 126
'new issues', see
      services, trade in
      intellectual property
      rights, foreign investment
      regulation
      see also,
      environmental standards
      labour standards
newly-industrialising
      countries (NICs), 29
non-trade barriers, see
      agriculture
North American Commission on
      the Environment (NACE),
      100

Organisation of Economic
      Cooperation and
      Development (OECD), 134,
      137, 144, 154, 223
Organisation of American
      States (OAS), 219

Pacific Economic Cooperation
      Council, 223
PAN (Partido de Acción Nacional)
      124, 210
      and advances in North, 215-6
Panama, 221
'parallel agreements', see
      environment, labour
      standards, sovereignty
      as NAFTA wrecking device,
      181-182
      shortcomings of, 123
perceptions of NAFTA, 125-6

Perot, Ross, 185
peso,
      results of appreciation, 17
political relations (US-Mexico),
      218-25
political system rigidity,
      (Mexico), 119, 210
      and economic reforms,
      209-10, 212-7
      and presidential
      authoritarianism, 124, 210-12
potential expansion of NAFTA,
      145-6, 209
preferential tariffs, 32, 34
PRD (Partido de la Revolución
      Democrática, 124, 210, 212
      216-8
PRI (Partido Revolucionario
      Institucional), 124,
      210, 212-4, 216
      and recomposition of
      political system, see
      also political system
      rigidity, 211-4
procedural protectionism,
      by USA, 15
Programa Nacional de
      Solidaridad (PRONASOL),
      72, 209, 212-3 see also
      adjustment costs,
      compensatory mechanisms,
public opinion, relative
      strengths of, 21

research & development (R&D),
      29
rules of origin, 31-4, 38,
      149, 157-60
      and Canada, 168
      and maquiladoras, 158-9
      and protectionism, 159
      and relocation, 158
      criteria of, 32
Regional Development Fund

(EC), 196
regional disparities,
    and transitional protection
    mechanisms, 122, 215
regional impact of
    implementation, 206, 216

Salinas de Gortari, President
    of Mexico, 80, 119, 120,
    129, 216, 220
Secretaría de Desarrollo Social
    (SEDESOL), 96, 108
    see also SEDUE
Secretaría de Desarrollo
    Urbano y Ecología (SEDUE),
    and environmental law
    enforcement, 193
    see also SEDESOL
sectors, see textiles,
    automobiles, agriculture,
    land transportation,
    financial services
sectoral effects (US), 187
sectoral disaggregation, 12
services, trade in, 21-3,
    30-1, 188-9, see also
    financial services
    and direct foreign
    investment, 35-6, 37
social disparity and cost, 120
sovereignty, 123, 218, 224
    and 'parallel agreements',
    195, 205, 219
    maintenance of, 5
'side payments', 18-20
side agreements, 205
    see also environment and
    labour

tariff classification, 33
tariff reduction schedules, 184
technological backwardness, 2
temporary imports, 31, 34-5, 38

Texas Center for Policy
    Studies, 102
textiles, 4
trade creation and diversion,
    see also capital flows,
    diversion of, 8, 133, 147
trade liberalisation, 11-12, 14
    and agriculture, 22, 69-71
    and insertion into
    international economy,
    222-5
    and protection, 183-5
    and state-business
    relations, 215-6
    in developing countries, 30
    in Mexico, 39-40, 204
    and domestic political change,
    210-8
    inter-firm, 11
    inter-industry, 11, 141
    Mexico and Japan, 153-7
    Mexico and OECD, 153-7
    modalities, timing and
    structure, 44, 48-56
    US-Mexican imbalance, 152
trade-related investment
    measures (TRIMs), 25
trade-related sanctions, 101
trading blocs, 2, 23
    and Japan, 150
trading partners,
    of US, 11
    and US-Mexican reciprocity,
    19
Treaty of Rome, 120
trilateral social
    interaction, 12

US Congress, 21, 98, 100, 107,
    123, 128, 145, 181, 196, 207
US International Trade
    Commission, 30, 143
United States (of America),
    and environmental-labour

alliance, 181
and foreign trade policy,
30, 180
and 'parallel agreements',
181-3, 191
and special location
advantage, 170
and trade postures, 178-81

Venezuela, 8

wage differentials, 205
water, 110
workplace conditions, see
labour standards
World Bank, 133, 197

Young, Allyn, 13